The British

The Library of Religious Beliefs and Practices
Edited by John Hinnells, University of Manchester, and Ninian Smart, Universities of Lancaster and Santa Barbara

Already published:

The Ancient Egyptians: Their Religious Beliefs and Practices
A. Rosalie David

Jews: Their Religious Beliefs and Practices
Alan Unterman

The Sikhs: Their Religious Beliefs and Practices
W. Owen Cole and Piara Singh Sambhi

Theravada Buddhism: A Social History from Ancient Benares to Modern Colombo
Richard F. Gombrich

Zoroastrians: Their Religious Beliefs and Practices
Mary Boyce

This series provides pioneering and scholarly introductions to different religions in a readable form. It is concerned with the beliefs and practices of religions in their social, cultural and historical setting. Authors come from a variety of backgrounds and approach the study of religious beliefs and practices from their different points of view. Some focus mainly on questions of history, teachings, customs and ritual practices. Others consider, within the context of a specific religion or geographical region, the inter-relationships between religions; the interaction of religion and the arts; religion and social organization; the involvement of religion in political affairs; and, for ancient cultures, the interpretation of archeological evidence. In this way the series brings out the multi-disciplinary nature of the study of religion. It is intended for students of religion, ideas, social sciences and history, and for the interested layperson. Books are in preparation on the Hindus, the Mahayan Buddhists and the Muslims.

The British

Their Religious Beliefs and Practices
1800–1986

Edited by
Terence Thomas

R

ROUTLEDGE
London and New York

First published in 1988 by
Routledge
11 New Fetter Lane, London EC4P 4EE

Published in the USA by
Routledge
a division of Routledge, Chapman and Hall, Inc.
29 West 35th Street, New York NY 10001

Phototypeset by Input Typesetting Ltd, London
Printed in Great Britain by
Richard Clay Ltd, Bungay, Suffolk

British Library Cataloguing in Publication Data
The British.
  1. Britons. Their religious beliefs and practices, 1800–1986
  I. Thomas, Terence   II. Series
  291'.0941

Library of Congress Cataloging in Publication Data
The British: their religious beliefs and practices.
  (Library of religious beliefs and practices)
  1. Great Britain—Religion.   I. Thomas, Terence.
BL980.G7B75   1988   291'.0941   88–11436

ISBN 0–415–01299–6 (c)
     0–415–01300–3 (p)

Contents

List of Contributors

Professor A. O. Dyson

Samuel Ferguson Professor of Social and Pastoral Theology in the University of Manchester

Revd Ieuan P. Ellis

Formerly Senior Lecturer and Head of Department of Theology, University of Hull

Dr Sheridan Gilley

Senior Lecturer in Theology, University of Durham

Dr David Hempton

Department of Modern History, The Queen's University of Belfast

Dr Kim Knott

Leverhulme Fellow, Community Religions Project, University of Leeds

Dr Terence Thomas

Senior Lecturer in Religious Studies, The Open University

Professor Kenneth Thompson

Professor of Sociology, Faculty of Social Sciences, The Open University

Introduction

In 1850 a painting was exhibited in the Royal Academy Exhibition which bore the title *A Converted British Family Sheltering a Christian Missionary from the Persecution of the Druids*. The action takes place in a hut which, being three-walled, looks more like a stage set except that where the footlights would have been on a stage a river laps the floor of the hut. The scene within the hut is heavy with Christian symbolism as might be expected from a Pre-Raphaelite painting. The action is a confusion of symbols, eucharistic, baptismal, even a fur-loinclothed John the Baptist character, and action resembling the deposition from the Cross. The roof is entwined with vines, and wheat and cabbages (a sign of Christian civilization?) grow in the field outside. Beyond the field there is a chief druid haranguing a mob and one unfortunate missionary has just been caught. Both he and the missionary being comforted within the hut are dressed in priestly, eucharistic vestments. The scene is set against the backdrop of an ancient stone circle, one of the stones being the main prop of the far hut wall and reredos upon which a cross has been painted in red. The painting was executed in a period of religious controversy concerning Romish developments in the Church of England, and as such is obviously a commentary on the controversy. After the Exhibition the painting came to rest in the home of a prominent High Churchman. The painter, William Holman Hunt, held that the scene depicted could

1

well have occurred historically. If so, then we have a depiction of one of the most significant 'moments' in the history of the religions of the British. Pity that such a pregnant 'moment' has been presented in what will appear to many a trivialized and somewhat 'corny' form.

The advent of Christianity to Britain is shrouded in lost history. It is possible that it arrived in the second century of the Common Era but its development in Britain is obscure until the Council of Arles (314) which was attended by three British bishops and a deacon. Before the advent of Christianity to Britain there was a period when the religion of Rome and the religion of the Celts existed side by side and co-mingled in places. The Celts of Britain shared in the same general religious milieu of pre-Roman Europe. There is evidence of a tenuous unification under the leadership of the Druids of Britain and continental Europe. There is also evidence of many gods being worshipped but not of an 'organized pantheon'.

The Celts were concerned to limit and, if possible, control the supernatural powers so that they worked in favour of humans rather than against them. By the beginning of the Roman period minor and major gods were acknowledged by the Celts but before that period the emphasis was on animism, sacrificial rites and a concern with the after-life. There is conflicting evidence concerning the Druidical priesthood, partly due to the influence of Roman sources of information and the opposition of Roman emperors whose opposition may have been based on the power, more social than political perhaps, exercised by the Druids. Whatever their true role it is clear that they exercised considerable religious authority over Gaul and Britain. Their religious practices involved magic using traditional oral sources and ritual. The cult activity associated with the cycle of fertility was their responsibility. Once a year they gathered in a large sacred assembly in the region of Carnutes (Chartres). According to Caesar, Britain was a centre for the training of Druids. They were associated with human sacrifice, mainly as a form of divination rather than as an appeasement of the gods. Their power waned with the advent of the Romans and they were banned by the emperor Claudius though he did not entirely wipe them out.

The evidence provided by archaeology from Neolithic times shows a succession of changes in the pattern of what we call religion. We will look later at the term religion itself. If we accept,

Introduction

for the moment, that the means of disposing of the dead and the materials which are found in association with the remains of the dead pointing to rituals of disposal, hint at beliefs in an after-life, and if we accept that all these evidences, and they are the main evidences in pre-history, are the evidences of religion in some form or other, then the history of religions in Britain is the history of change. Changes over perhaps a millennium, but changes neverthe-less and these changes must have been gradual so that at any one time there might have been different religious practices existing side by side, or interacting and producing syncretistic forms of religion. Neolithic remains give evidence of communal burials. The Bronze Age finds the presence of the Beaker folk from the Low Countries in Britain burying their dead in individual graves along with drinking vessels, hence the name given by archaeologists to these people. Later comes the period of the great henges with the wedding of astronomy with 'religion'. Shortly before invasion by Rome, Belgic tribes migrated to south-east Britain and we find that they cremated their dead. Over many of these periods there are also evidences of 'sacred spaces', usually open-air enclosures, where various rituals, including blood sacrifices, took place. Assuming, as has been suggested already, that changes did not immediately displace what existed previously, then there is hardly a period of any considerable length in pre- and early history that we can describe as anything but pluralistic.

The Roman cults were brought to Britain and there are extensive remains of their presence over a wide area. There are evidences of the presence of Jupiter worship and the other gods which had their place in the military calendar of festivals. Eastern cults were also present, especially the cult of Mithras. These Eastern cults with their myths of rebirth and personal communion with the gods are associated by some scholars with the idea of resurrection and baptismal rites in early Christianity. None of these Roman cults really penetrated the indigenous populace. They belonged mainly in military, commercial and metropolitan locations. One of the features of this period is that referred to as *interpretatio romana*, that is the ascription of a Roman name to a Celtic deity. One of the best known eclectic examples is the identification of Sulis, the Celtic goddess of the hot spring at Bath with Minerva, the Roman goddess, patroness of all the arts and crafts and inspirer of all that was wise and valiant, and the consequent embellishment of the shrine by the Romans. Thus the Romans appear not to have attempted to transform the Celtic gods and Romanize them nor suppress and displace them. Since the Roman gods were more or less confined to military and metropolitan areas, ordinary Celts to the west and north of Britain would not have spoken Latin and would have stayed with their indigenous gods. The broad picture of the period is that the Celtic gods remained in the areas little influenced by Rome. Cults introduced by the Romans predominated in military environs and the Celtic and Roman gods existed side by side or merged ecletically in metropolitan environs. Pluralism is the best way to describe the situation towards the end of the Roman period.

If Celtic religion remained alive in Britain in spite of the Roman invasions it is certain that Rome was deeply involved in the religion which did alter the religious map of Britain permanently by displacing the indigenous religion, that is Christianity. Reference has already been made to the presence of British bishops at Arles in 314. Alban was the first British martyr and gave his Christian name to the city of his birth, Verulamium. Tradition has it that he was baptized by a fugitive priest whom he sheltered. Perhaps the story is reflected in Hunt's painting. There are early fourth-century evidences on silver ware from Water Newton in Cambridgeshire. These evidences and later ones include the *chi-rho*, the Greek alphabetical symbols for the first two letters in the word Christ. There were churches known at Silchester in the fourth century and in Richborough in the fifth century. After the conversion of Kent by Augustine in 597, sent by Pope Gregory the Great to refound the Catholic Church in England, the Celtic Church having been forced westward by the Anglo-Saxon settlers, there existed for some time two Christian churches – the loosely formed Celtic Church and the more bureaucratically structured Roman Church. They occupied roughly different territories, the Romans in the south-east and the Celts in the west and north. There were some major differences relating to the Christian calendar and the Celtic Church had to come around to the Roman dating of Easter after some time. In time also the Celtic Church came more and more under the Roman influence through the activities of such as Theodore of Tarsus, the first archbishop to unify the English Church, who, in 672, forbade bishops from interfering in each others' dioceses and priests from moving about freely.

Introduction

The Celtic Church refused to be restricted to its enforced western domain and spread out from the west and Ireland to Scotland and the north of England. It was highly regarded for its missionary zeal, its scholarship and its asceticism, with its important centres in Iona and Lindisfarne. One of its most famous, or perhaps infamous, sons was the monk Pelagius, whose works are the oldest surviving by a British writer. He spent most of his life in Rome and Africa and the heresy he taught was not accepted in Britain until near his death where it persisted for some time and didn't disappear until the sixth century after condemnation at a number of church councils. There is still a sneaking admiration for him and for his humanistic leanings in Wales. The independence of the Celtic Church was virtually ended at the Synod of Whitby in 664. Pockets of the old religion persisted in many places even after the conversion of Sussex and the Isle of Wight, the last areas to be converted, in the late seventh century. Some areas had still not been turned at the time of the death of the Venerable Bede (735). Fairly soon thereafter, officially at least, the Church became faithful to Roman usage. It also began to send out missionaries to the Continent, to the Franks of Frisia and to the Germans.

Bede himself was an example of the fine scholarship which grew up very quickly within a century of Augustine's landing. Jarrow, where Bede did his work, boasted a fine monastery as did the earlier Wearmouth. By the tenth century many more monasteries of renown had been founded or refounded, including Glastonbury, Winchester, Ely and Peterborough. Churches such as St Lawrence at Bradford on Avon were built. Among our most precious art remains, the Book of Kells and the Lindisfarne Gospel belong to a slightly earlier period. Aethelwold, the bishop of Winchester in the late tenth century, composed a common monastic rule, the *Regularis Concordia*, based extensively on the continental Benedictine model and proposed as a rule to be observed by all British monasteries. Again there was a period of missionary activity, this time to Norway, Denmark and Sweden. David the Englishman is still the patron saint of the province of Västmanland in Sweden and what remains of his penitential cell has been incorporated into the structure of the parish church of Munktorp.

It was about the same time as David's mission to Sweden that William of Normandy defeated King Harold and this began a new chapter in the history of religion in Britain. The leading bishoprics went to continental clergy. An Italian, Lanfranc, became Archbishop of Canterbury. Church councils met to legislate for the English Church as did the councils of Normandy. William refused homage to the Pope and in this he was supported by Lanfranc. They claimed to be acting in accordance with English tradition. Later the period saw greater intervention by the papacy in the affairs of the English Church. Norman kings had introduced the institution of lay investiture, whereby ecclesiastical appointments were accompanied by the investing of abbots and bishops with symbols of their authority, symbols such as the ring and crozier in the case of a bishop, and the practice of paying homage to the sovereign. This institution was condemned by the papacy. When it was introduced into England, Anselm, one of the greatest scholars of his time, refused to pay homage to Henry I. A compromise was reached: Henry was not to interfere in episcopal elections but could receive homage and invest the bishops with their temporal possessions before consecration. By this time the clergy were more inclined to accept the authority of the Pope. The new monasteries such as the Cistercian houses of Fountains and Rievaulx had their origins on the Continent. The orders were Christian not British or English. England was very much a part of Europe with its kings ruling parts of France as well as their own country.

Over the next three hundred years things changed back and England became more nationalistic. Towards the end of the twelfth century the king, Richard I, was almost completely taken up with the Crusades and the attempt to recover Jerusalem from Islam. In the thirteenth century Henry III's patronage of aliens in his court and the way he allowed papal clerks to take over English benefices produced a reaction which resulted in victory over Henry by Simon de Montfort. Aggression against Wales and Scotland was a common feature of this period. In Wales the church did not feature prominently in the political struggles and the eventual subordination of the country. All that happened was that having been brought under English and European practice and organization in the twelfth century that domination was more firmly applied. In Scotland the Church retained more independence. At first it was successful in warding off the kind of organization which had been imposed in the rest of Britain. By the twelfth century a diocesan system began to emerge. In 1192 the Pope recognized the identity of the Scottish Church and its independence of all authority except that of Rome itself. This independence was a political strength and it served the Scottish kings well. They, in return, founded many new monasteries with vast estates. Henry II having received authority from Pope Adrian IV to invade Ireland, fought and obtained the homage of the King of Leinster in 1166. A few years later he was able to bind all the Irish kings in a dependent relationship. The anglicization of Ireland, including the Church, had begun. A feudal order was imposed on the Church and many new institutions were founded to strengthen the increasingly English character of the island. Trouble broke out on a number of occasions and complete anglicization failed. By the fourteenth century, war was frequent and the Church became bitterly divided into 'that among the English' and 'that among the Irish'.

The medieval period has the appearance of a stable time for the Church of Britain. It is the age of increasingly powerful monastic orders, especially the Franciscans and the Dominicans. But there was also a great deal of anti-clericalism, the laity objecting to the increasing wealth and power of the clergy both regular (i.e. monastic) and secular (i.e. parochial). Among the latter there was a vast gulf between the wealth and power of the bishops and the humble parish clergy. The Bishop of Ely in the late fourteenth century was spending £1,000 per annum on his household of about 80 persons while many of his clergy were probably having to exist on about £5 per annum or less. This was the age of some of the finest cathedrals, first in the Decorated style, e.g. Exeter and later the Perpendicular style, e.g. Winchester.

The period also had the first whiff of the doctrinal conflicts that were to follow full blown at the Reformation. John Wycliff was the English precursor of the later upheaval, the 'Morning Star of the Reformation'. He challenged the authority of the Pope on the grounds that it was not founded on Scripture. The Pope he regarded as Antichrist and monks he attacked for their life style. He also attacked certain Church institutions and rituals such as pilgrimage, the worship of saints and the holding of benefices in plurality. His most important doctrinal attacks were directed at the doctrine of transubstantiation in the eucharist, that is, the doctrine which holds that the bread and wine become the real body and blood of Christ. According to this doctrine the bread and wine retain the accidents of breadness and wineness but the substances become the real body and blood at the point of consecration. Wycliff argued that Christ was present in the eucharist not substantially nor corporeally, but virtually as a king is present in his realm. He also argued that the Bible, which contained the only criteria for belief, should be available for the faithful in English. He began a translation into English, a task which was carried on by his disciples. He was condemned on a number of occasions, the final condemnation coming after his death at the Council of Constance (1415) following which his works were burned and his bones dug up.

The continental Reformation is reckoned to have begun in 1520 with the papal ban on Martin Luther. In Britain the Reformation took on a different hue, being more tied up with royal politics than was the case in Germany. The break with Rome came over the refusal of the Pope to annul Henry VIII's marriage to Catherine of Aragon. The king was proclaimed the 'Supreme Head' of the Church of England. With Thomas Cromwell minister the king proceeded to dissolve the monasteries and the Church moved in a Protestant direction. This move was mainly signalled by the translation of the Bible and the provision of an official English version (1537). But further progress towards Protestantism was halted by the introduction of the Act of Six Articles and the fall of Cromwell. Henry tried to prove his 'catholicism' in this Act by supporting the doctrine of transubstantiation, communion in one kind (i.e. bread alone), clerical celibacy and vows of chastity, private masses and individual (auricular) confession and absolution.

The reign of Edward VI saw the introduction of new Prayer Books in the English language and the establishing of Protestant doctrines in the Church of England. In 1549 Cranmer's Prayer Book was established for use in the Church by Parliament under the Uniformity Act. The main changes were the use of English, a more evangelical emphasis on worship by the congregation and the eucharist was no longer to be a re-enactment of the sacrifice of Christ but a commemoration of his death and resurrection. In 1552 a more radical Act of Uniformity led to a second Prayer Book, this time the doctrine of transubstantiation was not only outlawed but belief in the 'real presence' of Christ in the sacrament was also denied. Such a move went further than the Lutheran position.

Following the brief reign of Mary I, when the Edwardian legislation, including that governing the Prayer Book of 1552, was repealed and Catholicism partially restored, Elizabeth I continued the movement of Protestantism and in the 'settlement' of 1559 restored royal supremacy, restored the Prayer Book of 1552 but, under pressure from 'catholicizing' bishops, modified the radical view of the 'real presence'. What remained is summed up in a verse that is held to have been crafted by Elizabeth herself:

> 'Twas God the Word that spake it,
> He took the Bread and brake it,
> And what the Word doth make it,
> That I believe and take it.

A 'visitation' designed to enforce the Settlement resulted in a few hundred clergy being removed from their benefices. Reinforcement of the Settlement came in the shape of 'The Thirty-Nine Articles of Religion'. These Articles re-affirmed many Protestant views but were not so radical in that while transubstantiation was condemned explicitly the purely commemorative doctrine of the eucharist was also condemned implicitly. The Calvinist doctrine of predestination also found its way into the Articles. The 'Puritan' element in the Church of England, that is the extreme Protestant element, remained in the Church for a time but as the refusal to radicalize the settlement hardened, many of them were forced to secede and the first signs of later nonconformity began to emerge. On the other hand many 'Catholic' clergy had no option but to remove themselves to the Continent where a seminary was organized and a mission to England founded. This movement did not see any great results for a few centuries. For a time there were strains in the national Church with 'admonitions' to Parliament which tried to turn the Church in a presbyterian direction on the one hand and the influence of Richard Hooker, the theologian of the Settlement, on the other.

In Wales, by now brought into an Act of Union with England (1536), the Reformation was an instrument of integration. The gentry became Protestants, the dissolution of the monasteries and chantries enlarged their estates, and eventually the statute of 1563 ordering the translation of the Bible and Book of Common Prayer into Welsh worked for the partial acceptance of the Church of England. Many Welsh people though, even down to the twentieth century, have thought of the Church of England as *yr hen estrones*, the old foreigner. There cannot be any doubt, however, that the translation of the scriptures, first by Richard Davies, and then by Bishop William Morgan (1588), not only saved the Welsh language, but also gave a standard to the Welsh language which is similar to that given to German by Luther's translation. The same cannot be said of the Prayer Book, which, though in full use until recently, was rather eccentrically translated by William Salesbury with an awkward style and too many Latinized words. The developments in Wales contrast with Ireland, where Henry VIII was declared king in 1541 but did not live long enough to enforce his new status. The Reformation Parliament of 1536–7 acknowledged him as supreme head of 'the whole church of Ireland' and later agreed to the dissolution of the monasteries. After the king's death, Ireland was effectively divided into English and Irish areas. There was no attempt to enforce religious reform. The plantation of Protestant settlers became a flood, especially in Ulster, English laws and customs spread but so also did Catholic influence under the impetus of the post-Tridentine reforms within the Catholic Church.

In Scotland, religious reform took a radically different line. The Scottish Church had for some centuries enjoyed a measure of independence. Continental Reformation influences had been entering Scotland since the days of Luther. These influences were resisted by James V and many Scottish reformers fled to England. The Reformation Parliament in Scotland (1541) merely served to impose reform within the Catholic Church. After James's death the regents of the infant Mary, Queen of Scots, were uncertain as to how to progress Church reform. Foreign policy veered between England and France. A number of marriages which successively alienated Mary from her Protestant lords led finally to another Reformation Parliament in 1560 and Scotland became Presbyterian and Protestant. Mass was abolished as was the authority of the Pope. Mary abdicated in favour of James VI in 1567. In spite of the Reformation Parliament the Stuart kings insisted on the Kirk being an episcopal institution. In 1584 pro-episcopal Acts were passed but in 1592 the Kirk regained power and Presbyterianism was ratified, only for the Scottish Parliament to establish episcopacy again in 1612. In 1637 the Glasgow General Assembly defied Charles I and again Presbyterianism replaced episcopate. After the outbreak of Civil War, when the episcopacy was abolished in England, the Scottish Covenanters in collaboration with the Long Parliament convened the Westminster Assembly which produced a number of Calvinistic and Presbyterian documents including the Westminster Confession which was accepted by the Kirk. After the Restoration of the monarchy the Kirk became episcopal again for a brief period until the Revolution of 1690 when it once again became Presbyterian and has remained so ever since.

As part of the process of the Restoration of the monarchy a new Act of Uniformity was required. This was accompanied by a new Prayer Book. The Act came into force in 1662 and the Prayer Book of that year was in use until the second half of our century. The implementation of the Act required that all ministers had to assent publicly to its exclusive use in worship by St Bartholomew's Day, about three months after the Royal Assent. Those who were not episcopally ordained by that date, that is those who took up their ministry during the Commonwealth, were to be deprived of their livings. In all about 2,000 Presbyterian ministers who refused to conform were so deprived.

These Presbyterians joined already existing groups of Christians who had withdrawn from the Church of England and became known as Dissenters. The first major group was formed about 1580 under the influence of Robert Browne. He established independent congregations in Norwich and elsewhere. These groups were known as 'Brownists' or Independents, a title which has lasted in some areas. Later Browne himself submitted to the Church of England but the groups who had initially followed him remained independent. They denied that the Church of England or any other Church not formed after their own model could be a true Church or possess valid sacraments and ordinances, and thus refused to allow their followers to join in communion with the Church of England. They are to be distinguished from the Presbyterian 'Puritans' of the Commonwealth who regarded them as sectaries. In 1633 the Independents were divided by the formation of separate congregations of Baptists who advocated the necessity of adult believers' baptism. This sect developed rapidly during the Commonwealth when about thirty ministers held Church livings. During this period the teachings of George Fox, a religious mystic, led to the formation of the Society of Friends, otherwise known as the Quakers. They denied the use of any external rites and advocated a total dependence on the Holy Spirit. Like other Dissenters they were persecuted by the Church but they also suffered at the hands of other Dissenters. The Toleration Act brought some relief for all Dissenters except Unitarians and Roman Catholics, so that during the early decades of the eighteenth century a large number of them conformed to the Church of England. Many others, however, turned to Arminianism, the counter-movement to strict Calvinism, and to Unitarianism which enjoyed some success in a period of popularity for Deistic views, generally associated with 'natural religion'. Later in the century the rise of Methodism, under the leadership of John Wesley in the 1730s gave a new vitality to Dissent and these bodies revived and grew. The Methodists themselves were eventually alienated from the Church of England and swelled the ranks of Dissent, though many Methodists would not really wish to be known as Dissenters, harbouring many of the doctrines and sentiments associated with the Church of England. Many of these dissenting groups were not given certain rights until well on into the nineteenth century. With the advent of the Industrial Revolution many of these Dissenting Churches made initial gains as they were more flexible than the national Church which was bound to existing parish boundaries and was not able to move with the new movements of population.

While the movements we have referred to in such a cursory manner here were taking place, movements which belong to the 'official' history of the Christian religion in Britain, at the local, 'popular' level there was a whole realm of 'alternative' religion being practised. In the middle ages the Church itself was involved in this 'alternative' religion viewing the realm of human existence as a realm of ghosts, demons and powers inimical to the living of a reasonable life, whether in terms of poverty and riches or health and sickness. To cope with the vicissitudes of life there was a whole complex of prayers, masses, rituals and incantations associated with the main services of the Church, especially the Mass, but also with the host of saints, the heroes and heroines of the faith who seemed to exist solely for the warding off of affliction and bad grace. Christianity seemed to have effectively displaced the gods and goddesses of the Celts and the Romans by an appeal to a religion which demanded faith in one God and offered salvation through the sacrifice of a pure being. What really happened was that the old gods and goddesses were reincarnated as saints. Some of them appeared at locations which were originally shrines to the old gods and goddesses. Wherever they were called upon they existed to give comfort and support against the rigours of life. Some of them were associated with the healing of particular diseases. Others were the patron saints of particular professions or crafts. Whatever their real status they existed for a long time as part of the structure of the local church and even evoked the support of high dignitaries.

With the advent of Protestanism the existence of these saints was threatened and while many of them disappeared the need for comfort and support did not. Though the saints themselves disappeared the customs associated with them carried on in folklore, tales of the unseen, folk cures for sickness, astrology and clairvoyance, witchcraft, incantations and myriad festivals and customs which persisted until fairly recently and have hardly passed from certain areas even now. One of the most persistent of these superstitions has been associated with taboos associated with the female. Taboos relating to menstruation and childbirth have persisted long after many other irrational fears have disappeared. There was some support for this in the official formularies of the Church until fairly recently. From 1552 the Prayer Book Service associated with childbirth had been known as 'The Thanksgiving of Women after Childbirth'. That was the influence of reform. However, the title goes on ' . . . commonly called the Churching of Women'. That title still promoted the notion of taboo since 'churching' assumes 'unchurching' on account of uncleanness, an idea which goes back to the Christian New Testament and beyond it to the Jewish Bible. It is also present in many other cultures. It is only very recently that not only has Prayer Book revision but also human custom changed this situation. One suspects that in some quarters, such as among those males who oppose the ordination of women, a remnant of the taboo lingers on. The main point to be made here is that while there have been movements in the history of religion in Britain, and by that for most of the history we mean the Christian religion, which have been recorded as advances in theology and church polity, underneath there have been alternative styles of religion which owe a great deal more to the older religions than most theologians and ecclesiastics are prepared to admit. The true picture of religion has, therefore, been one of complex plurality, always internally in the 'official' Church, externally in 'alternative' forms of religion, and then in the emergence of the dissenting sects which later became churches. In spite of all the written histories which have tended to take the 'official' line there never seems to have been a time when there was not a plurality of religious expression.

This leads us to a consideration of what constitutes religion. Is astrology a religious phenomenon? What about practices like healing? Are they really associated with faith, so called, or is there a remnant of magic left in it? Is one person's faith healing another person's magic and should both of them perhaps recognize the psychological truth that may underlie both? Kenneth Thompson deals with the problems of defining religion in Chapter Eight so I won't pursue this line of thought any further. David Hempton in Chapter Seven deals with 'popular' religion and also raises some of these definitional problems. You will see that in three chapters we refer to 'official' and 'popular' religion. The fact that these terms are printed within quotation marks is intended to show that the terms are not precise descriptions but rather flags to denote certain areas of the history of religions. The use of the terms reflects a rather arbitrary choice of terms by the editor. You may have noticed that I have, in any case, used the term 'alternative', on the pattern of 'alternative medicine', for that area or areas which are referred to as 'popular' elsewhere. Others might have gone for the straightforward 'unofficial' to point to this area. Yet others might have chosen 'mainstream' instead of the term 'official'. No one has yet come up with the definitive terms for what is described under these terms any more than anyone has come up with a definition of religion which satisfies everyone. We would claim no more than that what is dealt with in the following pages is generally the kind of activity which people would call religious and that there are internal differences in the field of religion which need to be generally distinguished from each other. It should be added that the study of what goes under 'popular' religion here is of very recent vintage and is the result of new attitudes in the study of history generally.

We have not tried to write a history of the Church in this volume nor have we tried to write the history of theology though you will find references to the history of the Church and to the history of theology. Neither is the work a history of religious ideas nor a work of the sociology of religion though you will find both aspects of study in the work. No religious beliefs are assumed nor do we aim to undervalue religious beliefs. We accept that religions have been and continue to be integral aspects of human existence. We do not say that religion is in decline nor do we claim any resurgence of religion. We have tried to report and discuss the religions as they have appeared in Britain in the nineteenth and twentieth centuries. You will not find everything about every religion in Britain during this period in the book. You may find that there is not a great deal of the detail of what has gone on under the name of religion in the period. The fact is that this book does not intend to be a history of religions in Britain in these two centuries. Rather it intends to be a study of the study of religions in the period. We hope that we have succeeded in the aim of the work, namely that it should present a report on 'the state of the art' of the study of religion in Britain over the period. We hope that readers of all kinds, the general reader and the student, will find in the text and the notes a mine of study resources which will invite and encourage a deeper study of the various aspects of the history of religions in the period.

It is incumbent on me to express my appreciation to a number of people who have contributed to the book. First, I must thank John Hinnells, the General Editor of the series, for the invitation to edit a work which has given me immense pleasure. I hope he is satisfied with the results. Then I must thank the scholars who have contributed the bulk of the material and who through their ready collaboration have made my task such an easy one. I wish to thank Macmillan & Co. and MARC Europe for permission to include the tables on pp. 217–26. Finally I wish to thank the staff of Routledge for their encouragement, patience and advice during the editing of the book.

Terence Thomas
Cardiff
March 1987

FURTHER READING

On Celtic Religion and Romano-Celtic Religion I am indebted to Miranda Green, *The Gods of the Celts*, Gloucester, Sutton, 1986. On other periods see:

Roman Britain:

Frere, S. S., *Britannia: A History of Roman Britain*, London, Routledge & Kegan Paul, 2nd ed., 1974.

Celtic Christianity:

Chadwick, Nora K. et al., *Studies in the Early British Church*, Cambridge University Press, 1958.
Thomas, C., *Christianity in Roman Britain to AD500*, London, Batsford, 1981.

Anglo-Saxon:

Mayr-Harting, H. *The Coming of Christianity to Anglo-Saxon England*, London, Batsford, 1972.

Medieval:

Duke, J. A., *History of the Church in Scotland to the Reformation*, Edinburgh, Oliver & Boyd, 1937.
Maynard Smith, H., *Pre-Reformation England*, (1938), London, Macmillan, 1968.
Watt, J. A., *The Church and the Two Nations in Medieval Ireland*, Cambridge University Press, 1970.
Williams, G., *The Welsh Church from Conquest to Reformation*, Cardiff, University of Wales Press, 1962.

The Protestant Reformation:

Chadwick, O., *The Reformation*, Pelican History of the Church, Vol. III, Harmondworth, Penguin, 1964.
Cowan, I. B., *The Scottish Reformation*, London, Weidenfeld & Nicolson, 1982.
Dickens, A. G., *The English Reformation*, Glasgow, Collins, 1969.
Parker, T. M., *The English Reformation to 1558*, Oxford University Press, 1966.
Ronan, M. V., *The Reformation in Ireland under Elizabeth 1558–1580*, London, Longmans & Co. 1930.
Thomas, K., *Religion and the Decline of Magic*, London, Weidenfeld & Nicolson, 1971, Harmondsworth, Peregrine, 1978 is especially good on the 'alternative' forms of religion.
Williams, G., *Welsh Reformation Essays*, Cardiff, University of Wales Press, 1967.

Seventeenth and Eighteenth Centuries:

Cragg, Gerald R., *The Church and the Age of Reason 1648–1784*, (The Pelican History of the Church, Vol. 4), Harmondsworth, Penguin, 1970.

PART 1

THE NINETEENTH CENTURY

CHAPTER ONE

'Official Religion'

Sheridan Gilley

Nineteenth-century Britain witnessed a renewed vitality to 'official' institutional Christianity, as more churches and chapels were built or restored than in any other period in the nation's history.[1] This expansion took place in part in response to an unprecedented rise in population which increased from ten and a half millions, excluding Ireland, in 1801, to thirty-seven millions in 1901, but it equally embodied the unbounded energies of a people engaged upon the creation of a global Empire, which was mistress of the seas and workshop of the world. The origins of the movement for national spiritual renewal lay in the simplified Evangelical Christianity of the Wesley brothers and George Whitefield, and of their Wesleyan and Calvinistic Methodists, who preached the need for repentance and salvation from sin through the grace won for man by Christ's death upon the Cross. Both the Wesleys were Anglican clergymen, and the full separation of the Wesleyan Methodists from the Church of England only took place in 1795, after John Wesley's death.[2]

The 1790s also saw the beginning of the mushroom growth of the other Evangelical Nonconformist Churches, at once expressed in missions abroad as well as at home, and continuing to outpace the general increase in population until 1851, when a unique national religious census in England and Wales revealed that the numbers attending Dissenting services almost equalled the worshippers of the Church of England: four and a half million Nonconformists to five and a quarter million Anglicans, including those who attended church or chapel more than once on a Sunday, in an adult population of about fifteen millions. The rate of Nonconformist growth fell after 1850, as the Church of England's vigour waxed, but chapel membership continued to rise in absolute terms until 1906, before entering on the long decline which has continued through this century.[3]

The Church of England after 1750 was too comfortably enmeshed with the squirearchal power structures of southern rural England to do anything to meet the religious needs of the fast-rising urban population, especially in the industrial towns of the north where parishes were large and churches few, and suffered increasing pastoral neglect.[4] The Anglican revival began among the Church of England's own Evangelicals in the 1790s under the aegis of Charles Simeon, Vicar of Holy Trinity, Cambridge, who during a ministry of half a century from 1783 inspired undergraduate ordinands with a double loyalty to Evangelical Christianity and to the Church of England.[5] The apostles of this reassertion of Protestant piety and principle in a partly corrupt and partly latitudinarian Church were later to be called the 'Clapham Sect', from the attendance of many of its leading figures on the ministry of John Venn in the leafy south London suburb of Clapham.[6] This was the place of residence of the philanthropist William Wilberforce, the arch-Evangelical crusader against the slave trade and every contemporary form of immorality and cruelty. Evangelicalism was vastly stimulated by the popular reaction against the atheistic impieties of the French Revolution, by offering Britain a path of conservative religious reform between the extremes of revolution and black reaction, and by pointing out the powerlessness of the eighteenth-century public religion of mere moral exhortation based on an appeal to prudential reason alone.[7]

The Anglican revival was also spurred among Protestant Tory High Churchmen by the educational, charitable and church-building activities of the High Church 'Hackney Phalanx' or 'Clapton Sect', centred on the ministry of Henry Handley Norris in the parish of South Hackney.[8] The Phalanx was the chief religious influence upon the fifteen-year Tory administration of Lord Liverpool, between 1812 and 1827, which out of concern for the breakdown of religion and public order, voted £1,000,000 in 1818 to build new churches in the first such measure since the reign of

Anne.[9] The beginnings of mass popular education were laid by the Phalanx's 'National Society for Promoting the Education of the Poor in the Principles of the Established Church', founded in 1811, which supplemented the activities of the predominantly Nonconformist British and Foreign School Society, established in 1814.[10] The great Anglican recovery, however, effectively dates from the administrative reforms of the Ecclesiastical Commission from 1835, which gradually ended the very worst eighteenth-century abuses of clerical pluralism, absenteeism and pastoral neglect,[11] and from the Oxford Movement, which began among a small group of clergymen dons in Oxford in the 1830s, and which placed a new emphasis on the Church's teaching on Ministry and Sacrament, restoring her corporate pride in her membership of the Body of Christ.[12] Under the impulse of this 'Church revival', the expansion of the Anglican ministry continued into the 1880s, and of congregations until the First World War.

The Roman Catholic revival at first paralleled the Nonconformist, as an English dissenting movement among the small minority of native Catholics, gentry and plebeian, some eighty thousand strong, mostly concentrated in northern England, especially in Lancashire. However, the Roman Church in England and Scotland acquired a new churchly and clerical character along lines more akin to the Anglican revival from the 1830s, in part through a huge influx of pauper Catholics from Ireland,[13] in part from a new continental 'Romantic' stress on devotion to the Virgin and saints, and on an appeal in the 'Ultramontane' movement to the authority of Rome, which lay *ultra montes*, beyond the mountains.[14]

Within all the Churches, the nineteenth-century revival saw the golden age of voluntary religious effort and voluntary religious association, beginning with the innumerable missionary, charitable and reforming societies which at the annual May Meetings in London from the early 1800s gave voice to the '10,000 compassions'[15] of popular Evangelicalism. Moreover, undergirding all the official forms of Christianity were increasingly rigorous public standards of moral behaviour and Sabbath observance, and a renewed attention to private Bible-reading and daily family prayer. It is in this sense that the solid substratum of Victorian 'official' Christianity can be called Protestant, and the formal and moderate temper of this kind of hearth-centred religion was defined by Wilberforce, the kindest of fathers and best of friends, who achieved a classical Christian blend of characteristics which could be summed up as 'holy worldliness': a spirit of self-sacrifice and the dutiful discharge of social obligation to inferiors and dependants; a firm belief in heaven, hell and judgement; a confidence in the powers of human effort under grace; and a delight in the 'holy joyousness' of a proper indulgence of the sober comforts of this world.[16]

In 1800, the religious initiative in England and Scotland clearly lay with the Evangelicals, and it appeared that a non-sectarian pan-Evangelicalism uniting large sections of the Anglican and Nonconformist churches might attain in England something of that national importance being achieved by Nonconformity in Wales[17] and Catholicism in Ireland.[18] This Protestant culture was to flourish and expand for the remainder of the century, defining the quality of much of the public and private life of the England of Victoria. Even in its more secular reaches, it sustained the Puritan ethic of industry, sobriety, thrift and suspicion of ungodly pleasure, both of the cruel sports of the eighteenth century and of novel reading and the theatre, and it could easily degenerate into a merely formal sexual hypocrisy, concern for respectable appearances and an urge to police the casual amusements of a semi-pagan working class. Yet Evangelicalism was also one of the principal channels for the expression of popular idealism and public emotion, as in the hymnody deriving from Isaac Watts and the Wesleys, in the preaching of pulpit giants of overwhelming spiritual power like the Baptist Charles Spurgeon and the Congregationalist Joseph Parker, and in the revivalist tradition, represented by the Evangelical Awakening in 1859,[19] in more quietist mood, from 1875, by the Keswick 'holiness' Conventions, and most spectacularly and successfully after 1880, by William Booth's Salvation Army, with its tens of thousands of working-class proselytes and evangelists throughout Britain.[20]

It was this ruthlessly self-giving and single-minded Victorian Christianity which made possible Florence Nightingale, Dr Barnardo and General Gordon, Josephine Butler, the crusader against the compulsory inspection of prostitutes, and the great Evangelical Earl of Shaftesbury, the leader of the fight against the long working hours of women and children in factories. Theirs was the dominant Victorian ethic, a moralistic Protestantism, which was in process of carrying all before it in the last years of Victoria's wicked uncles, the generation before Victoria; which wore the white flower of a blameless life at the court of the Queen and Consort; which defined the Briton's self understanding of Great Britain as a nation providentially guided or chosen by God; and which imbued Britons with the self-righteous moral energy to subdue a large portion of the earth.

There were, however, limits to this religious influence, for the power of Protestant Christianity was circumscribed by the social and political conditions which gave it form. The political conservatism of the dominant element in Evangelicalism before 1850 lost it the leadership of a significant portion of the working class at the crucial moment of its formation.[21] Indeed the nineteenth-century religious revival was to be a mostly middle-class affair: *malgré* Marx, the opium of the rich rather than the poor, committed to the preservation of social and political order and to the inculcation of values irrelevant to most of the urban proletariat, if attractive to the more 'respectable' working class, and easily imposable on the dependent pauper, women, children and agricultural labourers, especially in 'closed' villages controlled by Anglican landlords and among servants most influenced by habits of tradition and deference. Anglicanism was much weaker in the great new industrial towns, and was weakest among urban working-class men, but even the Nonconformists often repelled the poor. This was not so much by such specific practices as pew renting or the need to wear 'Sunday best' clothing to church, as by an ethos of optimistic upward aspiration and successful respectability which the poorest felt beyond their grasp. Not that the Churches were unconscious of the problem.[22] From Bishop Charles Blomfield's church-building in London in the 1830s through the evangelistic efforts of the non-denominational City Missions and Ragged Schools for the poorest children, to the university and public school settlements and the Salvation Army, the Protestant Churches achieved a central role in poor districts as dispensers of education, entertainment and charity. This was a position slowly surrendered to the new state Board Schools after 1870 and to municipal philanthropy and the modern welfare state, but it was only gradually lost in the opening decades of this century.[23]

Nor were the working classes anti-Christian secularists. The latter were a tiny educated minority. The radical enlightenment rationalist Deism of Tom Paine and Richard Carlile, with its rejection of Christian priestcraft as the ally of kingcraft, was an element in political radicalism at the beginning of the period, and in the 1820s, inspired those enemies of the Church who seemed to wish to strangle the king with the entrails of the Archbishop of Canterbury.[24] Some of the better educated artisan class were later to be influenced by the anti-religious writings of George Holyoake, while Charles Bradlaugh, who campaigned, in the end successfully, for his right as an atheist to sit in the House of Commons, had a large popular following.[25] Yet the Nonconformist influence within political liberalism, especially after 1850, inhibited the growth of anything resembling the anticlericalism of the Continent.[26] Most children passed through the often non-denominational Sunday Schools, which have been defended recently by an historian as intrinsically working-class institutions in both their staffs and clientele;[27] all day school education was conducted by the Churches before 1870, and even after 1870, the Board Schools imparted a basic knowledge of a firmly non-denominational Christianity and the Bible, which must have been at least as familiar to the population at large in the last years of the nineteenth century as in any earlier period of English history.

Yet even at the height of the Victorian religious experiment, this popular Christian culture was not translated into universal religious practice, as the 1851 religious census clearly showed. There were strong enclaves of working-class religion, the Primitive or revivalist Methodism of the mining villages of County Durham[28] and the mining and fishing villages of Cornwall and Wales, the Irish Catholicism of London and Liverpool, the host of backstreet Salems, Bethels and Ebenezers catering to the spiritual needs of sturdy minorities in English towns and villages.[29] But specifically political Churches, Chartist and Labour, in the 1840s and 1890s, were short-lived affairs, with a bias against the official Churches,[30] and the middle-class Anglican Christian Socialists – F. D. Maurice's circle in the 1850s and the Guild of St Matthew and Christian Social Union in the 1880s and 1890s – were better at interesting Christians in Socialism than in converting Socialists to Christianity.[31]

Indeed much of this so-called 'Socialism' was simply a benevolent paternalism under another name, and merely gave the existing social structure a more human face. The Church of England was not unfairly perceived to be the Tory Party at prayer, especially in its heartlands in southern rural England and the small provincial towns and better suburbs. The long crusade to preserve the Church's traditional privileges caused conflict with religious reformers of all kinds, Anglican liberals, radical Dissenters and Irish Catholics. These privileges were eroded during the half century from 1828 and 1829 with the repeal of the Test and Corporation Acts and Catholic Emancipation, which formalized the right of Dissenters to sit in the British Parliament, and admitted the Roman Catholics. Yet the Church revival after 1830 meant a more effective, aggressive and even oppressive parochial system reaching out to the entire population. The Anglican confessional state was an unconscionable time in dying, and the nineteenth century is littered with dates which mark its gradual decay:[32] the opening of municipal government to Dissenters in 1835; the commutation of church tithe in 1836 and abolition of church rate in 1868; the introduction of civil registration of births, marriages and deaths in 1836; the campaigns to end the Anglican monopoly in Oxford and Cambridge; and the attempt to win access to country churchyards for dead Dissenters and to exempt Dissenting children from Anglican teaching in village schools. But the official Church conceded nothing willingly, and even the worst efforts of Edward Miall's Nonconformist British Anti-State Church Association, afterwards the Liberation Society,[33] still left the Church of England an establishment with chaplaincies to the Crown, the courts, the ancient universities and the public schools, and with still the dominant religious influence in the services, prisons and workhouses even after the appointment of rival Catholic chaplains.

These were, then, ample grounds for conflict between Church and Chapel, even without the provocation of minority episcopal church establishments in Ireland and Wales.[34] The Whig Bill to abolish ten Irish bishoprics in 1833 provoked the reaction of the Oxford Movement, oddly enough, as events were to prove, in defence of the privileges of the highly Protestant Church of Ireland against a Roman Catholic population; the Irish Church was to be disestablished by Gladstone's Liberal administration in 1869. The struggle lasted longer in Wales, where a majority of the populace were Liberal Nonconformists: as a Welsh minister prayed of the Tory Disraeli; 'Kill him O lord, kill him. We cannot kill him without being hanged ourselves, but thou canst kill him.'[35] The Welsh Church was disestablished in 1920, after a campaign lasting more than half a century, and the division between Church and

Chapel after 1850 continued to reflect and reinforce the differences between Conservatives and Liberals.

There was, of course, some denominational cooperation between Churchmen and Dissenters, especially among the stronger Evangelicals in both camps: yet even here they found it difficult to run joint missionary and evangelistic societies like the urban City Missions. Again, Evangelicals could unite against Catholics, yet some Anglican Evangelicals refused to join the anti-Catholic Evangelical Alliance of 1846 out of loyalty to the Church of England.[36] So vehement an Evangelical as Dean Francis Close, for many years the so-called 'Black Pope' of that middle-class Anglican Evangelical paradise, Cheltenham, could simply forget the Nonconformist contribution in regretting the absence of church-building in Carlisle.[37] At a local level, in small rural communities, there was often tolerance and even friendship between Church and Chapel, but the wider energies of Anglicans and Nonconformists were all too often spent in conflict with each other.

Some part of that conflict must be ascribed to the more Catholic element in Anglicanism, as will be shown; the largest Nonconformist body, the Tory Wesleyan Connexion, defended the Established Church, until in the 1840s it was alienated from it by the rise of what all Protestants perceived as Anglican Popery.[38] Yet this point can only qualify the principle that there was little unity to a religion dedicated to upholding the dissidence of Dissent and the protesting elements in Protestantism. The internal dissidence of Protestantism might be regarded as a source of weakness or of strength: it certainly meant an imposing proliferation of competing religious buildings. In the 1820s, Anglican Evangelicalism underwent a major internal crisis, in a developing division between, on the one hand, the Clapham Sect moderates, who, almost in the spirit of the liberal apostles of progress, looked hopefully to the emergence of a Christian culture and a converted world, and on the other, the more pronouncedly Puritan and otherworldly Evangelicals, who despised such reliance on the arm of flesh, and on the basis of their literalist understanding of certain texts in Scripture, expected the imminent return of the Lord to usher in the Millennium to a darkening and sinful world.[39] The converts to this 'premillennial' view of the Second Advent were to include such leading figures of the Anglican Evangelical party as Edward Bickersteth and the seventh Earl of Shaftesbury. Another well-connected school of premillennial prophets, under the leadership of the great London Presbyterian preacher Edward Irving, revived the ancient Pentecostal practice of speaking in tongues[40] and founded the Catholic Apostolic Church, which adopted a new hierarchy of angels and apostles and a richly Catholic liturgy.[41] Yet another inspired visionary, the Church of Ireland clergyman John Nelson Darby, founder of the Plymouth Brethren,[42] with Irving laid the foundations of modern fundamentalism.[43] The circles around Irving and Darby[44] in the 1820s included aristocrats and bankers, and represented an old and powerful strand in the Protestant inheritance, but the result of their activity was ultimately to estrange a number of bright young Evangelicals from the Protestant tradition altogether and divide the movement at the very moment when it most appeared to be a success.

Irving and Darby were obviously extremists, but controversy within Churches was only the ecclesiastical norm. The largest Nonconformist body, the Wesleyan Methodist, was an optimistic-minded body open to reason[45] and immune to premillennial enthusiasm, and was dominated for half a century by its High Tory 'Pope', Jabez Bunting, who fought his own internal wars against ecclesiastical democrats and free-lance revivalists, enemies of the highly centralized Wesleyan bureaucracy and its strict internal discipline.[46] The official Connexion was disturbed or challenged by a whole series of internal and external revolts and protests against the official leadership, by the ecclesiastically democratic Kilhamite New Connexion in 1797, by the revivalist Primitives in 1811, by the Devonshire and Cornish Bible Christians in 1815,[47] and by opponents of organs and opponents of connexional dictatorship in the 1820s and 1830s. It underwent its major secession in the formation of the Wesleyan Reformers in 1849[48] which united with the Wesleyan Methodist Association to form the United Methodist Free Churches in 1857.

The divisions of Wesleyanism had little to do with theology, as the great majority of English Methodists held to John Wesley's Arminian belief that Christ had died for everyone and not only a pre-ordained elect. Arminianism, however, distinguished the bulk of Methodism from the largest of the Welsh denominations, the Calvinistic Methodists, and from the Calvinism of the other major Dissenting groups, though the Calvinism of the Congregationalists[49] and of the Particular Baptists was generally of a temperate and moderate kind, and there was a non-Methodist Arminian body, the General Baptists, as well as the hyper-Calvinist Baptist Strict and Particulars.[50] The divisions here were often as much social as religious: Congregationalist chapels had few labouring members and attracted a higher social class than the Baptists, who were deeply divided after 1830 over the issue of whether communion should be restricted to adults who had undergone believer's baptism. The division reflected the choices available to the chapel, as an assembly open to the society around it, or as a closed community which gave a sense of belonging by restricting membership to a remnant of the saved. Such divisions made difficult the development of a national Baptist Union, which had its beginnings in 1813 and was reorganized in 1831,[51] while the Congregational Union, founded in 1832, was badly split in the 1850s by controversy over an allegedly pantheist volume of very minor poems by an Independent minister. Congregations were jealous of their local autonomy, and though Congregationalism produced a domineering personality in the journalist-minister John Campbell, neither the Congregational nor the Baptist Unions had anything like the authoritarian power of the Wesleyan Connexion. This was a weakness, but it had the concomitant strength of allowing the popular Protestantism of town and village to choose among the various independent paths.

This Evangelical culture proved fertile soil for one American revival movement, the Mormons, who between 1837 and 1850, made 50,000 converts, who either migrated to America or lapsed in Britain when Brigham Young proclaimed polygamy in 1852. The much better educated and elitist Society of Friends, the Quakers, suffered from its own strict policy of expelling members who married outside the Society. It also came under Evangelical influence, and was disturbed by the Beaconite Evangelical schism in 1835. In all, Quaker membership declined from 20,000 in 1800 to 14,000 in 1870.[52] A similar division between the more and less Bible-oriented, and a similar decline, occurred among the English Presbyterians, most of whom, like many General Baptists, under the impact of religious rationalism, had become Unitarians by 1830.[53] Their peace was disturbed by Presbyterian attempts from 1816 to secure the endowments of once Presbyterian chapels and charities, a movement applauded by many British Evangelicals, especially the Wesleyans, and only defeated by government legislation in 1844. The Quakers were politically quietist before 1830, though productive of both social reformers like Elizabeth Fry and of manufacturers opposed to state factory legislation like John Bright, who, on other issues in the 1840s like the repeal of the Corn Laws, urged Quakers into radical politics. The Unitarians were already active political radicals,[54] but suffered increasing isolation from the Evangelical hostility of the rest of Nonconformity, which forced them to resign from the principal political organ of (pre-Methodist) Dissent, the Protestant Dissenting Deputies,[55] in 1836. The same decade saw the resurrection of the Presbyterian Church by Scottish Calvinist immigrants into northeast England and Lancashire, who kept aloof from the older English Presbyterian tradition and retained close ties with Scotland.

Indeed the greatest ecclesiastical schism of the century took place in Presbyterian Scotland, where the ultra-Calvinist rejection of ungodly government had created a tradition of secession from the official Presbyterian Church. The flourishing and increasingly dominant Evangelical party in the Church became increasingly restive after 1830 over the abuse of lay patronage in appointments to ministerial charges in defiance of the wishes of congregations.[56] A series of court decisions and mishandling by the English government led to the Disruption of 1843, when more than a third of the Church's ministers, under the leadership of Scotland's greatest divine, Thomas Chalmers,[57] left the establishment to form a new Free Church, not in opposition to the principle of establishment, in which Chalmers was a devout believer, but on the ground that secular intrusion in Church affairs was a violation of the Crown rights of the Redeemer. The Free Church was strongest, not in the western border countries, the ones with the most marked secessionist tradition, but in the cities where the new Church attracted a predominantly middle-class membership,[58] and in the Highlands, where congregations were overwhelmingly peasant. The reunion of two earlier seceder bodies to form the voluntarist United Presbyterians in 1847 left Scotland with three formally Calvinist Presbyterian Churches of roughly equal size, which built in often aggressive and inconvenient proximity to one another, and which yet proved collectively inadequate to the task of Christianizing the pauper proletarian offspring of Scotland's brilliant and brutal Industrial Revolution.

The Scottish Episcopalian remnant, which was strongest on the eastern seaboard, also underwent a marked nineteenth-century revival, partly as a result of the Anglicizing cultural and educational influence on the Scottish upper classes – three Archbishops of Canterbury in a century were to be of Scottish ancestry[59] – partly through the influence on Scotland of a higher churchmanship from the Church of England.[60] The still smaller Scottish Catholic population concentrated in Banffshire and the western Highlands and islands, was vastly reinforced by massive Irish immigration into the industrial towns of the western Scottish lowlands.[61] Both the Catholic and Irish influence caused great distress to Scottish Protestants, though the dominant Liberal tradition in Scottish society meant that Irish Catholicism did not encounter even in Glasgow the degree of Tory Orange bigotry long dominant in the politics of Liverpool.

It could also be said of England that after 1840, a new Catholicism, Roman or Anglican, achieved a wholly novel prominence in the nation's post-Reformation history. Of the four sons of the Evangelical 'Father of the Victorians', William Wilberforce, one, the famous 'Soapy Sam', was the High Church Bishop of Oxford and then Winchester; the other three became Roman Catholics.[62] Gladstone, the son of a Scots Presbyterian turned Anglican and Evangelical, passed from Evangelicalism to Anglican High Churchmanship,[63] while his closest erstwhile friend, Henry Edward Manning, another sometime Evangelical, ended his days as a Roman Cardinal.

The reasons for the Catholic movement, which flourished within the aristocracy and gentry and the professional rather than the commercial middle class, were partly political, partly institutional, partly intellectual. The Oxford Movement began as a defence of the privileges of the establishment and in the resistance to liberal political as well as academic reform in the traditionally High Church clerical environs of the University of Oxford.[64] Its initial novelty lay in the clarity and violence of its language and its willingness to shed the Erastian and Protestant elements in the older High Church tradition, and to redefine Anglicanism as a *via media* between Popery and Protestantism, rather than, as traditionally, between Popery and radical Protestantism or Puritanism. In the hands of the Vicar of St Mary the Virgin, John Henry Newman, it found a spokesman of genius; and after Newman's submission to Rome in 1845, the gifted rural poet-parson John Keble and the aristocratic Canon Professor of Hebrew at Christ Church, Edward Bouverie Pusey, encouraged its diffusion through the parishes, where it raised the sacramental tone and teaching of the clergy as well as their levels of dedication to their pastoral task.[65] The movement was called Tractarian, from its ninety tract manifestoes, published between 1833 and 1841; Puseyite, after Pusey; and Anglo-Catholic, to indicate its English and national character against the foreign internationalism of the Roman Catholics. In the 1840s Pusey revived the religious life within the English Church by establishing the first Anglican sisterhoods,[66] which were active and charitable rather than contemplative, dedicated to teaching, nursing and reclaiming prostitutes, and took as their models the burgeoning new female religious orders of Rome.[67] The Oxford Movement was, however, also laying down a pattern for the development of the other mainstream Churches, all of which spawned new clerical subcultures,[68] with more professional ministries increasingly trained in special theological colleges, with heightened and more clerical ecclesiologies and doctrines of priestly ministry and often more distinctive clerical dress and more formal and liturgical modes of worship. The symbol of the change was the ever-wider adoption of the Roman collar, insignium of the clergy of the diocese of Rome, first by the Catholic priesthood, then by High Churchmen and gradually in this century by the ministries of all the major Churches.

Intellectually, there was a growing Anglican unease at the lack of mental rigour in Evangelicalism, and this led to the quest for a greater theological complexity and a stronger institutional authority to meet the liberal challenge to a faith perceived to be all too vulnerable if based upon the Bible alone. One neo-Ultramontane radical, the gifted philosopher William George Ward, wanted a papal encyclical with his *Times* on the breakfast table every morning, and saw no mean between the anarchic wilderness of Protestant private judgement and the majestic infallibility of Rome. Thus the Catholic element in English Christianity benefited disproportionately from the Victorian 'crisis of faith', which led an ex-Evangelical like George Eliot into agnosticism, and the vigorously Protestant John Ruskin through unbelief into a greater sympathy for Catholicism. It was Anglo-Catholicism, and then Roman Catholicism, which won the allegiance of the century's greatest British theologian, Newman, who had been an Evangelical in

31

youth. Newman's subtle apologetic for a highly personal religion, synthesizing the intellectual, the institutional and the devotional, faith, reason, the conscience and the will, into a new understanding of Catholicism, was the nearest that the British mind achieved to a response to the all-corroding scepticism of liberalism in religion. The variety of sources for the Catholic revival are suggested by the many-sided personality of its principal architect, Nicholas Wiseman, the son of an Irish merchant family, born in Spain and educated in England and Rome. An internationally celebrated Syriac scholar in his twenties, in 1850, he became Cardinal Archbishop of Westminster at the head of the new Roman hierarchy of diocesan bishops for England.[69]

Yet the attraction of the new Catholicism was also an imaginative one. This was partly through the transposition into Catholic Christianity of an element of Evangelical conversionism and revivalism, as by the former Evangelical Frederick William Faber, founder of the Brompton Oratory, and by the Italian-inspired Redemptorist and Passionist orders, which conducted popular and successful public missions. Even the most pervasive of Protestant art-forms, hymnody, received a large Catholic component through the translation into English of great tracts of the Byzantine and medieval hymnals by the High Churchman, John Mason Neale, translations which won their way to the Anglican public with the appearance of *Hymns Ancient and Modern* in 1861, and thereby became a central part of the inheritance of middle-class England.

Catholicism also drew on the romanticism of the wider secular culture. Though as a stout Scots Protestant Episcopalian, Sir Walter Scott regarded the Middle Ages as an era of drivelling superstition, his fascination with the external forms of Catholic faith, like his love of the hymns of the Roman Breviary, helped to Catholicize the realm of the emotions, a task in which he was abetted by such latter-day apologists for a Protestant Church of England as the Poet Laureates Robert Southey and William Wordsworth. It was Scott's neo-medievalism which gave a form to the biggest church building boom in English history; the church builders craved aesthetic canons and an architectural creed, and this the Gothic Revival supplied. The Revival was partly picturesque or archaeological in origin, a desire for interesting sensation or for accurate information about medieval building,[70] and as a national style, it appeared in the new Houses of Parliament in the 1830s. But architects like the Catholic convert Augustus Pugin, who designed all the detail for the new Westminster, achieved their reputations by attempting to reproduce the spirit as well as the letter of medieval art. In the Roman Catholic Church, the Puginian Gothic crusade[71] was challenged by Wiseman's and Faber's preference for Italian Baroque, but Pugin's ideals achieved their widest outreach through one of the most influential undergraduate societies ever formed, the Cambridge Camden or Ecclesiological Society, founded by John Mason Neale and Benjamin Webb in 1839, as the Cambridge equivalent to the Oxford Movement, to give that movement its external clothing.[72] The Society made middle or Decorated Gothic *the* central Anglican architectural style, and enriched the religious culture with a new realm of symbolism in stained glass, pointed arches, brassware and coloured tiles,[73] ultimately displacing the neo-classical plainness of even many Nonconformist chapels.

There was hardly an Anglican church in the country unaffected by the change, which thrust the pulpit from its central Protestant position to the north side, restored chancels to use with a central altar; and increasingly, introduced a robed or surpliced choir and organ which might replace the rustic orchestra of fiddles in a western gallery.[74] If the cathedral suggested the musical model, the cathedrals themselves were gradually restored after 1850, while at Truro, the architect J. L. Pearson built the first Gothic Anglican cathedral in England since the Reformation. Indeed, of the mainstream Revival architects, the most prolific, Gilbert Scott, had been inspired by Pugin, G. E. Street and William Butterfield[75] were devout High Churchmen, while the extravagant William Burges did most of his finest work for two Roman converts, the Marquesses of Bute and Ripon.[76]

The extreme of the Anglo-Catholic movement, a small minority until the end of the century, attempted to introduce Roman Catholic ritual into Anglican churches, sometimes, as in Charles Lowder's St Peter's, London Docks, in an attempt to evangelize the unchurched poor through a non-verbal symbolism of coloured vestments, banners, candle-light and incense.[77] The outcome was often Protestant violence aided and abetted by the drunken Conservative mob. Even the wearing of the surplice caused riots in Exeter in 1845. A loftier ritual, described by the Evangelical Shaftesbury as the worship of Jupiter and Juno, aroused popular fury in 1859–60 in St George's-in-the-East, where local public house and brothel keepers had some reason to fear a more effective kind of religion.

The Anglo-Catholic reaction to militant Protestantism included the favourite Victorian resort to voluntary association, in the formation of the English Church Union in 1860. Protestants responded with the Church Association in 1865 to combat Catholic ritual irregularities, and after the Public Worship Regulation Act of 1874, five priests were gaoled for ritual offences against the law.[78] The principle involved was an important one; whether the full arousal of the senses in worship by the holiness of beauty was compatible with a truly 'spiritual religion'. However, the public attention and parliamentary time devoted to ritualism was out of all proportion to its incidence, and suggests the subversive attractiveness of an aesthetic, sometimes rather feminine Catholic devotionalism, in a hard, work-centred, often Philistine Protestant world.

All this was a far cry from the religious mood of the later eighteenth century. In 1790, Roman Catholicism looked like a vital but minor strand in the spectrum of non-established religion; in Birmingham, the Catholic priest was a close friend of the Unitarian Joseph Priestley, while in the 1820s the Stockton-Darlington railway was a Quaker-Catholic enterprise. The liveliest recent historian of the Catholicism of the early modern period, John Bossy, has defined it as a variety of non-Protestant Dissent, with the small, highly educated minorities of Quakers and Unitarians.[79] The Catholics were fortified, though only for a decade, by an inrush of seven thousand French refugee *émigré* clergy and religious, exiles from the Revolution,[80] who were actually subsidized by the Protestant State, which also granted money to Scottish Catholics and for the Maynooth seminary in Ireland. In fact, anti-Catholicism seems to have mounted, as Roman Catholicism became more self-confident, proselytising and Roman, and as England experienced the backwash of the mounting Evangelical crusade to convert the now turbulent Catholics of Ireland. In the 1830s, the Irish Anglican Evangelical Hugh McNeile ended in England's most Irish seaport, Liverpool, a notable experiment in interdenominational education, thereby consigning the city to a century of religious war.[81] Ultramontane and Gothic devotionalism also made Catholicism less English, as did Wiseman's crusade from the 1840s to Romanize the English Catholic Church, in defiance of its own native national 'Cisalpine' or Gallican tradition,[82] while the restoration of the Roman hierarchy in 1850, announced by Wiseman in a mood of insensitive flamboyance in a letter 'from out the Flaminian gate' of Rome, caused a 'No Popery' outcry led by Lord John Russell, the Whig Prime Minister. But Russell also used the occasion to declare his preference for the Roman enemy, who wore his uniform, over the Anglo-Catholic in disguise; and it was the Anglo-Catholics, who by introducing Popery into the very heart of the establishment, did far more than even Roman Catholics to inflame the passions of Victorian anti-Catholicism.

Anti-Catholicism also invoked English and Scottish anti-Irishness, which at a popular level, caused anti-Irish and anti-Catholic rioting, as at Stockport in 1852, in London and Birkenhead in 1862, and in the wake of 'No Popery' preachers like William Murphy in Birmingham in 1867 and Whitehaven in 1871. Yet Irish Catholics were no more despised as Catholics than English or foreign Catholics on the grounds of their Catholicism alone. Catholicism was unpopular as a living ideological force, being regarded with the same suspicion as modern Communism. Indeed conversion to Catholicism was, as W. H. Auden puts it, a disaster that could happen in the best of families, and the full force of anti-Catholic prejudice in such cases did not fall on the Irish. Some Protestant polemicists regarded Irish immigrants with more indulgence than either converts or nuns, as the Irish were at least in possibility converts to Protestantism. It was the nuns, rather than the Irish who were, if Professor Arnstein's recent book is to be believed,[83] the most unpopular single group in Victorian England. Nuns have at least as good a claim as prostitutes to be considered Victorian 'outcasts', even if unlike the prostitutes they were predominantly women of good family. Catholicism was regarded even by good Victorian liberals as foreign, exotic, dangerous, the religion of England's traditional enemies, France and Spain; the ally of reactionary governments, and the creed of superstitious peasants everywhere. The more Protestant-minded hated Rome as unscriptural and anti-Christian. The Irish were disliked as Catholics, as was the Duke of Norfolk, the head of the English peerage, the Queen of Spain and the local Italian organ-grinder. If Britain was by definition a Protestant nation, then Catholicism was the nation's foe.

Yet many English patriots were determined to distinguish the old English Catholic gentry, whose loyalty few doubted, from both the new Ultramontane priest and the new Irish rebel. The complication here was that an English radical and Liberal repelled by an Irishman's Catholicism might well rejoice in his radicalism or Liberalism; a High Churchman repelled by an Irishman's Liberalism might well respect his Catholicism. It is perhaps no accident that the greatest of nineteenth-century Englishmen, the English politician most wounded by the wrongs of Ireland, was both a Liberal and a High Churchman, William Ewart Gladstone. Gladstone was not quite the typical 'Victorian', because there is no such thing as a typical 'Victorian', though in his onslaught on the Pope after 1870, for denouncing the ideals of modern liberalism, he appeared to speak for the masses of his Protestant fellow-countrymen. In fact, his antipapal attitudes owed more to his sympathies with the Liberal Catholic and national Gallican traditions in Catholicism defeated when the first Vatican Council defined papal infallibility in 1870, in part at the urging of Gladstone's old friend Archbishop Manning; and Gladstone's crypto-Catholic antipapalism, like his sympathy for Ireland, points up the muddle and ambiguity of attitudes which defy too easy a summary.

Indeed for all its central place in popular prejudice, the 'No Popery' influence was, after 1850, arguably a declining one in the mainstream English Churches outside Lancashire. Though Nonconformity was predominantly Evangelical and anti-Catholic, the Irish Catholic crusades, for an end to the laws against Catholics, could count on the support of Protestant Dissenters also opposed to the privileges of the Church of England. Catholics and Dissenters were often united in their campaigns against the Church as by law established, and appealed to the rising forces of political Liberalism, in demanding the redress of their disabilities within the Anglican confessional state. Catholics and Nonconformists were, therefore, often on the same political side. Catholicism was at war with political Liberals on much of the Continent, but the most conservative British Catholics instinctively appealed to Liberal principles in their claim to legal equality with their fellow countrymen. Thus, on the religious level Catholics were outcasts in kind if not in degree with their non-Anglican Dissenting brethren, who were also, as Valentine Cunningham recently reminds us, 'everywhere spoken against'.[84] Catholics and Nonconformists shared in a common exclusion from the world of Anglican wealth and privilege, and in the same sense of being borne upwards to freedom by the triumphing Liberalism of the age.

What, however, cannot be said of Roman Catholicism was that it enjoyed an unusual freedom from the internal conflicts that racked the other major Churches. In the opening years of the century, the battle line was drawn between the stormy Bishop John Milner, a strong supporter of Roman authority and of his own, and the more national 'Cisalpine' school of the barrister Charles Butler and other leading laymen. There were tensions created by the influx of converts and the much greater influx of Irish, whose native priests were simply excluded from some dioceses, and who created controversial private fiefdoms in others. The growth of the Irish urban missions, however, confirmed the existing trend to insignificance of the chaplaincies to the gentry, and to the lessening of lay power in the Church. By 1850, the Bishops were firmly in control, and under Wiseman's direction, elaborated a large body of domestic legislation in a series of provincial synods. One major source of internal conflict remained: the competition to open new schools and missions exacerbated the ancient enmity between the secular priesthood and the religious orders, especially the Jesuits, who had been officially restored in 1829, in the teeth of Catholic episcopal as well as Protestant disapproval, and who with the Benedictines accounted for an unusually high percentage of the Church's clerical manpower.[85] The Jesuits, especially, were disliked by the Bishops for attracting so many priestly vocations to their own order, allegedly at the expense of the ordinary clergy, and for evangelizing the rich rather than the poor. Manning, who regarded them as a principal obstacle to the country's conversion to Catholicism, secured a decision in favour of the bishops' authority over the regulars in 1881, but not before tremendous episcopal efforts had been expended to establish an order here or prevent it there.

So called 'official' religion, then, was deeply divided, into rival denominations: between Church and Chapel; between Protestant and Catholic; and internally, by strains and schisms embodying both the vigour and the disunity of the age. A mark of this instability was the pilgrim-convert from one form of faith to another: like F. D. Maurice, moving from Unitarianism to a comprehensive establishmentarian Anglicanism; or his sisters, to Evangelicalism; or like the progress from Evangelicalism to Rome or Unitarianism and unbelief of Newman and his younger brothers.[86] This unsettlement was made worse by the emergence of a further division, between Orthodoxy and Liberalism, within Christianity, which was more slow to develop. Despite Christian ethical unease in the 1820s over the morality of divine behaviour in certain passages of the Old Testament, it was in the 1850s that the fluffy-minded Maurice achieved national notoriety for his denial that eternal punishment implied infinite duration. This was not a concern restricted to professed liberals, but ran through all the Churches, reducing the sheer quantity of preaching on damnation and reprobation, converting Calvinists to a belief in the annihilation rather than the penal torment of the wicked, and enlarging the bounds of purgatory for Roman and Anglo-Catholics.[87] But the public recognition, in the 1850s, of the emergence of a 'Broad Church' school within the establishment, beside the 'Low Church' Protestants and 'High Church' Anglo-Catholics, was sharpened by attacks in 1860 on *Essays and Reviews*, which popularized in England some of the findings of modern science and German Biblical Criticism.[88] The incident temporarily united the Protestant and Catholic wings of the Church under the leadership of Shaftesbury and E. B. Pusey, who happened to be cousins, to attack the new liberal heresy, in the envenomed atmosphere created by Darwin's *Origin of Species* of 1859, which inaugurated a new public awareness of the possibility of conflict between science and religion.[89]

If the Churches' response was in good part unintelligently defensive, Christian liberalism failed to produce a theologian of the first rank, to face a new host of middle-class intellectual ideologues opposed to Christianity, at least one of them a first-rate scientist, the inventor of agnosticism, T. H. Huxley.[90] It was also in the 1860s that the Roman Catholic Church denounced 'progress, liberalism and modern civilization', and in England suppressed Sir John Acton's school of Liberal Catholics, who wanted a greater freedom for Catholic historical scholarship;[91] and a Liberal Catholicism, with a kenotic Christology and a strong body of sacramental teaching, only reemerged in the 1880s in the Anglo-Catholic school of Charles Gore and its principal publication *Lux Mundi*.[92] The liberal tide flowed more smoothly through the world of Congregationalism, which remained predominantly orthodox but lacked an effective authority to check the drift from Calvinism and Biblical literalism as early as the 1850s, and after 1900, produced a rather flashy 'New Theology' in the preacher at the City Temple, R. J. Campbell. The more conservative Baptists were deeply divided by their 'Down Grade' controversy over the truth of their inherited Calvinism, and the Quakers lost their Evangelical imprint, retreating into a misty theism. The Unitarians produced one considerable theologian, James Martineau, while in Scotland, the Biblical theories of William Robertson Smith brought about his expulsion from his Free Church professorship. Victorian liberal optimism about the rosy future of humanity often found it easy to displace the Protestant Atonement theology with a largely exemplarist conception of a humane and gentle Jesus. This current was least successful among the Catholics, and in the first decade of this century, the attempt to reinterpret Catholicism in 'Modernist' categories, by the lay theologian Baron Friedrich von Hügel and the Anglo-Irish Jesuit George Tyrrell, was sternly put down by Rome.[93]

In this matter, St Pius X was wise in his generation: the stirrings of theological liberalism turned out to be, not the dawn of a new Christian era, but the eclipse of the fundamentally credal convictions which for a century had sustained the expansion of British Protestant Christianity, and with it the moral basis of the nation's self-confidence as an international power. The worst decline during the sixty years from 1900 was to be suffered by the Nonconformist chapels which were most receptive to the liberal message. The only major expanding religious body before 1960 were the British Catholics, who until the Second Vatican Council, conceded least to the *Zeitgeist*, though their congregations were also sustained by continuing immigration from an ever more Catholic Ireland. Despite the decline in the high Victorian levels of middle-class church-going, the establishment survived, both by becoming even more of an umbrella for rival internal denominations, one of them more Roman than Rome, and by drawing on its continuing resources of social prestige and financial power. The moral would appear to be a tautology, that a collective faith can best flourish here where it has least truck with liberal doubt, and the recent decline in Catholicism, and renaissance in Evangelicalism, suggests that of the two principal schools in modern British Christianity, the one which is always most successful is simply the one which most unambiguously believes. Yet all religious traditions have now to cope somehow with an increasingly amoral western European secularity which has still to show if it has an agreed collective value to offer to an ever more complex society. Much Victorian religion was crude and controversial, but it was also various and vital, rejoicing in many saints and not a few eccentrics, crackling with energy, a house with many mansions, a school of hard disciplines and tender family pieties, full of life. It has yet to be shown that the heart and centre of British society will hold for long after its decay.

NOTES

1 The best comprehensive survey is by Owen Chadwick, *The Victorian Church*, 2 parts, London, A. & C. Black, 1966 and 1970, though this is better on High Anglicans, the middle classes, English Catholics and the countryside than on Anglican Evangelicals, Nonconformists, the working classes, the Irish and urban religion. Also comprehensive is Horton Davies, *Worship and Theology in England*, 5 vols., New Jersey, University of Princeton, 1961–75, vol. III, *From Watts and Wesley to Maurice, 1690–1850*, and vol. IV, *From Newman to Martineau, 1850–1900*. From an older Anglican viewpoint an excellent narrative occurs in Francis Warre Cornish, *The English Church in the Nineteenth Century*, 2 parts, London, Macmillan, 1910.

2 R. E. Davies and E. G. Rupp (eds), *A History of the Methodist Church in Great Britain*, 3 vols., London, Epworth Press, 1965–83. On the wider Nonconformity, there are two invaluable collections of documents, D. M. Thompson (ed.), *Nonconformity in the Nineteenth Century*, London, Routledge & Kegan Paul, 1972; and J. H. Y. Briggs and I. Sellers (eds), *Victorian Nonconformity*, London, Arnold, 1973.

3 Robert Currie, Alan Gilbert, Lee Horsley, *Churches and Churchgoers: Patterns of Church Growth in the British Isles since 1700*, Oxford, Clarendon Press, 1977; John D. Gay, *The Geography of Religion in England*, London, Duckworth, 1971.

4 Alan D. Gilbert, *Religion and Society in Industrial England: Church, Chapel and Social Change, 1740–1914*, London, Longman, 1976.

5 Charles Smyth, *Simeon and Church Order*, Cambridge, Birkbeck Lectures, 1940; Arthur Pollard and Michael Hennell (eds), *Charles Simeon 1759–1836*, London, SPCK, 1959; Hugh E. Hopkins, *Charles Simeon of Cambridge*, London, Hodder & Stoughton, 1977.

6 Michael Hennell, *John Venn and the Clapham Sect*, London, Lutterworth Press, 1958.

7 E. M. Howse, *Saints in Politics: The 'Clapham Sect' and the Growth of Freedom*, University of Toronto, 1962; Ian Bradley, *The Call to*

Seriousness: The Evangelical Impact on the Victorians, London, Cape, 1976.

8   Yngve Brilioth, *The Anglican Revival*, London, Longmans, 1933; A. Webster, *Joshua Watson: the Story of a Layman, 1771–1855*, London, SPCK, 1954.

9   M. H. Port, *Six Hundred New Churches: A Study of the Church Building Commission, 1818–1856*, London, SPCK, 1961.

10 J. W. Adamson, *English Education, 1789–1902*, Cambridge University Press, 1930; H. J. Burgess, *Enterprise in Education: the Story of the Work of the Established Church in the Education of the People Prior to 1870*, London, SPCK, 1958.

11 Geoffrey Best, *Temporal Pillars: Queen Anne's Bounty, the Ecclesiastical Commissioners and the Church of England*, Cambridge University Press, 1964; Olive J. Brose, *Church and Parliament: The Reshaping of the Church of England, 1828–1860*, University of Stanford, 1959.

12 Geoffrey Rowell, *The Vision Glorious: Themes and Personalities of the Catholic Revival in Anglicanism*, Oxford University Press, 1983.

13 Roger Swift and Sheridan Gilley (eds), *The Irish in the Victorian City*, London, Croom Helm, 1985.

14 Edward Norman, *The English Catholic Church in the Nineteenth Century*, Oxford, Clarendon Press, 1984. Still unsuperseded for its period in its documentary detail is Bernard Ward, *The Dawn of the Catholic Revival in England 1781–1803: The Eve of Catholic Emancipation 1803–1829: The Sequel to Catholic Emancipation 1830–1850*, 7 vols., London, Longmans, Green & Co., 1909–15.

15 Ford K. Brown, *Fathers of the Victorians: The Age of Wilberforce*, Cambridge University Press, 1961; Roger H. Martin, *Evangelicals United: Ecumenical Stirrings in Pre-Victorian Britain, 1795–1830*, Metuchen, New Jersey, and London, The Scarecrow Press, 1983.

16 Michael Hennell, 'Evangelicalism and Worldliness, 1770–1870', in G. J. Cuming and Derek Baker (eds), *Popular Belief and Practice: Studies in Church History*, vol.8, Cambridge University Press, 1972, pp.229–36; Doreen M. Rosman, *Evangelicals and Culture*, London, Croom Helm, 1984.

17 M. W. Williams, *Creative Fellowship: an Outline of the History of Calvinistic Methodism in Wales*, Caernarvon, Calvinistic Methodist Book Agency, 1935; E. T. Davies, *Religion in the Industrial Revolution in South Wales*, Cardiff, University of Wales Press, 1965; David W. Bebbington, 'Religion and National Identity in Nineteenth-century Wales and Scotland' in Stuart Mews (ed.), *Religion and National Identity; Studies in Church History*, vol.18, Oxford, Blackwells, 1982, pp. 489–504.

18 S. J. Connolly, *Priests and People in Pre-Famine Ireland 1780–1845*, Dublin, Gill & Macmillan, 1982; Desmond J. Keenan, *The Catholic Church in Nineteenth-century Ireland: A Sociological Study*, Dublin, Gill & Macmillan, 1983.

19 J. Edwin Orr, *The Second Evangelical Awakening in Britain*, Edinburgh, Marshall, Morgan & Scott, 1949; John Kent, *Holding the Fort: Studies in Victorian Revivalism*, London, Epworth Press, 1978, is far more critical of the whole tradition.

20 R. Sandall and A. R. Wiggins, *The History of the Salvation Army 1865–1914*, 5 vols., London, Nelson, 1947–68.

21 W. R. Ward, *Religion and Society in England 1790–1850*, London, Batsford, 1982. For a full discussion of religion and working-class politics, see Hugh McLeod, *Religion and the Working Class in Nineteenth-Century Britain*, London, Macmillan, 1984.

22 K. S. Inglis, *Churches and the Working Classes in Victorian England*, London, Routledge & Kegan Paul, 1963; Hugh McLeod, *Class and Religion in the Late Victorian City*, London, Croom Helm, 1974. The classic pioneering statement of concern is E. R. Wickham's *Church and People in an Industrial City*, London, Lutterworth Press, 1957.

23 George Kitson Clark, *Churchmen and the Condition of England, 1832–1885*, London, Methuen, 1973; Jeffrey Cox, *The English Churches in a Secular Society: Lambeth, 1870–1930*, Oxford University Press, 1982.

24 Sheridan Gilley, 'Nationality and liberty, protestant and catholic; Robert Southey's *Book of the Church*', in Stuart Mews (ed.), *Religion and National Identity: Studies in Church History*, vol.18, Oxford, Blackwells, 1982, pp.409–32.

25 Edward Royle, *Victorian Infidels: the Origins of the British Secularist Movement, 1791–1866*, Manchester University Press, 1974; Edward Royle (ed.), *The Infidel Tradition from Paine to Bradlaugh*, London, Macmillan, 1976.

26 David W. Bebbington, *The Nonconformist Conscience: Chapel and Politics 1870–1914*, London, Allen & Unwin, 1982.

27 T. W. Laqueur, *Religion and Respectability: Sunday Schools and Working Class Culture, 1780–1850*, New Haven, Yale University Press, 1976.

28 Robert Moore, *Pit-Men, Preachers and Politics: The Effects of Methodism in a Durham Mining Community*, Cambridge University Press, 1974; Robert Colls, *The Collier's Rant*, London, Croom Helm, 1977.

29 Alan M. Everitt, *The Pattern of Rural Dissent: The Nineteenth Century*, Leicester University Press, 1972; James Obelkevich,

Religion and Rural Society: South Lindsey, 1825–1875, Oxford, Clarendon Press, 1976.

30 Stephen Mayor, *The Churches and the Labour Movement*, London, Independent Press, 1967.

31 E. R. Norman, *Church and Society in England, 1770–1970. A Historical Study*, Oxford, Clarendon Press, 1976; P. d'A. Jones, *The Christian Socialist Revival, 1877–1914*, New Jersey, University of Princeton, 1968, is less critical.

32 G. I. T. Machin, *Politics and the Churches in Great Britain, 1832 to 1868*, Oxford, Clarendon Press, 1977. There are also two valuable collections of documents in this area, David Nicholls, *Church and State in Britain since 1820*, London, Routledge & Kegan Paul, 1967 and R. P. Findall (ed.), *The Church of England, 1815–1948: a Documentary History*, London, SPCK, 1972.

33 W. H. Mackintosh, *Disestablishment and Liberation*, London, Epworth Press, 1972.

34 P. M. H. Bell, *Disestablishment in Ireland and Wales*, London, SPCK, 1969.

35 Cited David L. Edwards, *Christian England*, Vol. III, *From the Eighteenth Century to the First World War*, London, Collins, 1984, p.237, a useful survey. See also his introductory collection of biographies, *Leaders of the Church of England, 1828–1944*, London, Oxford University Press, 1971.

36 E. R. Norman, *Anti-Catholicism in Victorian England*, London, Allen & Unwin, 1968.

37 On Close, see Michael Hennell, *Sons of the Prophets*, London, SPCK, 1979, which describes the Evangelical leadership in the generation after Wilberforce.

38 David Hempton, *Methodism and Politics in British Society 1750–1850*, London, Hutchinson, 1984.

39 Iain H. Murray, *The Puritan Hope: a Study in Revival and the Interpretation of Prophecy*, Edinburgh, The Banner of Truth Trust, 1971.

40 Charles G. Strachan, *The Pentecostal Theology of Edward Irving*, London, Darton, Longman & Todd, 1973.

41 P. E. Shaw, *The Catholic Apostolic Church*, New York, King's Crown Press, 1946.

42 H. H. Rowdon, *The Origins of the Brethren, 1825–1850*, London, Pickering & Inglis, 1967; F. Roy Coad, *A History of the Brethren Movement*, Exeter, Paternoster Press, 1968.

43 Richard Carwardine, *Transatlantic Revivalism. Popular Evangelicalism in Britain and America, 1790–1865*, Westport, Connecticut, Greenwood Press, 1978.

44 A. L. Drummond, *Edward Irving and His Circle*, London, J. Clarke, 1938; J. F. C. Harrison, *The Second Coming*, London, Routledge & Kegan Paul, 1979, studies the millenarian tradition at a popular level.

45 Bernard Semmel, *The Methodist Revolution*, New York, Basic Books, 1974.

46 W. R. Ward (ed.), *The Early Correspondence of Jabez Bunting, 1820–1829*, London, Royal Historical Society: Camden Fourth Series, vol.11, 1972, and *Early Victorian Methodism: The Correspondence of Jabez Bunting, 1830–1858*, London, Oxford University Press, 1976.

47 Thomas Shaw, *The Bible Christians 1815–1907*, London, Epworth Press, 1965.

48 John Kent, *The Age of Disunity*, London, Epworth Press, 1966; R. Currie, *Methodism Divided: A Study in the Sociology of Ecumenicalism*, London, Faber, 1968.

49 R. Tudur Jones, *Congregationalism in England 1662–1962*, London, Independent Press, 1962; Clyde Binfield, *So Down to Prayers; Studies in English Nonconformity 1780–1920*, London and New Jersey, J. M. Dent and Rowman & Littlefield, 1977.

50 A. C. Underwood, *A History of the English Baptists*, London, Baptist Union Publication Department, 1947.

51 E. A. Payne, *The Baptist Union: A Short History*, London, Baptist Union Publication Department, 1959.

52 Elizabeth Isichei, *Victorian Quakers*, Oxford University Press, 1970.

53 C. G. Bolam et al., *The English Presbyterians: from Elizabethan Puritanism to Modern Unitarianism*, London, Allen & Unwin, 1968.

54 R. V. Holt, *The Unitarian Contribution to Social Progress in England*, London, Allen & Unwin, 1938; Ursula Henriques, *Religious Toleration in England, 1787–1833*, London, Routledge & Kegan Paul, 1961, shows the wider contexts.

55 Bernard Manning and O. Greenwood, *The Protestant Dissenting Deputies*, Cambridge University Press, 1952.

56 J. H. S. Burleigh, *A Church History of Scotland*, Oxford University Press, 1960; A. L. Drummond and J. Bulloch, *The Scottish Church, 1688–1843: The Age of the Moderates*, Edinburgh, St Andrew Press, 1975; A. L. Drummond and J. Bulloch, *The Church in Victorian Scotland, 1843–1874*, Edinburgh, St Andrew Press, 1975; A. L. Drummond and J. Bulloch, *The Church in Late Victorian Scotland 1874–1900*, Edinburgh, St Andrew Press, 1978.

57 Stewart J. Brown, *Thomas Chalmers and the Godly Commonwealth in Scotland*, Oxford University Press, 1982.

58 A. A. MacLaren, *Religion and Social Class: The Disruption Years in Aberdeen*, London, Routledge & Kegan Paul, 1974.

59 A. C. Tait, Randall Davidson, Cosmo Gordon Lang. Davidson was

Tait's son-in-law. Edward Carpenter, *Cantuar: the Archbishops in their Office*, London, Cassell, 1971.

60 Marion C. Lochhead, *Episcopal Scotland in the Nineteenth Century*, London, John Murray, 1966.

61 David McRoberts (ed.), *Modern Scottish Catholicism 1878–1978*, Glasgow, Burns, 1979; Christine Johnson, *Developments in the Roman Catholic Church in Scotland 1789–1829*, Edinburgh, John Donald, 1983.

62 David Newsome, *The Parting of Friends: A Study of the Wilberforces and Henry Manning*, London, John Murray, 1966.

63 Perry Butler, *Gladstone: Church, State and Tractarianism*, Oxford, Clarendon Press, 1982.

64 W. R. Ward, *Victorian Oxford*, London, Cassell, 1965.

65 Alf Härdelin, *The Tractarian Understanding of the Eucharist*, University of Uppsala, 1965; Owen Chadwick (ed.), *The Mind of the Oxford Movement*, London, A. & C. Black, 1960; Eugene R. Fairweather (ed.), *The Oxford Movement*, New York, Oxford University Press, 1964.

66 Peter F. Anson, *The Call of the Cloister: Religious Communities and Kindred Bodies in the Anglican Communion*, London, SPCK, 1955.

67 J. N. Murphy, *Terra Incognita or the Convents of the United Kingdom*, London, Longmans, Green & Co., 1873. There are many individual histories, but no more up-to-date survey.

68 Anthony Russell, *The Clerical Profession*, London, SPCK, 1980.

69 Richard J. Schiefen, *Nicholas Wiseman and the Transformation of English Catholicism*, Shepherdstown, Patmos Press, 1984.

70 Kenneth Clark, *The Gothic Revival*, London, Constable, 1928; Georg Germann, *Gothic Revival in Europe and Britain: Sources, Influences and Ideas*, London, Lund Humphries & the Architectural Association, 1972.

71 Denis Gwynn, *Lord Shrewsbury, Pugin and the Catholic Revival*, London, Hollis & Carter, 1946.

72 James F. White, *The Cambridge Movement: the Ecclesiologists and the Gothic Revival*, Cambridge University Press, 1962.

73 Basil Clarke, *Church Builders of the Nineteenth Century*, London, SPCK, 1938; Stefan Muthesius, *The High Victorian Movement in Architecture 1850–1870*, London, Routledge & Kegan Paul, 1972.

74 G. W. O. Addleshaw and Frederick Etchells, *The Architectural Setting of Anglican Worship*, London, Faber, 1948; Arthur Hutchings, *Church Music in the Nineteenth Century*, London, Herbert Jenkins, 1967; Bernarr Rainbow, *The Choral Revival in the Anglican Church, 1839–1872*, London, Barrie & Jenkins, 1970.

75 Paul Thompson, *William Butterfield*, London, Routledge & Kegan Paul, 1971.

76 J. Mordaunt Crook, *William Burges and the High Victorian Dream*, London, John Murray, 1981.

77 Lida E. Ellsworth, *Charles Lowder and the Ritualist Movement*, London, Darton, Longman & Todd, 1982.

78 James E. Bentley, *Ritualism and Politics in Victorian Britain*, Oxford University Press, 1978.

79 John Bossy, *The English Catholic Community, 1570–1850*, London, Darton, Longman & Todd, 1975.

80 Dominic Bellenger, 'The *Emigré* Clergy and the English Church 1789–1815', *Journal of Ecclesiastical History*, vol.34, July 1983, pp.392–410; *The French Exiled Clergy in the British Isles after 1789*, Downside Abbey, 1986.

81 James Murphy, *The Religious Problem in English Education; the Crucial Experiment*, Liverpool University Press, 1959; Philip Waller, *Democracy and Sectarianism: a political and social history of Liverpool, 1868–1939*, Liverpool University Press, 1981.

82 J. Derek Holmes, *More Roman than Rome: English Catholicism in the Nineteenth Century*, London and Shepherdstown, Patmos Press, 1978.

83 Walter L. Arnstein, *Protestant versus Catholic in mid-Victorian England: Mr. Newdegate and the Nuns*, Columbia and London, University of Missouri Press, 1982.

84 Valentine Cunningham, *Everywhere Spoken Against: Dissent in the Victorian Novel*, Oxford, Clarendon Press, 1975.

85 Bernard Basset, *The English Jesuits: From Campion to Martindale*, London, Burns & Oates, 1967; Francis Edwards, *The Jesuits in England: From 1580 to the Present Day*, London, Burns & Oates, 1985.

86 William Robbins, *The Newman Brothers: an Essay in Comparative Intellectual Biography*, London, Heinemann, 1966. John Henry Newman's *Letters and Diaries*, London and Oxford, Nelson and Clarendon Press, 1961–, now nearing completion, show his vigorous dialectic with his brothers Charles (an atheist) and Frank (a Unitarian).

87 Geoffrey Rowell, *Hell and the Victorians*, Oxford, Clarendon Press, 1974. For the visual aspect of death, see John Morley, *Death, Heaven and the Victorians*, London, Studio Vista, 1971.

88 Ieuan Ellis, *Seven Against Christ: a Study of 'Essays and Reviews'*, Leiden, Brill, 1980; B. M. G. Reardon, *From Coleridge to Gore: A Century of Religious Thought in Britain*, London, Longman, 1971.

89 James R. Moore, *The Post-Darwinian Controversies*, Cambridge University Press, 1979.

90 Sheridan Gilley and Ann Loades, 'Thomas Henry Huxley: the war between science and religion', *The Journal of Religion*, vol.61, July 1981, pp. 185–308, with an extensive bibliography.
91 Josef Altholz, *The Liberal Catholic Movement in England: The 'Rambler' and Its Contributors 1848–1864*, London, Burns & Oates, 1962.
92 J. A. Carpenter, *Gore: a study in Liberal Catholic Thought*, London, Faith Press, 1960; A. M. Ramsey, *From Gore to Temple*, London, Burns & Oates, 1960.
93 Lawrence F. Barmann, *Baron Friedrich von Hügel and the Modernist Crisis in England*, Cambridge University Press, 1972; David G. Schultenover, *George Tyrrell: In Search of Catholicism*, Shepherdstown, Patmos Press, 1981; Gabriel Daly, *Transcendence and Immanence: A Study in Catholic Modernism and Integralism*, Oxford, Clarendon Press, 1980.

CHAPTER TWO

The Intellectual Challenge to 'Official Religion'

Ieuan Ellis

'What is this nineteenth-century religion for which all things have been preparing?'[1] Richard William Church's question, half-ironic, half-puzzled, reflected the state of debate in the churches in the 1860s. The question was prompted by a reading of, among other things, *Essays and Reviews*, a book which claimed that the atmosphere of religion had altered entirely, and a new age of meaning had dawned. As Benjamin Jowett, its inspirer and principal contributor, had said,

> The truth seems to be, not that Christianity has lost its power, but that we are seeking to propagate Christianity under circumstances which, during the eighteen centuries of its existence, it has never yet encountered.[2]

That was the belief of at least some members of the so-called 'Broad Church party' about the fortunes of theology in the middle years of the nineteenth century. Although the outward profession of religion apparently flourished, the intellectual convictions of Christianity were being undermined. This challenge to faith had been openly discussed in other parts of the religious world, particularly in Germany, for the past fifty years; Britain could no longer be isolated from it.

The obvious facts about this era of religious change are well known. The Enlightenment of the eighteenth century had asserted the need to free knowledge from the dominance of traditional metaphysics and theology. The 'dogmatic' and 'unscientific' in religion must be swept away, and history must be seen in terms of the progress of civilization, rather than the narrow picture contained in the Bible. In the nineteenth century these ideas, combined with rapid advances in many fields of knowledge, affected the whole outlook of theology. The Church in a growingly pluralistic society lost its position at the centre of affairs as the authorized interpreter of an accepted and universal tradition of revelation and natural law; religion was seen as an individual matter and not a public one; theology was required to recognize the rights of man and the autonomy of conscience and private judgment.

Thinkers who were unfriendly to religion in this manner were numerous and active in the nineteenth century. John Henry Newman was a worthy apologist for Christianity, but his brother Frank moved in an opposite direction, from faith to doubt, and kept up a continuous attack on the pretensions of the official churches and their moral and intellectual hollowness. Henry Thomas Buckle wrote an influential *History of Civilisation* in 1857 which mapped society's growth in naturalistic terms as an emancipation from religious dogma and bigotry towards a higher ethical state. 'The signs of the times are all around,' he declared, 'the handwriting is on the wall, the dominion of superstition, already decaying, shall break away'.[3] Herbert Spencer's *First Principles*, in 1862, and W.E.H. Lecky's *History of the Rise and Influence of the Spirit of Rationalism*, in 1865, had a similar message. G. H. Lewes predicted a total subversion of historic Christianity, a process which his companion, George Eliot, had assisted by translating Strauss's rationalistic *Life of Jesus* and Feuerbach's *The Essence of Christianity*. Leslie Stephen published in 1876 – a year after his final renunciation of his Anglican orders and denial of Christianity – a *History of English Thought in the Eighteenth Century* which showed secular culture emerging into the clear light of day. John Morley used his editorship of the *Fortnightly Review* to detail the religious doubts which his contemporaries faced. Mill, Huxley and Froude provided other examples of leaders of intellectual life who eschewed official Christianity. Thirty secular societies were active in the London area alone between 1837 and 1866, and they recruited members under the banners of secularism, materialism, free inquiry, and free thought propaganda.[4] Other signs of the times were the Church rate agitation in Parliament, which rumbled for many years, the discrediting of the blasphemy laws, and the refusal of the Privy Council Judicial Committee to uphold rigid interpretations of doctrine. Charles Bradlaugh, a noted secularist, eventually entered Parliament in 1886, after a long fight to affirm instead of swearing on the Bible. The electors of Northampton stubbornly returned him time after time until his rights in this matter were conceded.

All this was evidence of a changed climate for the churches and provided the context for a growing questioning of faith. However, a simple perspective of a withdrawal of religion in a secular age would be a mistaken one. The secularists in Victorian Britain were, in fact, in a minority, and 'honest doubt' was not atheism. The Victorians, delighting as many did, in their new Gothic churches and chapels, filled with stained glass, with vested clergy and choirs, and enhanced ritual, had only to look back at the eighteenth century, and ask which was the truer unreligious age, 'the last century, a time when love was cold' as Newman put it in one of his felicitous phrases.[5] A glance at the eighteenth century, such as was provided by Mark Pattison in *Essays and Reviews*, puts both Victorian religious fervour and doubt in a particular light.[6]

Theological evolution in the nineteenth century is best portrayed in the changes undergone by religious men themselves, rather than simply the pressures of a hostile world. In the non-Catholic churches the changes were implicit in the nature of the Protestant faith, in its appeal to the Bible, the primacy of conscience, the direct access to God without the mediation of the saints or the sacraments, and the foreshortened historical perspective regarding the institution of the Church. The energy in these ideas had not been dormant in the eighteenth century, at least in the period up to 1750, but many observers felt that theology had become moribund by the beginning of the nineteenth century, and a new spirit was needed. On other fronts in the Church there were stirrings of reform, e.g., the evangelical revival and the Tractarian movement (the latter more revolutionary in its bearings than has often been understood); a theological revival concerned with questions relating to scripture and doctrine could not long be delayed. Catholics underwent other changes, but these also were conditioned by the inner life of the Christian community. A merely external history of the challenge to faith would not explain why the religious upheavals of the nineteenth century were so far-reaching or felt so acutely. The sense of inner conflict and personal crisis is often palpable in the works of authors like E. B. Pusey, Stopford Brooke, F. W. Robertson and Matthew Arnold, to mention only four. Thus, the approach in this chapter will be to illustrate the challenge to belief in its internal dimension as much as its outward manifestations.

Change was slow at first, but by the 1880s the signs of theological realignment were plain to see. A convenient date for the watershed in theology seems to be 1860, when *Essays and Reviews* was launched as the manifesto of the radical wing of the Liberal or Broad Church Party. Though it was an historical curiosity by the end of the century, *Essays and Reviews* at the time of its publication provoked the worst crisis since the reformation, according to the then Archbishop of Canterbury.[7] Its programme for the remaking of English theology accepted biblical criticism, evolutionary theory, and revelation in other religions, all under the aegis of a vastly enlarged Church of England, so that it was truly a 'national church' on the best Hegelian models. But from our point of view an equally significant volume might have been the English translation of the life and letters of Friedrich Schleiermacher in that same year of 1860. In Schleiermacher (1768–1834) theology found a new exponent whom some placed on a level with Luther. Religion did not need the buttress of an infallible Bible, or a system of morality, or the certainty of historical tradition – all of which were under attack, anyway – its real authority lay within, in the individual's sense of his absolute dependence on God. In the event, no one in Britain was prepared to be as radical as that, though there were admirers, F. D. Maurice and the Congregationalist scholar, J. D. Morell, among them. However, the translation was a sign of change in itself, suggesting the beginning of a slow percolation of ideas from the Continent. In the earlier period to be interested in German theology was a sure mark of heterodoxy, which meant doubting the Bible or traditional metaphysics; but by 1892 Harnack was claiming that there was no longer any distinction between German and English theology.[8]

The shift in theological perspectives could be illustrated in many ways. One way is to see how Bishop Butler and William Paley fell into disfavour in the nineteenth century. They summed up the best in eighteenth-century divinity, the appeal to reason, the continuity in human experience, the assumption of a common intellectual discourse in which men of religion and men of science shared. But by 1860 Pattison was complaining in *Essays and Reviews* of Butler's limitations, and the fact that his proofs for religion were less persuasive than his Victorian defenders believed. Butler's anthropomorphic conception of God as the 'governor of the universe' excluded all that was poetical in life and sublime in religious speculation.[9] Many thinkers, Newman and Gladstone among them, claimed to be indebted to Butler, but usually tempered their praise with some qualification. The reversal of Paley's fortunes can be seen in the fall in the sales of his *Natural Theology*. It had gone into twenty editions by 1820, and there were seven more by 1848; but after 1848 there seemed to be little demand for it, and it was not reissued until 1879 and then 'revised to harmonize with modern science', by F. le Gros Clark. Paley's was an harmonious universe, a living textbook of general revelation for all men to see, which was calm, ordered and dependable. There was little mystery, nothing to jar the clear mind. The thinking religious man by 1860 felt that this was facile, and its view of God left much to be desired. According to Leslie Stephen it became the fashion to speak of Paley and his mechanical religion with contempt, 'partly because of his utter inability to be obscure'.[10]

The reading habits of clergymen show how a difference in outlook developed. In a clerical lending library in Lincolnshire the commonest withdrawals in the period 1838–41 were systematic theology and doctrine. There was also an interest in Church history; the Church as a divine institution, of course, not an historical product. But by the end of the century there seemed to be little vogue for Church history, at least of the classical kind, and the preoccupation of the clergy was no longer systematics or doctrine, but the Bible, its history and criticism; and so the most frequent withdrawals in 1897–1901 were commentaries on scripture. (In 1897, as in 1838, hardly anyone, apparently, took out books on the philosophy of religion.)[11]

This change was a response to an alteration in Biblical studies as a whole. An example of the crop of new books about scripture available in 1897 was S. R. Driver's commentary on Deuteronomy, published two years earlier as part of the new *International Critical Commentary* series. Driver accepted the Graf-Wellhausen redating of the Old Testament and the probability that Deuteronomy corresponded to the law-book found in the temple in Josiah's reign, which had been much influenced by the prophetic understanding of Israelite religion. In other words, Moses was not the author of the book, and the prophets had preceded the law, and not vice-versa. In 1891, T. K. Cheyne's commentary on the Psalter held that David was not the author of most of the psalms; indeed, many of them were no older than two centuries before Christ. Other commentaries during these years showed that the redating of the Old Testament was part of a larger question about history generally. For some liberal theologians the whole of world history was the object of revelation – God revealing himself in the universal evolution of Spirit, or in the gradual disclosure of the immanent Trinity. That suggested that the Bible, strictly speaking, was not revelation but a record of, or response to, revelation. So God had 'two great books', the book of the Bible and the book of nature, which meant, inevitably, a revaluation of scripture's uniqueness and inspiration.[12] The relation of biblical revelation and universal history was a matter of great debate on the Continent, but its implications were clearly understood by some British scholars, notably William Robertson Smith. Smith saw Christ as the central point of all history, but his *Religion of the Semites* (1889) did not hide the fact that the Jews shared much in common with their non-Jewish neighbours in Old Testament times, and their religion had undergone much change and development.

'The bible is like any other book.' That principle was announced in *Essays and Reviews* by Jowett, and it summed up for many religious readers the heresy of the nineteenth century, the so-called secular hermeneutic of scripture. The fact that God's word had, nonetheless, been written in human language and obeyed the laws of grammar and syntax and that its texts had evolved and had been transmitted like other documents, had never been taken for the obvious truth that it was. The tools applied to other literary monuments surely had their use here. Toland, Lessing, Coleridge, even two bishops (Marsh of Ely, in 1818, and Hampden, later Bishop of Hereford, in 1833),[13] had said this much earlier, but its real import was not felt until the mid-nineteenth century. Needless to say it was the foundation stone of Schleiermacher's new outline of theology when it appeared in English in 1850: the New Testament critic, he said, was both bound to follow 'the same rules, and entitled to make use of the same means' as were applicable else-where in literary study.[14]

When put into practice, the principle had some far-reaching results. The two Cambridge scholars, F. J. A. Hort and B. F. Westcott, brought out a new text of the New Testament in 1881 which showed how faulty and of late date was the 'received text' on which the Authorized Version had been founded. Many of the thousands of alterations were minute, but twelve verses were lost from the end of Mark which now concluded with an apparently incomplete account of the resurrection, at verse eight. Mark received even more radical attention from other researchers. In 1835 Karl Lachmann, on the premise that gospel material evolved like other written material, held that Mark was nearer the original order of events than Matthew and Luke. At least one English journal quickly noted the logical consequence of this when in 1867 another German scholar, H. J. Holtzmann, proposed the theory of the priority of Mark – his was the first gospel and Matthew and Luke used him as their main source, altering as they thought fit, and adding material of their own. 'Markan priority' was a great step forward, unlocking a whole series of vistas into the meaning and purpose of the 'synoptic gospels', and much of it seemed obvious when the documents were laid side by side.

H. B. Wilson, who had already achieved notoriety as editor of *Essays and Reviews*, described Holtzmann's revolutionary work as a 'very temperate essay' on the present state of the gospel ques-tion,[15] but conservative readers thought differently. Mark now seemed a primitive author, whose deficiencies had to be made up by Matthew and Luke. The contradictions, inconsistencies, and actual mistakes, in all the 'sacred evangelists' were unsparingly exposed. Moreover, the theological criterion by which the Church had placed Matthew first in the canon was now displaced by an historical criterion. This reversal of the gospel chronology was as far-reaching in its implications as the change in the Old Testament chronology, in which the prophets came before the law. And where was the fourth gospel in all this? The 'spiritual gospel' of the fathers, Luther's favourite gospel, the ultimate authority for the divinity and uniqueness of Christ, suddenly changed status. Wilson, quoting F. C. Baur, held that John was a late second-century work, and its testimony questionable.

This, then, was the advent of the new or 'higher' criticism. In the event, most British biblical scholars drew back from any extreme application of the historical method, and conducted their exegesis with reverence. Even Jowett, in some ways the most radical of them all, retained the view of history of a man of letters, and seemed to be interested in literary effect rather than what happened for its own sake.[16] But the possibility of a biblical criticism free of Church control was always there. In no area was this better demonstrated than the 'quest for the historical Jesus'. The Christ of the creeds was secure in the churches, but when the gospels were treated as historical documents another figure appeared. He was the preacher of a universal religion which was larger than Christianity, and the property of all mankind and not simply the Church. He spoke not with the accents of divinity but of conscience, of the principle of private judgment, and of eternal moral truths.

As Ernest Renan portrayed him, he was the hero of an historical romance, and Christianity was 'love for Jesus' (his disciples 'loved him to madness'), an essentially humanist doctrine and not a supernatural one. Renan's *Vie de Jésus* went into eight editions in the year in which it was published, 1863, and an English translation was available by 1864. The sister work, on *The Apostles*, published in English in 1869, contrasted Jesus with his followers and saw the history of the Church as a record of 'treacheries to which the idea of Jesus will be exposed'. We would better understand how great the 'illustrious Nazarene' was by seeing how paltry were his disciples.[17] Other lives of Jesus followed in quick succession, once the market was established; the most popular example in English was written by F. W. Farrar in 1874, and though the author was an archdeacon and soon to be a dean, and a favourite preacher of the Queen's, his biography of Christ was a liberalizing work in which Jesus looked more like a Greek than a Jew and who, though he worked miracles, captured the imagination through the beauty of his character and his moral appeal. Farrar, the orthodox Anglican, had obviously learned from Renan. Farrar's Bampton Lectures in 1885, on the *History of Interpretation* suggested why it was left to the nineteenth century to produce such books about Jesus: only now, after centuries of mistaken exegesis, was a proper historical, contextual approach to the Bible a possibility.[18]

Accommodation and adjustment to biblical criticism was a slow process and, often, a painful one. The religious public needed a great deal of reassurance, and only a book like *Lux Mundi*, in 1889, because of the impeccable credentials of its authors, could safely suggest a lower level of inspiration in the Old Testament (the word 'myth' was used) and a fresh look at the question of historicity. Charles Gore, the editor of *Lux Mundi*, and his colleagues had realized that most people, however, were prepared for change, unwilling though they might be to admit it. Church- and chapel-goers were affected like everyone else by the sense of development and progress so strongly felt in the Victorian era – what Tennyson called the consciousness of being the 'heir of all the ages, in the foremost files of time'. It was difficult to resort to an a-historical theology if that was the case, particularly if you believed in the primacy of scripture and the implicit interest in foundations and origins which went with it.

The same need to bridge the gap between present experience and a past theology – this time the 'rational' theology of the previous century – explains another development in religious thought in Britain in this period. Thomas Arnold saw the reason for the change as early as 1843 and, appropriately, resorted to German to define it, 'It is what we call the *Time-Spirit* which is sapping the proof from miracles – it is the *Zeitgeist* itself.'[19] The atmosphere of official religion in the eighteenth century had been unfriendly towards emotion, 'enthusiasm', subjectivity. Locke's dictum about the claims of a cool head and a clear mind set the tone for the age: reason was natural revelation, and revelation was natural reason enlarged by a new set of discoveries communicated by God immediately, the truth of which, however, was vouched for by reason. 'So that he that takes away reason to make way for revel- ation puts out the light of both.' The works of Butler and Paley exemplified this attitude, and it lingered on in the account of Chris- tianity presented by Archbishop Whately, a formidable logician and scholar, in 1861.[20] There were obvious difficulties in such a theology which above all assumed that Christianity could be proved to be true.

In one aspect in particular this 'rational' religion became vulner- able. In the desire to present an external attestation of faith, Paley and others had given great weight to the miracles or 'evidences' of Christianity. Rather than their theological character, it was the 'scientific' nature of the proof for the miracles that was the interest: the honest inquirer, accepting that the gospels contained eye-witness accounts, and that the apostles did not mean to deceive, must believe in the miracles of Christ and, therefore, concede his supernatural status and the claim made for him. It was not even necessary (so some argued) that all the miracles of Jesus need be cited; the case could be supported on half a dozen only. There was certainly no need to refer to 'ecclesiastical miracles', i.e., those claimed for the saints, which the sturdy Protestant would suspect anyway.

The doubts raised by this evidential Christianity by the 1850s were not simply inspired by Hume or a rationalist critic of the gospels like Paulus, they rose from within. The fact was that to the churchman and nonchurchman alike, an externally attested Christianity on eighteenth-century lines seemed altogether too abstract, or facile, or simply irrelevant, in the changed atmosphere of Victorian Britain. This was an age of profound subjectivity, of a poetry of the heart, of an art which depicted the emotions, of a philosophy which searched for the meaning within. There need be nothing specifically religious about this, there was ample secular sentiment and rhapsodysing about the inner self; but religious men also felt it, and often felt it acutely. So the values which the divines of the previous century had rejected or relegated to the 'enthusiasts' made their return, sometimes spectacularly – hymns, sermons, tracts, celebrated mystery, inwardness, the life of the soul, the beauty of holiness. 'Heart speaking to heart', said Newman, that was the essential dialogue of religion. The heart was to be contrasted with the head, love with the intellect. In sermons preached while he was still an Anglican in 1843, Newman denied that any intellectual act was necessary for right faith besides itself.

> The safeguard of Faith is a right state of heart . . . we believe because we love . . . Why, o men, deface with your minute and arbitrary philosophy the simplicity, the reality, the glorious liberty of the inspired teaching?[21]

From another, very different, quarter came Schleiermacher's dictum, 'Religion resigns . . . all claim on anything that belongs either to science or morality.' The seat of religion was within, and that constituted its best explanation and defence.

However, to point out the wrongs of a mere evidential theology was one thing, to replace it with something more suitable was another. The danger of an appeal to the heart was a dualism which related the world of fact and sense to one part of human experience, and the world of value and spirit to another. At least the old theology claimed to integrate the two. The historical critics were aware of a similar difficulty. When Lessing in 1777 announced the need for proper historical inquiry, he also bequeathed a problem, the 'ugly wide ditch' between the 'incidental truths of history' and the 'necessary truths of reason'. The historical sense was an ambiguous gift. If everything was contingent, subject to the flux of historical change, where was certainty to be found? The obvious answer to some liberal theologians in the nineteenth century was to point to the conscience, or to some moral principle which was universal in application and eternal in scope. The words of Jesus, said Jowett, were of the most universal import. 'They do not relate to the circumstances of the time, but to the common life of all mankind.'[22] To cut the Gordian knot like that did not make the quest for an alternative to the evidential argument any easier. The period between 1860 and 1890 saw various attempts to answer the problem.

In *Essays and Reviews* Baden Powell addressed himself specifically to the evidences, on the grounds that the modern advocates of Paley 'betray an almost entire unconsciousness of the advance of opinion around them.' His own labours, as a distinguished scientist (Savilian Professor of Geometry at Oxford) and clergyman, were a lifelong attempt to evolve a true theology of creation in which God was perceived as the supreme mind in the universe, not, however, in terms of physical causes but moral ones. By 1860 his dislike of any arguments which appealed to miracles and divine intervention was extreme. He could see no solution to the problem except to believe that 'the more knowledge advances, the more it has been, and will be, acknowledged that Christianity, as a real religion, must be viewed apart from connection with physical things'. Faith concerned 'points of less definite character' and ended in 'such assurance as may be most satisfactory to each earnest individual inquirer's own mind'.[23] It was obvious that this was only an interim answer, but Powell died a few weeks after it appeared, and the fuller statement was never forthcoming.

In 1884 Frederick Temple, once a contributor to *Essays and Reviews*, and now Bishop of Exeter, returned to the problem, in the Bampton Lectures on *The Relations between Religion and Science*. At Oxford, Temple had been a pioneer in teaching Kant to undergraduates, and he saw the difficulty in the contrast between a 'world of mere phenomena' and a 'world of spirits', which meant that our scientific faculties imposed on us one belief, our spiritual faculties another. However, 'though the strictly spiritual in religion cannot be got out of phenomena at all', he went further than Powell: miracle, though rare, was possible, and our knowledge of science was still incomplete; and a spiritual purpose could be seen if the two worlds were considered together.[24] In *Lux Mundi* there was no article on the evidences, and the eighteenth-century reliance on a narrow interpretation of miracles was rejected. Faith did not need proof, but the source of faith was not in man's self-consciousness but in the activity of God immanent in the world. 'You can no more shut up faith to the compartment of feeling than reason to the compartment of the intellect.'[25]

To withdraw from a world of proof and mere factual knowledge must affect the doctrines of revelation, and this was the next question to which Victorian theology on its voyage of discovery addressed itself. Without going to the lengths of denying 'this fiction of an external revelation', as some of the authors of *Essays and Reviews* did, many felt increasingly the need for a restatement. Some were aware of the problem of knowledge raised by Kant, which had serious implications for the traditional approach, and focused attention in particular on the part which man played in the understanding of revelation. One of the prime agents in unsettlement was Maurice, from his first book, *The Kingdom of Christ*, in 1838, onwards. For Maurice, revelation was not static or propositional, it was personal, historic, and it must be universal in scope. He saw it as an act of love arising out of the life of the Trinity. Others in the Maurice circle took up the question of how man's apprehension of revelation was conditioned by his growth and development.

Enlarging on this theme Westcott spoke of the finite and unfinished nature of doctrinal propositions. 'As long as experience is incomplete, there can be no finality in the definition of doctrine.' The change from earlier ideas could be seen in two contrasted statements: in 1865 H. P. Liddon proclaimed that 'a particular intellectual presentation of Truth may be modified, but nothing of the kind is possible with any article of the Christian Faith.' J. R. Illingworth in 1889 thought very differently: 'Christian truth, in virtue of its very vitality . . . must be for ever outgrowing the clothes with which successive ages invest it.'[26]

By 1846, in his Boyle lectures, Maurice was examining how his belief in the universal revelation of divine order affected one's understanding of the non-Christian religions. Christ, as the root of humanity, had taken the nature of man, not that of a European only. So all man's religion was evidence of God's work – 'wonderful testimony to be borne from the ends of the earth' – and one could truly speak of the Mohammedan, Hindu, and Buddhist sides of Christianity, and the lessons to be derived from these great religions.

> We are debtors to all these in a double sense . . . we owe them the deepest gratitude if they have led us to ask ourselves whether there is any faith, and what kind of faith it is, which must belong, not to races or nations, but to mankind.[27]

Maurice's was a theological assessment, not simply a liberal theologian's belief that universal principles of morality and justice transcended all religions, and it was not widely understood or copied; but the lectures were evidence of a new awareness of the phenomenon of man's religion. That interest increased as the century wore on, in the work of Rowland Williams, Max Müller, Monier Williams, and others. Jowett, in his commentary on St Paul's epistles, spoke of the change in theology which must follow on the increasing knowledge of the religions of mankind.[28] Boyd-Carpenter's Bampton Lectures on the *Permanent Element in Religion* (1888) envisaged the study of comparative religion, a recommendation made more positively in Robertson Smith's *Religion of the Semites*.

To allow that other religions might be a medium for God's disclosure of himself was a profound revulsion from the traditional teaching that they were the product of the Fall. In other ways also the rewriting of doctrine in these years began to show the influence of a wider interpretation of revelation, and the subjective matter of man's role in relating it to his own experience. Thus, by the 1850s, in the name of morality, men and women began to question the accepted 'formal' theory of the Atonement. This had stood the West well since Anselm in the eleventh century, and it had received a magnificent expression in Calvin's *Institutes* which was rigorously argued and carefully related to scripture. But a series of works found its substitutionary ideas indefensible or lacking in some way;

there were objections from McLeod Campbell (*The Nature of the Atonement*, 1856), Maurice, Horace Bushnell, and others still later. The stress on sin, on punishment and expiation, seemed to be excessive, and the theory was too external; too little was said about man's response. From another angle, A. M. Fairbairn criticized the notion of the impassibility of God in the traditional teaching, while Arthur Lyttelton in *Lux Mundi* objected to the isolation of the truth of the Atonement from other aspects of doctrine. Maurice's *Theological Essays* in 1853 loosened another stone in the traditional structure – the doctrine of the everlasting punishment of sinners. Maurice opposed such an understanding as unworthy of God; so did F. W. Farrar in a celebrated series of sermons in Westminster Abbey in 1877; and others followed. A more liberal and less offensive understanding of original sin was another preoccupation in these years.

The long decline of Calvinism in the nineteenth century ('that awful and immoral system', as *Lux Mundi* described it) has often been commented on, but it should be understood carefully. It was not so much Calvin whom the Victorians rejected – often a crude version, anyway, of what Calvin was alleged to have taught – but what he stood for, the idea of a coherent and essentially objective and external body of truth. The damage was not simply to the outlying parts but to the interlocking and harmonious nature of the system; no part could be withdrawn or altered without changing the balance of the whole structure, and by 1890 there seemed to be signs of internal collapse. It was not surprising that there were various attempts by the liberals to relax clergymen's subscription to the Articles and tests of belief. A controversy over the Athanasian creed engaged the convocations of the Church of England in the early 1870s, and it was realized that the damnatory clauses in the creed no longer had the force (sending offenders to hell) that their framers believed; they were to be understood instead like similar warnings in scripture. 'Moreover, the Church doth not herein pronounce judgment on any particular person or persons, God alone being the judge of all.'[29] That disavowal was noted by various commentators.

The theological inheritance of the past also faced nineteenth-century churchmen with the problem of adjusting to 'science'. Cartoons of bewhiskered bishops ridiculing an ape-like Darwin for his theory of natural selection, the 'clash' between Huxley and

Wilberforce at the British Association meeting in Oxford in 1860, Tyndall's presidential address at the British Association in 1874, attacking the claims of an 'absolute knowledge' (theology) which sought to control science – all this is material for the usual scenario of the Victorian 'war between science and religion'. In actual fact, the truth is rather more complicated than this. The theology of the eighteenth century bequeathed among other things a belief in the fixity of nature, which was seen as a vast mechanism ruled by laws, the processes of which could be traced by induction, and suggested a great designer. This was the familiar world of natural theology which has already been mentioned, and which the young Darwin perfectly exemplified: he 'hardly ever admired a book more than Paley's *Natural Theology.*'[30]

It was Darwin's recourse to natural selection which brought this world into doubt, destroying the possibility of ultimate certainty through inductive inference, and the fixity of biological species. Whether, however, this was a challenge to original Christian belief, and not simply to a particular phase in theological evolution, was open to question. It was possible to argue that Baconian induction and a belief in special creation were a relatively late development in the Christian view of science, and a return to a patristic and immanentist understanding of nature was more orthodox and biblical. This was the view of Aubrey Moore and others, later to be enshrined by him in *Lux Mundi*. Thus it was perfectly possible to be a Darwinian and also a conservative. On the other hand, one could also embrace evolutionary ideas in the service of a larger whole, of that progressive and organic view of reality proposed in the Idealist philosophy which followed Kant. In that case, to be an 'evolutionist' was also to be a liberal theologian. (We have already seen this operating in the Bampton Lectures of Temple in 1884.) Whichever solution one adopted (and the first was nearer to Darwin's own world of thought than the second), the 'warfare' or 'conflict' between science and religion was unnecessary. Indeed, one could claim that Darwinism afforded theology the possibility of reform and renewal just as much as in science it made great new advances in understanding possible. Moore surely meant this, as well as a good deal else, when he said that 'Darwinism under the disguise of a foe did the work of a friend.'[31] Victorian theology, in its process of reconstruction and change, would have had to challenge, sooner or later, the 'exploded scientific theory', as Moore called it, on which eighteenth-century theology rested, and Darwin came as an aid to this. Thus the change came about not simply because of pressure from outside. Part of the 'romanticism' of nineteenth-century theology was an attempt to return to the past where the springs of a truer understanding of nature were believed to be present.

However, Moore spoke from the vantage point of 1889 when the question could be seen in a clearer perspective. In the years immediately after the publication of the *Origin of Species* the quest for theological renewal, to which the new science would contribute, took second place. Churchmen felt insecure, familiar landmarks were disappearing, and the Paleyian teleology was in ruins. Their uncertainty was reflected in a concentration on the internal doctrinal consequences of evolutionary theory, which seemed far more dangerous than the supposed collision with Archbishop Ussher's chronology (the creation of the world in 4004 BC), or a literal understanding of Genesis 1 and 2. The problem was the Bible's own pre-Darwinian point of view, which the apostles, and Christ himself, shared. Thus, the theory of 'corporate personality', as it is now known, had to be reassessed. St Paul's theology depended on an antithesis between the first Adam and the second which was admittedly a sophisticated matter but seemed to require the actual historic existence of the first man. As a by no means unintelligent reviewer in the High Church newspaper, *The Guardian*, asked in 1860, if man originated not from one but many sources,

> what becomes of the headship of our race in Adam and again in the antitype, the second Adam? What becomes of the Incarnation in all its deeper bearings and significances? What of the Atonement? . . . What of our Justification? What of the general resurrection, if we be in no real sense members of a risen Head?[32]

Darwin was probably surprised that such implications could be read into his work.

The theory of evolution seemed to undermine Christology from another angle. How could Christ be definitive, the norm against which everything was measured, if he belonged to an earlier stage in man's growth? Renan, having read Darwin, pointed out sensibly that Christ did not know mathematics or geometry, he did not speak Latin or Greek, and he was unversed in philosophy. Renan's solution, that he was a countryman at heart and his teaching reflected a pastoral idyll, the beauty of an innocent agrarian life, hardly offered a satisfactory substitute.

Many churchmen, therefore, despaired of a reconciliation with the new science. Much ingenuity and effort was spent in harmonizing Genesis and geology, and reinterpreting the 'days' of creation, and so forth; the writers of *Essays and Reviews* dismissed them as childish and futile. The religious public had forgotten the counsel of Newman, writing in his Anglican days when the unease about science began to be felt: Newman spoke of the age being

> all light; therefore the Church is bound to be – we will not say dark, for that is an ill-omened, forbidding word – but we will say deep, impenetrable, occult in her views and character . . . We are now assailed by science, and we must protect ourselves by mystery . . . mystery fits in with this age exactly; it suits it; it is just what the age wants.[33]

The 'melancholy, long withdrawing roar' of the sea of faith, of which Matthew Arnold spoke, supplies the background to the phenomenon of theological reaction in the period, of which some examples have already been given. If churchmen had simply to contend with the assaults of an atheistic state, or a changed university establishment, while remaining unaffected themselves, the story would have been different. A unified Christianity would have met the forces of unbelief head on. As it was, a great deal of religious effort was expended in heresy hunts and trials of belief within the churches. These were encouraged by party politics – High Churchmen used 'liberalism' as a stick to beat the Broad Churchmen and settle old scores, and Evangelicals used other tactics for their own advantage – but they were also motivated by the fear of the enemy within the gates, in one's congregation, or home, or even in one's soul. Bishop Wilberforce bewailed having to deal with unbelievers (i.e., liberal clergymen) in his own diocese of Oxford, but he also experienced the personal crises of faith within his own family, as his three brothers in turn left the Evangelical certainty of their upbringing and succumbed to the lure of Rome. Finally, in 1868, his daughter became a Roman Catholic. Others found beloved sons and daughters turning to unbelief, and feared the whisperings of the infidel even nearer at hand. Indeed, the story of Victorian religion is sometimes better told in these spiritual odysseys than in accounts of theological movements and intellectual developments: the apologias and biographies of the Newman brothers, Maurice, James Martineau, and others, were popular reading with their contemporaries, who found reflected in them their own internal struggles in the quest for faith and security.

This personal involvement explains better than almost anything else the sheer scale of Victorian religious reaction. Otherwise, one might be tempted to dismiss it as mere bigotry or even a pathological phenomenon. It certainly rivals the excesses of the worst periods of Church history. Monster petitions were circulated, 11,000 laymen signed one against *Essays and Reviews*, 7,000 another at the height of the controversy over the Athanasian creed; effigies of offending professors were burnt in public; enormous profits were made by publishers from controversial books and pamphlets – 400 such works appeared between 1860 and 1864. The reaction produced some astonishing examples of intellectual crudity: thus, J. W. Burgon, fellow of New College, Oxford, proclaimed from the university pulpit in 1861, a doctrine of complete literalism, to the effect that the books, sentences, words, syllables – 'aye, and the very letters' – of the sacred text were absolutely infallible.[34] As a result of this, in inverse proportion to the growth of liberal ideas in the country at large, many churchmen between 1850 and 1880 became more conservative as they grew older, and abandoned the freer convictions of earlier days. Fright and panic completed the retreat for others.

Reaction was the dark side of this internal struggle. It cannot be disregarded in any assessment of Victorian religion, and as it developed it actually affected the form and character of the churches. In the Church of England in the 1860s conservative bishops were appointed, and the complexion of the episcopate was changed, according to bishop Tait, a friend of Temple, and other liberals.[35] Church support for the Tory party was canvassed by Disraeli in the 1865 election on the grounds that they were the better defenders of the faith. Pattison held that before the appearance of *Essays and Reviews* the Church was poised to effect a final reconciliation between Christianity and science, faith and philosophy, but the tide had entirely changed (Pattison's diagnosis could, of course, be challenged).[36] The chief casualty in this process was the Broad Church party which by the 1870s was extinct. Alleged representatives of the Broad Church like Maurice and Jowett (who actually held little in common), were hounded for their beliefs; Maurice lost his chair at King's College, London in 1853, as a result of one such campaign.

In the Scottish churches, a *cause célèbre* was the dismissal in 1881, on the grounds of unsound teaching, of Robertson Smith, from his Old Testament professorship at the Free Church College in Aberdeen. Earlier, John Tulloch and George Gilfillan both experienced opposition for their criticism of traditional theology for its dogmatic and objective basis, rather than an approach that was more empirical and dynamic in accordance with the spirit of the age. The radical Welsh clergyman, Rowland Williams, Vice-Principal of St David's College, Lampeter, was condemned by a Welsh bishop in 1857, and after his move to an English parish the clergy petitioned another bishop to dismiss him for his views on the inspiration of scripture. His living was actually legally revoked but restored under appeal. In the English Free Churches the Congregationalist 'higher critic', Samuel Davidson, was forced out of his post at Lancashire Independent College in 1857, and was still the object of odium twenty years later. The Congregationalist *British Quarterly Review*, which openly admitted its 'loathing' for Renan and others of his sort, still held to the Mosaic authorship of the Pentateuch in 1884, and its attacks on Wellhausen were echoed by the Methodist *London Quarterly Review* as late as 1890.[37] However, a new spirit in the Free Churches was signalled by the publication of R. F. Horton's *Inspiration and the Bible* in 1888, and the work of the Methodist scholars W. T. Davison and A. S. Peake.

In the church of Rome the movement of reaction benefitted the Ultramontanes as against the 'liberals'. Thus, H. E. Manning, Cardinal Archbishop of Westminster, who had started life as an evangelical Anglican, became a fervent supporter of Pius IX in his crusade against modern error. Manning would doubtless have agreed with W. G. Ward, also a former Anglican, who declared his wish to have a papal bull on his breakfast table each morning, and it was Manning who was a fierce critic of *Essays and Reviews*, as indicating the inroads of unbelief in the established religion. (It would not have escaped his notice that the condemnation of *Essays and Reviews* by the convocations of the Church of England, for containing teaching contrary to that received by the Church of

England 'in common with the whole Catholic Church of Christ', appeared in the same year, 1864, as Pius IX's 'syllabus of errors' which denied that the 'Roman pontiff can and ought to reconcile himself and reach agreement with progress, liberalism, and modern civilization'.) Manning's Ultramontanism saw in the Pope, stripped of his possessions by the Italian *Risorgimento*, and forced to retreat into the Vatican, the symbol of Christ's threatened Church, at odds with a hostile and irreligious world. Father Faber, as another convert, gave a psychic, mystical quality to Pius IX, in sermons on *Devotion to the Pope* and *Devotion to the Church*, and expressed in his appallingly sentimental (but highly popular) poetry the emotional force of Ultramontanism.[38] For such minds, the Pope, as a prisoner in the Vatican, could be likened to Christ the prisoner in the tabernacle. Newman said that he knew of nothing more calculated to make him into an infidel, but Newman was suspected of liberalism; and others, like Lord Acton, who advocated in *The Rambler* the cause of an intellectual Catholicism in the modern world, were in bad odour with the hierarchy. *The Rambler* was succeeded by the *Home and Foreign Review*, which ceased publication in 1864 to avoid ecclesiastical censure.

Pius's successors continued this trend in which the Church's authority was centralized and the papacy strengthened to combat the enemy. Leo XIII brought Catholic philosophy under the supreme control of St Thomas Aquinas' teaching, against Kant and modern tendencies of thought, and Pius X silenced the 'Modernist' movement which had among its alleged leaders the English Catholic George Tyrrell. Up to the second Vatican Council, indeed, the Roman Catholic Church was a citadel church with a mentality shaped by the crisis of religion in the nineteenth century. But it might be said that, to a lesser degree, all the major denominations in Britain were touched by this mentality. The legacy was a conservative wing throughout the Church which has persisted until today.

Reaction notwithstanding, religious thought in Britain in 1900 looked very different from its form in 1800. An instance of this was the vogue in some quarters for the teachings of the German scholar Albrecht Ritschl (1822–89). Westcott and Hort knew of his work on the New Testament and early Christian history. His great book on *The Doctrine of Justification and Reconciliation* was translated into English in 1872, and several studies were devoted to him, including a large volume in 1899 by A. E. Garvie.[39] Young men from the Scottish universities were sent to study the Ritschlian theology as it had developed under Harnack and Herrmann. The attraction of Ritschl was a 'theology without metaphysics', without talk of the 'five proofs' or external verification, free of reliance on miracle, rejecting scholasticism and its pre-Kantian view of knowledge. The closed formal nature of theology was a thing of the past, it must be more free and open. The Ritschlians claimed to make full use of biblical criticism in elucidating the historic Jesus and his ethical ideal of the kingdom of God.

In other quarters, the change from the old ways could be summed up in one word, immanence. Traditional theology had placed too much emphasis on God's transcendence and had seen its own province, consequently, in the light of an *imperium* or dominance over human knowledge. In *Lux Mundi* the approach was very different. When coupled with Gore's Bamptons on *The Incarnation of the Son of God*, a persuasive case for a theology of divine immanence in the modern world was the result – indeed Moore in a striking phrase spoke of a 'higher pantheism'.

The authors of *Lux Mundi* admitted that theology needed 'disencumbering, reinterpreting, explaining', without jettisoning the past (there were 200 patristic references and many respectful allusions to Aquinas, Butler, and others). They used the language of contemporary religious philosophy in speaking of the moral will as the ultimate and elemental self, going back behind reason. Consequently Christianity was not tied to any particular intellectual position and would always be engaged in a search for the suitable expression and formulation of its beliefs. Faith could not be described as if it were a theory, and the scientific temper was impotent in matters of moral feeling and practice. The 'knowledge' vouchsafed in faith was entirely different from scientific knowledge. The titles of God used in metaphysics, Infinite, Absolute, First Cause, etc., had no meaning for the religious consciousness.

What was significant about *Lux Mundi* was the extent to which Gore and his colleagues admitted the province of modern thought. The nineteenth century, they held, was not simply another epoch of thought while the Church remained unchanged; its peculiar principle affected the very being of the Church within.

Great scientific discoveries . . . are not merely facts to be assimilated, they involve new ways of looking at things. And this has been pre-eminently the case with the law of Evolution . . . Evolution is in the air. It is the category of the age . . . a necessary consequence of our wider field of comparison. We cannot place ourselves outside it, or limit the scope of its operation.[40]

A particular instance of this was the Christological problem mentioned earlier. Gore held that evolution did not simply challenge the authenticity of scripture, it made possible a new understanding of Christian truth. Christ thought that Moses *had* written the Pentateuch, but this was not because he was fallible or incorrect, but because 'the Incarnation is a self-emptying of God'. The Christology demanded by evolution must be a kenotic one. Christ chose not to know, 'He *used* human nature, its relation to God, its conditions of experience, its growth in knowledge, its limitations of knowledge'.

Other contributors spoke of the renewal in theology which was now in being. Darwin had forced us to realize that God was either nowhere in creation, or he was everywhere. So the coming of evolutionary theory was providential. 'It remains then for Christianity to claim the new truth and meet the new demand by a fearless reassertion of its doctrine of God.'[41]

What *Lux Mundi* and similar restatements did for the end of nineteenth-century theology should not be exaggerated. The modern reader will not find much evidence of an ecumenical vision of theology, of Christians in an altered world being drawn together to discover the common sources of faith. Here, perhaps, the loss of the Broad Church party was felt most keenly, for it had envisaged such a possibility and saw great hopes in a united liberal scholarship. Rather, what one finds in this final phase is a theology of transition; its achievement was to provide the conditions for the continued development and vitality of theology in the twentieth century.

NOTES

1   M. C. Church, *Life and Letters of Dean Church*, sec. edn. London, Macmillan, 1897, p. 202.
2   B. Jowett, *The Epistles of St. Paul*, sec. edn. London, 1859, vol. II, p. 519.

3   H. T. Buckle, *History of Civilisation in England*, new edn. London, 1904, vol. III, pp. 484–5.
4   Figures in E. Royle, *Victorian Infidels*, Manchester University Press, 1974, pp. 300–1.
5   Owen Chadwick, *The Mind of the Oxford Movement*, London, A. & C. Black, 1960, p. 79.
6   *Essays and Reviews*, eighth edn. London, Longman Green, 1861, pp. 254–329.
7   Parliamentary Debates, vol. 176, p. 1551.
8   L. E. Elliott-Binns, *English Thought 1860–1900. The Theological Aspect*, London, Longman Green, 1956, p. 339.
9   *Essays and Reviews*, pp. 286–97.
10 M. L. Clarke, *Paley: Evidences for the Man*, London, SPCK, 1974, p. 134.
11 Owen Chadwick, *The Victorian Church*. Part II, London, A. & C. Black, 1970, pp. 60 and 108–9.
12 So B. Jowett, F. W. Farrar, A. F. Kirkpatrick; see A. F. Kirkpatrick, *The Divine Library of the Old Testament*, London, 1891, p. 105.
13 Ieuan Ellis, *Seven Against Christ*, Leiden, E. J. Brill, 1980, pp. 310–11.
14 F. D. E. Schleiermacher, *Brief Outline of the Study of Theology*, Edinburgh, 1850, pp. 137, 143.
15 *Westminster Review*, new series, vol. XXXII, October 1867, p. 542.
16 J. B. Bury, quoted in T. W. Heyck, *The Transformation of Intellectual Life in Victorian England*, London, Croom Helm, 1982, p. 146.
17 E. Renan, *The Apostles*, London, Trübner, 1869, p. 78.
18 F. W. Farrar, *The History of Interpretation*, London, Macmillan, 1886, pp. vii, xxv, 328 ff.
19 A. P. Stanley, *Life and Correspondence of Thomas Arnold*, eighth edn London, 1858, vol. 1, p. 252.
20 R. Whately, *Dr. Paley's Works. A Lecture*, London, 1861.
21 Owen Chadwick, *The Mind of the Oxford Movement*, pp. 91–2.
22 *Essays and Reviews*, pp. 413, 428.
23 Ibid., pp. 128, 144.
24 F. Temple, *The Relations between Religion and Science*, London, Macmillan, 1884, pp. 41, 59 f., 62.
25 *Lux Mundi*, tenth edn. London, John Murray, 1890, p. 76.
26 L. E. Elliott-Binns, op. cit. p. 221.
27 F. D. Maurice, *The Religions of the World*, sixth edn London, Macmillan, 1886, pp. 211, 241, 244.
28 B. Jowett, op. cit. vol. II, p. 186.
29 F. Warre Cornish, *A History of the English Church in the Nineteenth Century*, London, Macmillan, 1910, vol. II, p. 166.

30 J. R. Moore, *The Post-Darwinian Controversies*, Cambridge University Press, 1979, p. 309. I am greatly indebted to Dr Moore's work in this section.
31 *Lux Mundi*, p. 99.
32 The *Guardian*, February 1860, p. 134.
33 Ieuan Ellis, op. cit. p. 221.
34 J. W. Burgon, *Inspiration and Interpretation*, Oxford, 1861, p. 76.
35 Ieuan Ellis, op. cit. p. 168.
36 *National Review*, January 1863, p. 197.
37 *British Quarterly Review*, vol. XXXVIII, 1863, pp. 207ff., 304; vol. LXXIX, 1884, pp. 115–43, and W. B. Glover, *Evangelical Nonconformists and Higher Criticism in the Nineteenth Century*, London, Independent Press, 1954, pp. 44ff., 110, 176.
38 Cf. Anthony Archer, *The Two Catholic Churches*, London, SCM Press, 1986, pp. 22ff.
39 A. E. Garvie, *The Ritschlian Theology*, second ed. Edinburgh, T. & T. Clark, 1902, pp. 26, 31.
40 *Lux Mundi*, pp. 30, 47, 65, 191.
41 Ibid. pp. 102, 360.

BIBLIOGRAPHY

In addition to the works cited in the Notes see also:

Chadwick, Owen, *The Secularization of the European Mind in the Nineteenth Century*, Cambridge University Press, 1975.

Cowling, M., *Religion and Public Doctrine in Modern England*, Vol. I, Cambridge University Press, 1985.

Cupitt, D., *The Sea of Faith*, London, BBC Publications, 1984.

Jay, Elisabeth, *Faith and Doubt in Victorian Britain*, London, Macmillan, 1986.

Kent, John H. S., *The End of the Line?*, London, SCM Press, 1982.

Mozley, J. K. *Some Tendencies in British Theology*, London, SPCK, 1951.

Reardon, B.M.G., *From Coleridge to Gore*, London, Longman, 1971.

Rogerson, John, *Old Testament Criticism in the Nineteenth Century*, London, SPCK, 1984.

Vidler, A. R., *The Church in an Age of Revolution*, London, Pelican, 1961.

CHAPTER THREE

East Comes West

Terence Thomas

In the nineteenth century the Christian religion, as we have seen in Chapter Two, was facing challenges from various aspects of modernity. In addition to these forces of a broadly secular nature there were other challenges which were religious in nature and came from older and alien forms of religion and culture. They were a challenge especially for Christian apologists and propagandists, including those engaged in the missionary work of the churches. In saying that the East came West I am referring to a movement of knowledge rather than of people. For reasons of space the East will, in the main, be confined to India, remembering that in the period we are dealing with India was possibly pre-eminently the East as far as most people in Britain were concerned. This movement of knowledge occurred for a variety of reasons. First, there is the influence of the Enlightenment, especially on the continent of Europe with philosophers such as Schopenhauer taking a strong interest in Hindu philosophy. It became fashionable in certain quarters to study Eastern philosophies. Second, as far as Britain especially was concerned, there was the expansion in trade and imperialism which brought with it obligations as well as benefits, obligations to learn something about the new empire. Beginning in the 1870s the Glasgow publishers Trübner & Co. published over sixty titles in their 'Oriental Series'. *The Times* in reviewing the series had this to say:

A knowledge of the commonplace, at least, of Oriental literature, philosophy and religion is as necessary to the general
reader of the present day as an acquaintance with the Latin
and Greek classics was a generation or two ago. Immense
strides have been made within the present century in these
branches of learning; Sanskrit has been brought within the
range of accurate philology, and its valuable ancient literature
thoroughly investigated . . . but the results of all the scholarship that has been devoted to these subjects have been almost
inaccessible to the public because they were contained for
the most part in learned or expensive works, or scattered
throughout the numbers of scientific journals. Messrs.
Trübner & Co., in a spirit of enterprise which does them
infinite credit, have determined to supply the constantly-
increasing want, and to give in a popular or, at least, a comprehensive form, all this mass of knowledge to the world.[1]

In the early 1870s, R. W. Church, Dean of St Paul's Cathedral,
was responsible for introducing a series of evening lectures in the
Cathedral on Buddhism, Islam and Hinduism. The latter he delivered himself under the title *The Sacred Poetry of Early Religions*.[2]
He admitted to speaking on matters about which he had no first-
hand knowledge but acknowledged his debt to scholars such as
Friedrich Max Müller who, in essays published in *The Times* and
other widely read periodicals, had made his readers familiar with
his most important achievements. This is the position at the beginning of the final quarter of the nineteenth century. When the
century opened matters were rather different.

At the beginning of the century Islam was the main challenge to
Christianity as it had been for many centuries. It was the only
religion which had challenged Christianity both politically and
ideologically on the Continent. On the other hand many Europeans
had a highly romantic view of Islam. The political threat had
receded and by the opening of the nineteenth century, Christianity
under the imperial banner was in the ascendancy in many lands
where Islam had hitherto ruled unchallenged and Islam itself was
undergoing a crisis of faith and identity. The volume of literature
attacking Islam, however, seemed to continue unabated. There is
another side to the encounter with Islam by this time in that it had
become an object of academic study along with studies in Arabic

73

and Persian. Although much of the material available was the result of translations from Danish and French, the Qur'an had been available in a good English translation – the work of George Sale – since 1734.[3]

As the century opens we are faced with a fair body of knowledge about other religions in addition to Islam. The two most obvious ones were Hinduism and Buddhism. By this time many people were disregarding Dr Samuel Johnson's view that 'There are two objects of curiosity, the Christian world, and the Mahometan world: all the rest may be considered as barbarous.'[4] Indeed there must have been many who would have agreed with Matthew Arnold that 'The wise man knows that Mahometanism, and Brahmanism and Buddhism are not what the Missionaries call them; and he knows too, how really unfit the Missionaries are to cope with them.' On the other hand there were missionaries who were able to cope with these religions. One of the first two non-Roman Catholic missionaries to enter India, Bartholomew Ziegenbalg, a German, made a detailed study of the religious beliefs of South Indians only to be told by his superiors in Europe that his task was to root out Hinduism in India, and not propagate heathen superstition in Europe.[5] There is a diversity of responses to the knowledge of these religions. Some took the line that they were totally devoid of anything approaching the truth as found in Christianity, others, in a fashion which appears quite astonishing to us today, found remnants of the earlier influence of the Hebrew patriarchs over a large area of Asia. William Jones, jurist and great Orientalist, was one of those who laboured hard to reconcile Hindu chronology with that of the Bible. Traces of such Christian symbols as the Trinity were claimed for Buddhism and Chinese religion. As the century progressed many of the speculations of the end of the eighteenth century had to be rapidly jettisonned and more rational examination began. Generally speaking, the more intellectual aspects of Hinduism and Buddhism were viewed quite sympathetically while the idolatrous aspects of both religions were generally condemned, with only an occasional liberal appreciation of the sacramental view of the use of idols or images expressed.

Much of the story of the increased interest in other religions in the nineteenth century is as yet unresearched let alone written about. A few important landmarks are regarded as significant. Among the lesser events given regular attention are the lectures of

F. D. Maurice, *On the Religions of the World* (1846)[6] while the greatest single event is probably the translation and publication of *The Sacred Books of the East* under the editorship of Friedrich Max Müller, from 1879 onwards.[7] The picture as we have it has many blank areas which need to be filled in though in this chapter we can still only achieve a bare sketch.[8]

The literature we shall examine is divided into two main types. There is the apologetic type in which the intention is to prove the supremacy of Christianity over other religions. Such apologetic material divides into two sub-types, one of a rather polemical nature, the other of a more eirenic nature. The former is based on a fairly conservative approach to Christian belief, the latter tends to come from the more liberal attitude to Christian belief. Both kinds of apologetic, which had been directed almost exclusively against Islam for many centuries, were now directed in addition against Hinduism especially and to a lesser extent against Buddhism. There is surprisingly little literature directed at Judaism as a living religion, in spite of the increasing number of adherents in Britain as the century went on. Judaism received much attention in the popular press, in magazines and periodicals,[9] but in the kind of literature of a specifically religious, and scholarly, kind such as we will examine in this chapter, it would appear that Judaism was, on the whole, marginalized in the nineteenth century, and was not considered as an important object of concern for the Christian apologist.

The second type was the literature on religion of a scientific nature which had been growing as the century wore on. By that is meant an objective study of religions free of credal or confessional pressures. (Of course such studies were often made to serve the missionary demands of the churches.) The earlier material for the most part is simply a presentation of information and some analysis of the information. True, as has been suggested already, some of the analysis was anything but scientific, but as we shall see, scholars were coming to grips with the material and by the second half of the century were giving us results which have served us well to this day.

The literature shows a considerable leap in understanding between the final quarter of the eighteenth century and the 1830s and another leap between the 1830s and the 1860s and 1870s. The results of the earlier studies are found in monographs and in the transactions of journals of learned societies such as the Royal

Asiatic Society and the Asiatic Society of Bengal founded by William Jones within months of his arrival in Calcutta in 1783. Publications included *Asiatic Researches* and *Calcutta Review*. This storehouse of information has recently been referred to, rather unkindly to my mind, as 'largely bits and pieces of information and misinformation about other religions reported by travellers and missionaries.'[10] Though much of the work was done by amateurs they were very gifted amateurs. The names included British, French, German and, very occasionally, Indian scholars.

In addition to the two main categories of literature there was the unusual, occasionally eccentric, but in many ways prophetic, contribution.

The transmission of the information and the reporting of the studies took a variety of forms. In 1833 The Society for the Diffusion of Useful Knowledge began to publish *The Penny Cyclopaedia*, which ran to twenty-seven hefty volumes. The article on Buddhism in Volume 5 (1836) was one of the sources of F. D. Maurice's information. The *Cyclopaedia* contained articles which showed the state of knowledge of other religions at the time. In the case of Hinduism such knowledge is found in a lengthy entry on Hindustan, with excellent sections on philosophy and religion, including the caste system. In the entry under 'Mohammed, Abul Kasem Ibn Abdollah' we are given a brief biography of the Prophet, the state of Arabia before his rise and a brief treatment of the 'principles' of Islam, 'whose precepts even now are zealously followed from the Ganges to the Atlantic by more than a hundred and twenty millions of people'. Each entry though presented in popular form shows considerable scholarship on the part of the author. The sources of information are carefully noted and advice on further, more detailed sources are also given. The sources include French and German authors, sometimes in translation, as well as native English authors. While the authors of the *Cyclopaedia* articles show their dependence for much of their work on others they sometimes show their own competence by engaging in discussion of disputed knowledge such as that surrounding the dates of the Buddha. While Dr Pritchard, the author of this entry according to Maurice, comes down on the side of a date much earlier than that acknowledged today, or even by T. W. Rhys Davids forty years later, he avoids some of the wilder speculation of the previous generation.[11]

Pritchard is well aware of the poor state of knowledge of Buddhism at the time:

> Though much has been written upon Buddhism, a critical investigation of its origin, its system of doctrines, and the history of its diffusion among so large a portion of mankind, is still a desideratum. Hardly any of the original authentic documents, which were written in Sanskrit, have yet been fully examined, and the information which we now possess respecting its dogmas is almost exclusively derived from sources of secondary rank. We think it right, therefore, to warn our readers not to receive with too implicit faith the statements respecting Buddhism, which we shall endeavour to condense within the limits of the present article.[12]

Two works written early in the century are quite different in their style and approach but both are sympathetic towards Islam and go to great lengths to vindicate the work of the Prophet and the resulting history. The earlier of the works is by the Revd Charles Forster, a Rector of Sisted in the Church of England. In 1829 he published *Mahometanism Unveiled*, being 'an inquiry, in which that arch-heresy, its diffusion and continuance are examined on a new principle tending to confirm the evidences . . . of the Christian faith.' On the surface this appears to be just another apologia for the supremacy of Christianity. That it is not is evidenced by the way it was attacked by those claiming an orthodox defence of Christianity.

The cause of the attack was Forster's defence of Islam as a religion which existed according to the will of God. His argument was that as Christianity was descended from Judaism through Abraham's son Jacob, so Islam was descended from Abraham's son Ishmael. By the terms of the

> prophetic promise to Abraham . . . a blessing is annexed to the posterity of each; and on Ishmael, as well as on Isaac, this blessing is pronounced, because he was Abraham's seed, and as a special mark of the divine favour. (Gen. 17:20; 21:13) This last consideration is worth attending to; since a promise to Ishmael, thus connected by Jehovah himself with his descent from the father of the faithful, seems to lead the mind naturally beyond the idea of a mere temporal fulfilment. *Some sufficient*

fulfilment we are certainly authorised and bound to expect for each branch of the original promise.[13]

As if this view of the origins of both religions would not anger the 'orthodox' sufficiently he goes on to argue that they should coexist until the day of 'consummation spoken of in Scripture prophecy, when the one true religion shall universally prevail, and "the knowledge of the Lord shall cover the earth, as the waters cover the sea." '

Forster's complete argument is that Islam has a valid prophetic existence, that its success in the world (a factor that always worried Christian apologists), was testimony to the validity of its existence, that it was in a 'joint operation' with Christianity 'acting co-ordinately, upon a vast scale, on the civil and social relations of mankind, and on their moral and spiritual interests and affections' until the final day. Though it had this joint role Islam was, nevertheless, the subordinate partner, but:

> . . . they hold so many fundamentals in common, that in the judgment of the most unexceptionable authorities, they contain a natural and necessary tendency to convergence; the imperfect scheme, when its providential work shall have been accomplished, becoming absorbed in the perfect, and the moon of Mahomet resigning its borrowed rays, to melt in the undivided light of the everlasting Gospel.[14]

In 1840, Thomas Carlyle delivered a number of lectures in London which were published under the title *On Heroes, Hero-Worship and the Heroic in History*.[15] Three of the heroes referred to figures in religion. The first lecture was titled 'The Hero as Divinity'. The god figure in question was, interestingly, not Jesus Christ, but Odin a figure in Scandinavian mythology. Martin Luther and John Knox were featured as 'The Priest as Hero'. When he came to choose an example of a prophet as hero he chose Muhammad. His reason for the choice was not that he was 'the most eminent prophet; but . . . the one we are freest to speak of.'[16]

Carlyle was well aware of the vilification of Muhammad that had gone on for centuries in the Christian West and mounts not only a vigorous defence of the Prophet, but presents him as a figure of virtue and his religion as superior to Christianity in many ways. 'Withal I like Mahomet for his total freedom from cant.' There is 'no dilettantism in this Mahomet', and while 'we will not praise Mahomet's moral precepts as always of the superfinest soot; yet . . . there is always a tendency to good in them.'[17] Muhammad's creed was far superior to that of

> those miserable Syrian Sects, with their janglings about *Homoiousion* and *Homoousion* . . . Islam devoured all these vain jangling sects; and I think had right to do so. It was a Reality, direct from the great Heart of Nature once more. Arab idolatries, Syrian formulas, whatsoever was not equally real, had to go up in flame, – more dead *fuel*, in various senses, for this which was *fire*.[18]

Not only does Muhammad compare favourably with notable Christian Fathers he far outranks certain English thinkers of a previous generation such as Bentham and Paley. 'If you ask me which gives, Mahomet or they the beggarlier and falser view of Man and his Destinies in this Universe, I will answer, it is not Mahomet!'[19]

Carlyle's view of the Qur'an was that it was an incredibly difficult book to read, not because it was unintelligible but because it read like a 'State-Paper Office, unreadable masses of lumber'. Nevertheless, 'One would say that the primary character of the Koran is this of its *genuineness*, of its being a bona fide book . . . coming from the heart and speaking to other hearts.' Such fulsome praises and more, as when he refers to Muhammad as 'this deep-hearted son of the Wilderness, with his beaming black eyes and open social deep soul,' might raise an eyebrow or two were it not for the fact that the work is obviously based on deep scholarship.

Nineteenth-century commentators thought that Carlyle was so committed to his picture of Muhammad because it reflected in great measure his own brand of religion, and he was in sympathy with 'stern, gloomy geniuses, somewhat of his own mould.'[20] F. D. Maurice actually sat and listened to the lecture and wrote to his wife that he thought Carlyle would have been '*more* kind and tolerant toward the truth in all forms of faith and opinion' if he accepted the truths of the Christian faith in a more orthodox fashion rather than treating them 'as only one of the mythical vestures in which certain actions – which, without such a vesture, he secretly knows and confesses to be good-for-nothing abstractions – have wrapped themselves up.' Maurice also accused Carlyle of 'miserable vagueness' and 'silly rant'.[21] But he failed to acknowledge that

Carlyle had done his groundwork well, something that could not always be said of Maurice and the accusation of vagueness comes ill from a writer whom many of his contemporaries thought very woolly. Carlyle's main source was Sale's translation of the Qur'an but he was also deeply read in German scholarship. Ruth apRoberts has recently demonstrated the extent of Carlyle's researches and the respect that was shown towards him by such a figure as Goethe.[22] A twentieth-century Islamic scholar has said that 'In its essence Carlyle's conception of Muhammad is a true one, and one that is still of value in its broad outlines to the historian of today.'[23]

In 1847 F. D. Maurice published his work, *On the Religions of the World*. In the same year Rowland Williams, Fellow of King's College, Cambridge was awarded the Muir Prize for an essay which met the test of being 'the best refutation of Hinduism, and State- ment of the evidence of Christianity in a form suited to the Hindus.'[24] John Muir had been a member of the Bengal Civil Service and insisted that Hinduism was to be treated fairly in establishing 'the exclusive claims and authority of Christianity as an object of faith and rule of life to the whole of mankind.' Part of the prize was withheld pending the publication of an expanded version of the essay as a substantial volume. This appeared in 1856. These two works are viewed together because Maurice's work was also in a sense commissioned, since it was the publication of the Boyle lectures, funded under the terms of the will of the late Robert Boyle, the seventeenth-century scientist, 'for proving the Christian Religion against notorious Infidels, to wit, Atheists, Theists, Pagans, Jews and Mahometans.' The aim of the lectures was not only to refute the claims of other religions but also to be 'assisting to all companies, and encouraging them in any undertaking for propagating the Christian Religion to foreign parts.'[25]

Maurice's lectures were in two parts. In the first he set out to examine the main characteristics of the major world faiths and to see what good might be found in them that was worth preserving.[26] In the second part he set out to answer the questions: 'In what relation does Christianity stand to these different faiths? If there be a faith which is meant for mankind, is this the one or must we look for another?'[27] It has been claimed that Maurice worked on the principle that 'there is some truth, but not the same truth, in every religion, and that whatever truth they exhibit must come from the source of all truth.'[28] It is further claimed that Maurice saw in Judaism, Christianity and Islam 'an assertion of the divine initiative which is lacking in other religions.'[29] Given that Maurice, at best, is not easy to understand it can just as easily be claimed, and possibly with more justification, that he is, on the whole more concerned with what is good in other religions than with what is true, and that even in dealing with Judaism and Islam, which along with Christianity look to God for the initiative unlike 'the Hindoo manner', the divine initiative is easily extinguished. With regard to Islam it is not even clear that what the Prophet was responding to was divine initiative. He defends Muhammad against the charge of plagiarism but then goes on to say that he acquired what existed already in Judaism and Christianity and so absorbed it as to make it his own. The Jews might believe that they still behaved according to the belief that God spoke to their fathers, but 'Systems, rabbinical and philosophical, may choke that belief; money-getting habits may almost extinguish it.'[30] This last argument is an interesting example of anti-semitism on the lips of an otherwise nineteenth-century 'liberal'. In terms of truth Maurice seems to say that the Jews originally had it and lost it while the Muslims latched on to it for a time but were never really assimilated to the truth.

His evaluation of Hinduism and Buddhism is even more negative. In both religions he finds analogies with Christianity. In Hinduism he finds the notion of priesthood and of being twice-born. The concept of wisdom in Hinduism recalls memories of Wisdom in Judaism and its later manifestation in the Logos of the Fourth Gospel. It is in the areas of Incarnation and Sacrifice, however, that the 'controversy with Hindooism turns'. In Hinduism he sees only the terrifying aspects of the propitiation of Siva, 'ready at any moment to come forth in a form of terrifying wickedness, in the likeness of some Man-God.' He contrasts with this the sacrifice of the Cross of Christ, 'the sacrifice of the God-Man'.[31] In Buddhism Maurice again finds analogies, more particularly in notions of Spirit. Buddhism and its relationship to Hinduism is viewed as an analogy of Christianity's break with Judaism and the importance of Pentecost. In Buddhism he finds 'a profound feeling of reverence for the human spirit'. This spirit according to Buddhism has great capacity, is not confined to one class or race and is in some sense divine. He also sees 'the privilege of the divine man to contemplate the Divinity in His purity'. Although these beliefs are admirable, indeed reflect a Buddhist side of Christianity, he even speaks of 'Christian Buddhism', nevertheless he sees no more revelation in Buddhism than he sees in Hinduism.[32]

He finally addresses the question whether Christianity as a revelation must give way to any other religion. The answer is predictable. In respect of the alternative for India and England [sic] it is 'whether we hold a system of opinions or a revelation from God.'[33] All religions demand a ground other than the purely human. Quite what that ground might be in the other religions he never makes quite clear. We are presented with the rather illogical notion that different truths, some originating with God, some from the human alone, come from the same source of truth. Muddled though this may be his final assertion is clear enough:

> Is not Christianity the consistent assertor of [that] higher ground? Does it not distinctly and consistently refer every human feeling and consciousness to that ground? Is it not *for this reason* able to interpret and reconcile the other religions of the earth? Does it not in this way prove itself to be *not* a human system, but *the* Revelation, which human beings require?[34]

It was said that Maurice's book was a work that could not have been written before his age.[35] That may be true, though we have seen something more radical in the work of Forster. Be that as it may Maurice's work is still marred by inadequate knowledge of the religions concerned, allowing the worst in other religions to be compared with the best in Christianity, and depending on assertion rather than open discussion to dictate his final opinion.

Much the same can be said about the work of Rowland Williams but he does offer a more rigorous examination of other religions, in his case just Hinduism and Buddhism. There is at least a hint that Williams was more radical than Maurice in his approach to the other religions. After 1860 Williams was one of two clergy deprived of their livings temporarily as a result of litigation over the publication of *Essays and Reviews*. (See Chapter Two.) He was primarily known in his earlier days as a linguist in Hebrew and Chaldee but had also been known for his radical theological views through the publication of sermons under the title *Rational Godliness* in 1855. The work he published in the following year has been almost universally neglected though at the time it was hailed by the

Sanskrit scholar H. H. Wilson as the standard reference for the Hindu speculative systems[36] and by the Dean of Westminster, A. P. Stanley, as 'one of the best manuals for dealing with the difficulties of heathen India'.[37]

Williams' book is in the form of a dialogue between two English Christians, two Hindus, a Nepalese Buddhist and a European, not English, materialist named Wolff! The work expresses Williams' strong interest in history. He analyses the imprecise dating of Hindu and Buddhist sacred texts, their variety of interpretations of the sacred and their internal inconsistencies. In the final analysis this treatment counts against Hinduism and Buddhism and for the superiority of Christianity. While this kind of conclusion puts him in the same class as Maurice there are important differences both with regard to how one should approach other religions and with what kind of theology the approach should be made.

His theology was based very much on the Person of Jesus Christ and in a sermon preached in 1855 he summed up this theology thus:

(Christ) concentrates and exhibits in his life, in his doctrine, in his death, and in the Holy Spirit whereby he ever lives, and wherewith He animates the whole of His Church, the Divine perfection of those excellences, of which fragments, and shadows, and images, are scattered throughout the world elsewhere.[38]

In this passage Williams seems to be expressing some form of Logos doctrine by which those qualities which were manifest in the Christ are to be found in historical and geographical contexts unconnected with the Gospel story. This interpretation is reinforced by a statement published in a later work, the controversial Review of 1860.

We cannot encourage a remorseless criticism of Gentile histories and escape its contagion when we approach Hebrew annals; nor acknowledge a Providence in Jewry without owning that it may have comprehended sanctities elsewhere. But the moment we examine fairly the religions of India and of Arabia . . . we find they appealed to the better side of our nature and their essential strength lay in the elements of good which they contained, rather than in any satanic corruption.[39]

The latter part of this statement corresponds with much that can be found in Maurice. The key difference would appear in the notion that the 'Providence' we find in Judaism might be manifest in other 'sanctities'; i.e. in other holy contexts. This is a radical difference between him and Maurice. It seems clear that Williams did see something of the divine and not merely human aspiration in Hinduism and Buddhism.

Such a conclusion is affirmed by his statements through the mouth of one of the participants in dialogue, Blancome, who so nearly represents Williams' own views as to be taken for Williams himself. In dealing with Hinduism he discusses the concept of *vach*, the Word proceeding from Brahma, the Supreme Principle. Blancome says:

> With submission at least to wiser people, I do not think it a greater tampering with mixture of distinct systems, than the early Church doctors permitted themselves in setting forth the life of Christ after the phrase of Plato, if I say that your Vach appears as a prophecy, or expression, of the everliving Word of God.[40]

Moreover Blancome does not deny it when Wolff suggests that his view of revelation abandons the usual 'positive' position and approaches 'something that more nearly resembles some Indian theories of the Divine spirit pervading and elevating humanity.'[41]

Williams was no less critical than Maurice in his approach to Hinduism and Buddhism. The former religion is based on scriptures which are unreliable in respect of dating and inner contradictions while the latter is condemned for something which is still held against Buddhism by Westerners to this day, namely its alleged doctrine of 'total perishableness' or *nihilisme absolu*, such a 'dreary prospect' according to Williams.[42]

Finally Williams would urge the Hindus to cast away their idols and associate 'whatever is best in [Hinduism] with the purer faith we bring them' and so be led into 'the entire truth'.[43] This attitude towards Hinduism is later put in an even more positive way. Having rejected Hinduism on the grounds of bad historical evidence and a confusion of divinities Blancome nevertheless acknowledges that it is not unlikely that the Spirit of God which *'bloweth where it listeth'* has given Hindus a 'good hope for eternal life', and a hope of being delivered:

Such a hope perchance you have; but it is Christ which brings us the deliverance, and gives us the gift. Might I not then say, your prophecies, or at least your desires, are fulfilled in Him.[44]

In the history of inter-religious encounter J. N. Farquhar, who flourished half a century after Williams, has been made the author of the advocacy of Christ as the Crown *and fulfilment* of Hinduism.[45] So far this early expression of the idea by Williams has gone unacknowledged though it points to an advanced approach to inter-religious encounter such as is not found in Maurice, for instance, though it is Maurice, having written the more popular book, who gets the praise for the advance in Christian response to other religions in the first half of the nineteenth century.[46]

In the published version of his lectures F. D. Maurice included the following footnotes:

I understand that a young German, now in London, whose knowledge of Sanscrit is profound, and his industry *plus quam Germanica*, has it in contemplation to publish and translate all the Vedas. English money it is to be hoped will not be wanting, when the other and more indispensable requisite is supplied by a foreigner.[47]

The young German was the 23-year-old Friedrich Max Müller. After a couple of years in London Max Müller moved to Oxford to supervise the printing of his six-volume translation of the *Rig-Veda*. He received appointments in Oxford and by 1858 he was a Fellow of All Souls. He was friendly with the contributors to *Essays and Reviews* and would, albeit reluctantly, have contributed an essay on Eastern religions to its successor volume if it had been published.[48] In 1860 he was in contention for the Chair of Sanskrit in the University but he lost to the more 'orthodox' M. Monier-Williams, perhaps because of his association with the contributors to *Essays and Reviews*. Subsequent history has neglected Monier-Williams in favour of Max Müller and although the latter was responsible for such monumental work as the translation of Oriental documents in the series *The Sacred Books of the East*, it is easy to forget Monier-Williams' important contribution to the study of Indian religions and his influence in the last quarter of the century, through a number of publications in the 1870s and 1880s. Succeeding generations of scholars are still indebted to him for his

Sanskrit-English Dictionary.[49] Although there were those such as E. B. Pusey in the Oxford of 1860 who thought that the work of Max Müller would directly aid the work of Christian missionaries, Monier-Williams was more obviously committed to such a programme. His inaugural lecture in Oxford was a plea for missionary organizations to arrange for their missionaries to learn Sanskrit so that they could engage in intellectual discussions with Hindu *pandits*. This was not his finest contribution to Indian studies. In other works he looked not only at Hinduism but also at Buddhism and Islam within the Indian context and in relationship to Christianity.

Monier-Williams' contribution to the study of Indian religions is important because he combined his knowledge of the religious texts with descriptions of localized religious ritual and practice gained from his visits to India, Sri Lanka and Tibet. His best known book was his *Hinduism*, a volume in the series published by the Society for the Promotion of Christian Knowledge under the general title of 'Non-Christian Religious Systems'.[50] Published in 1877 by 1899 the book had gone through thirteen impressions. Its popularity was due to a number of factors. The series itself was marketed as a popular series. There was the popular format of the book, produced, as were the other volumes in the series, in a pocket-book size and the volumes were sold for 2s 6d. But beyond that it is difficult to see how the book, and the others in the series for that matter, could be so popular. It is not an easy book to read. It does not pander to a popular readership, indeed the text in places is quite difficult with the inclusion of technical Sanskrit terms.

As an introduction to the study of Hinduism it has in most of its parts stood the test of time very well. A more recent work would probably not show the aversion the author has for certain aspects of Hinduism such as 'idolatry', or the use of images in worship. Also a more recent author would probably not regard the main philosophical traditions of Hinduism in quite the same way or hold that the Sanskrit language gives unity to Hinduism. He doesn't actually use the term 'system' of Hinduism as the title of the series suggests but the role he bestows on Sanskrit along with the normative role given to traditional philosophy and the non-dualism of Shankara comes pretty near to the formulation of a system.

Monier-Williams accepts the non-dualist approach as the authentic interpretation of the Vedas and the Upanishads and its discipline of the path of wisdom and meditation (*jnana marga*) as 'the highest way of salvation'. The other two paths he regards as inferior ways belonging to 'popular Hinduism'. He regarded the challenge to *jnana marga* by *karma marga*, the way of pious works, and *bhakti marga*, the way of personal devotion to God, as belonging to 'popular Hinduism', a sort of concession to the masses. In fact the latter form of Hindu expression is the majority approach. As such it is in a sense 'popular' but not necessarily 'populist'. The non-dualist approach is followed by a small number of intellectual Hindus and while it enjoys a certain elite status this does not mean that it is superior to the other two paths. The reality of Hinduism is that these ways are not exclusively practised by different groups of believers. The *Bhagavad Gita* has exercised a unifying influence so that all three paths are practised at one time or other or even simultaneously by the same person. Unfortunately the pre-eminence given to the Advaitin position by such scholars as Monier-Williams has led to a distorted picture of Hinduism being presented in the Western classroom by succeeding generations of teachers.

Another major criticism centres on the final two and a half pages of the book. Here objectivity gives way to Christian propaganda. He predicts the final end of Hinduism and calls for a Christian mission to fill the vaccuum and ward off Islam. If that were all that could be said about this work it would be rather sad. However, it can be said that it is the equal of any other work that sets out to introduce the general reader to a study of Hinduism, and can still be used with profit. In one respect at least it is superior to nearly all other books of a general nature in the field, even those produced in recent times. It gives a comprehensive account of Hinduism as a living religion rather than just a historical description based on literary sources. The final chapter, apart from the final two and a half pages, is an incredibly detailed description of Hindu holy places, divinities and festivals. Most of the information obviously comes from his own observations with insights into quite localized activities. In his opening chapter he warned his reader that the subject of his book was such that 'no description of Hinduism can be exhaustive which does not touch on almost every religious and philosophical idea that the world has ever known.' Far from being the ordered structure which certain studies based on a study of

documentary Hinduism makes it, Monier-Williams saw the structure of Hinduism as 'a huge polygon, or irregular multilateral
figure'.[51] His conclusion is that the Hindus 'are a profoundly
religious people' having a religion which 'will stir the depths of the
heart, and give room for the exercise of faith and love,'[52] It has
been said that he reacted angrily if Hindus were referred to as
'heathen' and that he humorously claimed to be 'half a Hindu'.[53]
This reflects his treatment of Hinduism and one wonders at the
statements he goes on to make about the decline of Hinduism and
the rather militant remarks about the Christian mission. He was,
in this respect, rather typical of many scholars of his period though
it should not detract from his scholarship and the debt that students
of Hinduism owe him.

In the preface to his Dictionary written but a short time before
his death he speaks autobiographically of his work in Oxford where
he remained Boden Professor until he died in 1899. It will be
recalled that he was in competition for the Chair with Max Müller
who was later given the Chair of Comparative Philology. In many
ways they remained in competition, Max Müller concentrating on
the translation of texts and formulating theories based on the
reading of texts, Monier-Williams maintaining his studies of a more
immediately empirical nature. This contrast comes out in Monier-
Williams' last words. He believed that his Indian journeys, while
delaying the final publication of the Dictionary, provided him with
valuable material to produce a better Dictionary than might otherwise have been the case. He went on to recall that critics had
expressed surprise that he had spent his life in:

> the dry, dreary and thankless drudgery of writing Dictionaries
> and Grammars, and to practical researches carried on among
> the Pandits of India in their own country, rather than to the
> duty of proving the profundity of my learning and my fitness
> to occupy a high Professorial position by editing or translating
> obscure Sanskrit texts which have never been edited or trans
> lated before.[54]

This passage carries a footnote in which he compares the task of
translating obscure texts to climbing hitherto unclimbed mountains
however comparatively insignificant. He ends by suggesting that
anyone who regards such an activity as a criterion of scholarship
to 'associate with Indian Pandits in their own country and . . . find

out that far severer proofs of his knowledge and acquirements will be required of him there.'[55] This somewhat testy statement shows the tension which possibly existed between him and Max Müller. It also shows something of the trend that was to ensue in the study of religions for a very long time. In the contrasting styles of Monier-Williams and Max Müller the latter won out and the study of the so-called 'high religions' became almost exclusively the study of texts and Hinduism was caricatured for nearly a century as almost exclusively Advaita Vedanta or Neo-Vedanta, with any other form of Hinduism being 'popular' or debased and not worth scholarly study. Even though Monier-Williams appears to support such a valuation of Advaita Vedanta he nevertheless applied his scholarly attention to all forms of Hinduism.

Friedrich Max Müller, by comparison, was more involved with some of the wider issues of the study of religions. He devoted more time to speculating on the origins of religion which he decided were to be found in the development of language. He also devoted much time to speculation on the development of myth as a vehicle for religion. Much of what he had to say on both language and myth hardly survived his own life. He came in for a lot of criticism from anthropologists influenced by the theories of Charles Darwin which he himself rejected. Much of his writing, originally lectures on a variety of allied subjects, makes interesting antiquarian reading but has little value beyond his own time. His importance for us is the immense work that he did in developing the study of religion as an academic study free from credal demands. Although the term 'science of religion' was not original to him its continued use and the practice of what the term stands for even today owes a great deal to him.

The study of religions has advanced in format and content far beyond his own and some of that advance has been in the areas which cover anthropological, sociological and phenomenological studies of religions. His hope for the science of religion was expressed in terms which are typical of him with its emphasis on literary sources, and underlines the contrast between him and Monier-Williams:

By a proper division of labour, the materials which are still wanting, will be collected and published and translated, and when that is done, surely man will never rest until he has discovered the purpose that runs through the religions of mankind, and till he has reconstructed the true Civitas Dei on foundations as wide as the ends of the world. The Science of Religion may be the last of the sciences which man is destined to elaborate; but when it is elaborated, it will change the aspect of the world, and give new life to Christianity itself.[56]

He accurately, though unintentionally, describes the position in the study of world religions a century later. There has been a division of labour but it involves the collection and interpretation of a great deal more material of a non-documentary kind than he envisaged. His emphasis is purely on documents. Furthermore the search for the purpose, if any, that runs through the religions of mankind and the reconstruction of Civitas Dei is very much a minority interest among those who engage in the study of religions and the giving of new life to Christianity has not, at least yet, taken place. What is important is the vision that the task is enormous, involves all religious traditions and needs teams of scholars to do the work adequately. The work does involve the translation of the key documents however much the exclusive concentration on this aspect of the work may be criticized. The community of scholars he gathered for the work of translating *The Sacred Books of the East* was the first sign of a new spirit of encounter between the scholars of different religions which gave substance to the new discipline of comparative religion and became an important aspect of later dialogue between adherents of different religions.

Max Müller was a member of the Church of England and believed that Christianity would benefit from the wider study of religions. However, there was another side to him in that he thought that the religion of the future, the 'true religion', would be the fulfilment of all the religions of the past. Such a view was bound to bring him into conflict with more 'orthodox' upholders of the Christian faith. His most doughty opposer in this was the Right Revd R. Caldwell, at one time Assistant Bishop of Madras.

The bishop's attack was provoked by a lecture delivered by Max Müller to the Aryan Section of the International Congress of Orientalists in London in September 1874. A few weeks later the bishop addressed a church congress in Brighton and excused himself from talking about missionary matters in view of the importance that the relationship between Christianity and Oriental religious systems had lately assumed. The bishop acknowledged that Max Müller had praised missionaries, yet:

> if Christianity should come to be regarded, not as a divine gift to mankind, not as a divinely-ordained remedy for sin and errors, but virtually as a human invention, as springing equally with all other religions, from what is termed 'the sacred soil of the human heart' then missions would soon die.[57]

The phrase quoted was taken from Max Müller's lecture. This was not the first time for him to be attacked by missionaries. In the lecture attacked by Caldwell he defended himself against missionaries at home who had abused him 'in unmeasured language' while appreciating that missionaries abroad had thanked him for what he had said about them and their work in a lecture in Westminster Abbey the previous December.[58] Caldwell's attack was twofold. On the one hand he detected an undermining of the exclusiveness and superiority of Christianity and on the other hand he was unhappy with the favourable way Hinduism was described. 'We are called upon, not only to respect that which is good [in Hinduism], which is perfectly fair and right, but also to ignore that which is evil, or to forget that the evil is greatly in excess of the good.'[59] He also attacked Monier-Williams for this alleged lack of honesty in showing forth the true picture of Hinduism. He referred to his book *Indian Wisdom* and suggested that from the same sources could be compiled many more volumes entitled *Indian Folly*.[60] Caldwell was not the most extreme type of Christian apologist. He did see some good in Hinduism arising both from the purely human spirit and a 'higher element' which could only be regarded as divine but there was much more which could only be described as diabolical, for example 'the sensual worship of Krishna in imitation of the love of the Divine Saviour'.[61] He did not object to the comparative study of religion if only the comparisons were fairly made in which case Christianity could not but gain. Given that both Max Müller and Monier-Williams were consciously attempting to do what the bishop condemned them for not doing it is difficult to know what the bishop's real concern was. Monier-Williams especially in the Preface to *Indian Wisdom* thought that what he was doing was contributing knowledge which could be used to advantage in the spread of 'the regenerating influences of Christianity . . . through the length and breadth of the land [of

India]'.[62] It would seem that the bishop's missionary zeal might have been offended by a comparative study which assumed no superiority of one religion over another, rather than a study which began with the assumption of the superiority of Christianity.

Bishop Caldwell, though not technically a missionary himself, is not untypical of missionary reaction to the 'scientific' study of religions. It must be remembered that the history of Protestant Christianity in India, and in this I include the Anglicans, was in the early days a constant struggle, first to get into India in the face of the opposition of the East India Company, and then to actually be allowed to proselytize in the Company's territories and later in government territory. The reaction of one Revd Joseph Mullens of the London Missionary Society in Calcutta to Queen Victoria's Proclamation in the wake of 'the Sepoy outbreak', the Indian Mutiny of English history books and the First War of Independence of modern Indian history is an example of the frustrations felt by missionaries generally. Mr Mullens quotes a passage from the Royal Proclamation:

Firmly relying ourselves on the truth of Christianity, and acknowledging with gratitude the solace of religion, we disclaim the right and the desire to impose our convictions on any of our subjects. We declare it to be our royal will and pleasure, that none be in anywise favoured, none molested or disquieted, by reason of their religious faith or observances; but that all shall alike enjoy the equal and impartial protection of the law. And we do strictly charge and enjoin all those who may be in authority under us, that they abstain from all interference with the religious belief, or worship, of any of our subjects on pain of our severest displeasure.

Mullens acknowledged with gratitude the Queen's confession of her own faith and the solace enjoyed in that faith but he would have liked to have seen Christianity proclaimed more clearly as 'the only revelation from heaven' and the solace derived not from some vague religious belief 'but from the doctrines and promises of the Bible specially named.' He then proceeded to criticize the government for giving way to the demands of caste in Hindu society and for allowing Hindus and Muslims time off to enjoy their own religious festivals.

It must strike all thinking men, that to give holiday from public duties on days of heathen festivals, gives honour to the festivals, and associates with them notions of rest and enjoyment; their observance therefore tends to honour the idols celebrated as the days return.

Mullens was one of those, like Rowland Williams but with far less charity, who wrote a refutation of Hinduism for a prize. His disdain and scorn for Hinduism is very clear in such an essay but his sharpest invective was reserved for the government of India for its liberal attitude towards the rights of Hindus to practise their faith.

> What a shame all this is! How unprincipled are these efforts to encourage the natives of India in maintaining religions which the government must believe to be false! How cowardly the attempt to hide from them the religion which the government has, in official documents, acknowledged to be its own! How insulting to the God of heaven and earth that they should disavow the glorious truths to which England owes all its greatness, and truckle to false religions which rob Him of his honour! How could the government hope to prosper; how with such a spirit could it otherwise than look for the heavy chastisement which have well-nigh brought the empire to ruin?[63]

So the Sepoys' rising had about it the ring of God's wrath for disobedience. Though this was a particular attack on the government for refusing to declare its Christian faith thereby giving the 'natives' succour against the missionaries, the general tenor of the sentiments are not that untypical of missionary attitudes during the nineteenth century and indeed it is not surprising nor necessarily culpable in people whose very reason for existence was the elimination of other religions and the establishing of the Christian religion for all humanity.

So far we have paid a great deal more attention to scholars engaged in the study of Hinduism, though Monier-Williams did refer to Buddhism in one or two of his works. The leading name in the study of Buddhism in the last quarter of the nineteenth century and, according to recent scholars, the author of the first scholarly book on the religion in English is Thomas Williams Rhys

Davids. He qualified as a barrister-at-law and for a time served in the Ceylon Civil Service. Like Monier-Williams he not only studied the documentary evidence, he also based much of his teaching on personal observations during his time in Sri Lanka and India. He was teaching the Pali language, the language of the Buddhist religious texts, as early as 1876. His contribution to the series published by the SPCK, a companion to Monier-Williams' volume, *Buddhism: being a Sketch of the Life and Teachings of Gautama, the Buddha* went to 22,000 copies by 1910 and is regarded as still worth reading.[64] In 1881 he founded the Pali Society for the publication of the main Buddhist texts. It is still the major institution for the study of Buddhist Pali texts. In 1904 Rhys Davids became the first holder of the Chair of Comparative Religion in the University of Manchester. In 1891 he had followed in the steps of Max Müller in delivering a series of Hibbert Lectures on the subject of the origin and growth of religion as illustrated by the history of Indian Buddhism.

The first thing one notes about Rhys Davids' standard work is the advance which has taken place since the publication of *The Penny Cyclopaedia*. We are not comparing the depth of treatment so much as what has come to be known in the intervening forty years. Rhys Davids still admits that little is known of the books of the Northern Canon and so he limits the book to 'a consideration of Buddhism as it appears in the earliest records; with a rapid summary of the principal lines along which in after-times the most vital changes, and the most essential development took place'.[65] In other words he is basing his study on early primary rather than secondary sources. (In Rhys Davids division of Buddhists Southern Buddhists refer to those usually referred to today as Theravada, while the Northerns, from Tibet to Japan, are those usually referred to today as Mahayana.) He reflects the interest of the *Cyclopaedia* in numbers and goes on to point out that the vast numbers of Buddhists does not mean that every individual Buddhist follows the identical form of religion. 'Not one of the five hundred millions who offer flowers now and then on Buddhist shrines, who are more or less moulded by Buddhist teaching, is only or altogether a Buddhist.'[66] In spite of this statement he still argues the case for referring to Buddhism as a 'system'. His argument is that even though in Buddhism there exist side by side inconsistent and even antagonistic beliefs 'each of these beliefs breathes more or less of the spirit of the system out of which they all alike have grown, and can only be rightly understood by those who have first realized what the system really was.'[67] The basic teaching of the Buddha, the *dhamma*, is probably the most systematic basis of any religion so one can appreciate why Rhys Davids would use the term 'system' for that teaching which gave rise to Buddhism. However it is in allowing this 'system' to overide the dynamic diversity of Buddhism that he probably differs most from the treatment of Buddhism in our own times.

Given that his book was so popular it is surprising that what he has to say about a key element in Buddhist doctrine and belief, the notion of *nirvana* (in Pali *nibbana*), has been so widely ignored and distorted in Western teaching on Buddhism. We saw how Rowland Williams labelled Buddhism as a religion of 'total perishableness', *un nihilisme absolu*. It is obvious from the space devoted to the discussion of Nirvana that Rhys Davids is aware of the common interpretation of the concept among his contemporaries. He acknowledges that the word means 'simply going out, extinction' but he argues very persuasively, as Buddhists themselves do, that the statements in the scriptures which refer to Nirvana point to anything but extinction of the human individual. He gives the following as one such example:

> They who, by steadfast mind have become exempt from evil desire, and well trained in the teachings of the Gautama; they having obtained the fruit of the fourth Path [i.e. having reached the stage of Arahat], and immersed themselves in that ambrosia, have received without price, and are in the enjoyment of Nirvana. Their old karma is exhausted, no new karma is being produced . . . [68]

Accepting that the word Nirvana means extinction Rhys Davids suggests that from the above evidence it does not mean extinction of the soul:

> *It is the extinction of that sinful, grasping condition of mind and heart, which would otherwise, according to the great mystery of Karma, be the cause of renewed individual existence.* . . . Nirvana is therefore the same thing as a *sinless, calm state of mind;* and if translated at all, may best, perhaps, be rendered

'holiness' – holiness, that is, in the Buddhist sense, *perfect peace, goodness, and wisdom.*[69]

Note the hesitant way he offers a translation. He devotes the next paragraph to a discussion of the pitfalls in the way of translating concepts from one cultural context to another and advises that it is better to stick to the term Nirvana with a full understanding of its Buddhist meanings rather than try to translate it.

Looking back at the work of Rhys Davids in the very early days of comparative religion one cannot but be impressed by the techniques and style of teaching a religion which is not easy for a Western mind to grasp. His methods were somehow largely ignored after his generation and have had to be recovered in our own generation. Within the Christian churches the study of other religions was suppressed and even in university teaching a lack of objectivity and sympathy in respect of other religions often entered in. In the Hibbert Lectures of 1881 he takes several opportunities to compare aspects of Buddhism with aspects of Christianity. Faced with the question of whether or not Buddhism is a religion devoid of hope he doesn't try to argue to the contrary but asks:

> Must we have a belief in some personal happiness that we ourselves are to enjoy hereafter? Is it not enough to hope that our self-denials and our struggles will add to the happiness of others? Surely we have even so a gain far beyond our deserts; for we receive more, infinitely more, than we can ever give. We inherit the result of the Karma of the countless multitudes who have lived and died, who have struggled and suffered, in the long ages of the past. And if we can sometimes catch a glimpse of the glories that certainly lie hid behind the veil of the infinite future, is not that enough, and more than enough, to fill our hearts with an abiding faith and hope stronger, deeper, truer, than any selfishness can give?[70]

Quite what his hearers made of this, all that talk of Karma, of self-denials for the sake of others, of a hope stronger than selfishness can give, is hard to imagine. It shows how one scholar faced the ideas which were coming from the East into the West towards the end of the nineteenth century. I have suggested that the immediate fruits were largely rejected, that the study of religions took a path which insulated the students from the realities of the other religions, that within Christian circles the very thought of other religions was largely cast aside, so that in the second half of the twentieth century we were scarcely ready for the encounters which were to take place and which will be discussed in Chapters Five and Six. In our time we hear a call for a Copernican Revolution in inter-religious encounter and dialogue. It will not be inappropriate to end this chapter, sketchy and incomplete though it be, with a similar call from Rhys Davids:

> We can . . . rejoice that the cultivated world [sic] is beginning to enter upon the fruits of Oriental research in Indian matters, and that the habit of Western historians of considering all things at a distance from the basin of the Mediterranean as beneath notice, and of thus practically ignoring the existence of about two-thirds of the human race, is beginning to be broken through. It would be useless to attempt to predict the measure of the influence which this change of standpoint will eventually have upon our ideas of history: but it may be compared to the results which followed inevitably on the discovery that this earth was not the centre of the universe. And when we call to mind how closely intertwined are religious with historical beliefs and arguments, we may realize in some degree what effect may follow upon the unveiling of a long history of civilization, independent of Egyptian, Jewish, or Greek thought; upon the curtain being drawn back from a new drama of struggling races and rival religions, filled with ideas strangely familiar and as curiously strange. It is not too much to say that a New World has been once more discovered . . . and that the inhabitants of the Old World cannot, if they would, go back again to the quiet times when the New World was not, because it was unknown.[71]

Rhys Davids said it was useless to predict any possible change. He was right to be cautious. The prediction may at last be coming true a century after these words were uttered.

NOTES

1 A. Barth, *Religions of India*, Glasgow, Trübner's, 1889, Frontispiece.
2 R.W. Church, *The Sacred Poetry of Early Religions*, London, Macmillan, 1874.
3 For a full treatment of the situation in the previous centuries see

D.A. Pailin, *Attitudes to Other Religions: Comparative Religion in Seventeenth- and Eighteenth-century Britain*, Manchester University Press, 1984. See also P.J. Marshall and Glyndwr Williams, *The Great Map of Mankind, British Perceptions of the World in the Age of Enlightenment*, London, Dent & Sons, 1982.

4   C. Forster, *Mahometanism Unveiled*, London, Privately published, 1829, frontispiece.

5   S. Neill, *A History of Christian Missions*, Harmondsworth, Penguin, 1964, p.230.

6   F.D. Maurice, *On the Religions of the World and their Relation to Christianity*, Cambridge, Macmillan & Co., third edn revised, 1852. (Orig. pub. 1846.)

7   F. Max Müller, *The Sacred Books of the East*, trans. by various Oriental scholars, Oxford, The Clarendon Press, 1879 onwards.

8   For general treatments of the subject of this chapter see: E.J. Sharpe, *Comparative Religion: A History*, London, Duckworth, 1975; C. Welch, *Protestant Thought in the Nineteenth Century*, Vol.2, New Haven and London, Yale University Press, 1972, ch. 4; L.E. Elliott-Binns, *English Thought 1860–1900*, London, Longmans Green & Co., 1956, ch.9; N. Smart et al., eds, *Nineteenth Century Religious Thought in the West*, Vol.III, Cambridge University Press, 1985, ch.6, 'Friedrich Max Müller and the Comparative Study of Religion'.

9   See A. & R. Cowen, *Victorian Jews through British Eyes*, Oxford University Press, 1986.

10 Welch, op.cit., p.106.

11 William Jones thought that since many of the images of the Buddha show him with hair of a 'curled or woolly appearance' he and his religion were of African descent. *The Penny Cyclopaedia*, Vol.5, Library of Useful Knowledge, London, C. King, 1836, p.526, col.1.

12 Ibid.

13 Forster, op.cit., p.78.

14 Ibid., p.109.

15 T. Carlyle, *On Heroes, Hero-Worship, and the Heroic in History*, Minerva Library of Famous Books, London, Ward Lock, 1891 (ed. and with Critical Introduction by G.T. Bettany). (Orig. pub. 1841.)

16 Ibid., p.43.

17 Ibid., p.53.

18 Ibid., pp.46–7.

19 Ibid., p.55.

20 Bettany, ibid., p.ix.

21 F. Maurice, *Life and Letters of F.D. Maurice*, 2 vols., London, Macmillan, 1884, Vol.1, p.282.

22 Ruth apRoberts, 'Mahomet, or Leaning to the East', paper read at a

Conference on 'Victorian Learning' at City University New York, May, 1986, soon to be published in Browning Institute Essays.

23 G. Montgomery Watt, 'Carlyle on Muhammad', in *The Hibbert Journal*, Vol.53, (April, 1955), pp.247–54. Cited by apRoberts.

24 E. Williams, *The Life and Letters of Rowland Williams, D.D.*, London, Henry S. King & Co., 1874, Appendix B, p.388.

25 Maurice, *On the Religions of the World*, p.1.

26 Ibid., p.10.

27 Ibid.

28 H.G. Wood, *Frederick Denison Maurice*, Cambridge University Press, 1950, p.77.

29 Ibid.

30 Op.cit., p.155.

31 Ibid., p.182.

32 Ibid., pp.198–213.

33 Ibid., p.184.

34 Ibid., p.247.

35 A.P. Stanley, 'Theology of the Nineteenth Century', in *Frasers Magazine*, February, 1865, p.257.

36 I. Ellis, *Seven Against Christ: A Study of 'Essays and Reviews'*, Leiden, Brill, 1980, p.27.

37 Stanley, op.cit., ibid.

38 Rowland Williams, *Rational Godliness*, Cambridge, Deighton, Bell, & Co., London, Bell & Daldy, 1855, p.395.

39 *Essays and Reviews*, fourth edn., London, Longman, Green, Longman, & Roberts, 1861, p.51.

40 Rowland Williams, *A Dialogue of the Supreme Lord, in Which are Compared the Claims of Christianity and Hinduism*, Cambridge, Deighton, Bell and Co., London, Bell and Daldy, 1856, p.554.

41 Ibid., p.522.

42 Ibid., p.528.

43 Ibid., p.525.

44 Ibid., p.541.

45 Sharpe, op.cit., p.153.

46 John Tulloch, *Movements in Religious Thought*, 1885 (Reprint Leicester University Press, 1971), p.274.

47 Op.cit., p.xiv.

48 Ellis, op.cit., p.239.

49 Sir M. Monier-Williams, *A Sanskrit-English Dictionary*, Oxford, Clarendon Press, 1899.

50 M. Williams, *Hinduism*, London, SPCK, 1877.

51 Ibid., p.12.

52 Ibid., p.184.

53 O. Chadwick, *The Victorian Church*, Part II, London, Adam & Charles Black, second edn, 1972, p.38.
54 *A Sanskrit-English Dictionary*, p.ix.
55 Ibid.
56 F. Max Müller, *Chips from a German Workshop*, I, London, Oxford University Press, 1867, p.xix. Cited in Sharpe, op.cit.
57 R. Caldwell, *The Relation of Christianity to Hinduism*, London, R. Clay, Sons, & Taylor, 1874, p.4.
58 Caldwell, op.cit., Appendix, 'The Inaugural Address of Professor Max Müller to the Aryan Section of the International Congress of Orientalists, London, September, 1874.
59 Ibid.
60 Ibid., p.5.
61 Ibid., p.7.
62 M. Williams, *Indian Wisdom*, second edn, London, Wm H. Allen & Co., 1875, p.x.
63 J. Mullens, *The Queen's Government and the Religions of India*, London, Ward & Co., 1859, pp.11, 21 and 9.
64 T.W. Rhys Davids, *Buddhism*, London, SPCK, 1877; Heinz Bechert and Richard Gombrich, eds, *The World of Buddhism*, London, Thames & Hudson, 1984, p.10.
65 Rhys Davids, *Buddhism.*, p.8.
66 Ibid., p.7.
67 Ibid., p.8.
68 Ibid., p.111.
69 Ibid., pp.111–12.
70 T.W. Rhys Davids, *Lectures on the Origin and Growth of Religion as Illustrated . . . in Indian Buddhism*, second edn, London, Williams & Norgate, 1891, p.215.
71 Ibid., p.216.

PART 2

THE TWENTIETH CENTURY

CHAPTER FOUR

The Christian Religion

Anthony Dyson

THE TWO DECLENSIONS

The Pre-Raphaelite Brotherhood, in the years immediately after 1848, was intent on a radical aesthetic revolution.[1] Art had to be able to mediate a genuine emotional engagement, a moral relevance and a unified metaphysic of reality. The art of the Pre-Raphaelites had therefore to reflect, amid an increasingly mechanized society, a sacramental view of life in which 'the concrete substance of everyday living was matched always to a symbolic register'.[2]

John Everett Millais's *Autumn Leaves* (1856), perhaps his last acceptably Pre-Raphaelite painting, embodies a parable of the quest for an authentic iconography which is instructive also for thinking about the Christian religion. How, amid the multiple convulsions of modern times, are the mysteries of a religious tradition, or the distinctively Christian apprehension of infinity within time, to be fixed in communal iconic images which are also faithful to nature and life? *Autumn Leaves* was intended by Millais to carry a Christian and a religious meaning about mortality. Many people, then and subsequently, have interpreted it as no more than a homely children's scene, a 'genre' painting which, as such, was not altogether successful.[3] It was too stilted and solemn. Thus it is not surprising that Millais should write: 'I have always felt insulted when people have regarded the picture as a simple little domestic episode, chosen for effect, and colour, as I intended the picture to awaken by its solemnity the deepest religious reflection.[4]

In this 'moment's monument' – the phrase is D. G. Rossetti's – set in the garden of Annat Lodge, near Perth in Scotland, several kinds of icons rub shoulders, with personal, religious and possibly socio-political implications. The end of summer and the end of the day, with the wisps of smoke, point to human decay, transience, the end of life. (This may also communicate Millais's own sense of loss as the unity of the original Brotherhood was broken by circumstances.) Two of the girls in Millais's painting, modelled by two sisters-in-law, are palpably children of the well-heeled middle classes. The other two girls, recruited in Perth, betray their circumstances by their dresses; one wears the uniform of a school attended only by the very poor. So mortality is the destiny of all, poor and rich alike. This mood is compounded by the dull aftermath of the sunken sun, by the dark mist in the valley beyond, by the few, stark, denuded poplars, by the children's faces on the shadow side, by their 'strange impassivity', 'awfully still and composed', as if they knew themselves to be instruments of fate, and by the stiff, almost hieratic movements of the two chief figures – animated gesture held in suspense – 'an exquisite pause in time'.[5] But the natural religious iconography is supplemented by two icons belonging to the Christian tradition. In the left middle background, heavily shrouded in evening mist, rises the spire of St John's Kirk, Perth, and in the right foreground one of the four children holds an apple. The apple, in Christian iconography, has contrasting referents – Eve, sin, sexual shame, but also salvation (cf. the painting *Adam and Eve* of the circle of Albrecht Altdorfer).

The varied iconography presupposes that those who view the painting will have the capacity to pass from natural and human phenomena to a religious awareness. The observer is not expected to read off a story, but to grasp a non-narrative, metaphorical moment of a transcendent kind, but rooted in history.

That the Pre-Raphaelites did not always achieve success in their choice and treatment of emblems was not merely their own correctable fault, but also a structural feature of their culture which had little vision of the interconnectedness of spirit and matter which is the necessary precondition if icons are to mediate between everyday fact and implicit values.[6] So the Pre-Raphaelite painters constantly ran the risk either of *declension into abstraction* where the precariousness and specificity of the momentary vision is lost, or of *declension into genre* where the special animation, the allusive subject matter, the intense consciousness of the present into which also a momentous past and future has been condensed, are all absent.[7] In this chapter I shall examine six important emblems or icons of modern British Christianity, namely the institutional churches, the ecumenical movement, Christian public witness, theology, worship and women's participation. In briefly exploring these icons, I shall use the notions of '*declension (or falling-away) into abstraction*' and '*declension into genre*' as heuristic devices which will allow us to relate historical phenomena to theological values. *Declension into abstraction* involves a withdrawal from the realism and particularity of a culture, a preoccupation with timeless truths at the expense of the compromises and complexities of lived existence. *Declension into genre* involves a complicity with the culturally given, a false automatic ascription of highest value to the social-political-religious status quo.

THE INSTITUTIONAL CHURCHES

There is no shortage of dire statements attesting to the decline, and possibly the fall, of the Christian churches in Britain (and in the wider European context too).

In *The End of an Era* Elliott Kendall looks at Christian Britain from the standpoint of a Third World once missionized by Britain. One of the assumptions of the missionary movement was that Christians in the West had got used to the idea that 'they were living in a Christendom in which most of the world's Christians were to be found'.[8]

> But it is now less obvious that there is a Christian West at all. The West is increasingly secular and as far as religion is concerned is developing into pluralistic societies. Moreover the numerical strength of Christianity is no longer here.[9]

Kendall specifically notes the disruption and conflict in Ireland in recent years, and the inability of Christian people and churches 'to make a decisive impact upon the barbarism'.[10] Again, 'foreign church visitors to Britain often comment on the lethargy and ennui of the typical Christian congregation in Britain. There is an air of weariness after 200 years of world mission'.[11]

John Kent, in *The End of the Line?*, exploring the misfit between traditional theology and contemporary experience, asks whether 'all that the critical theology of the last two hundred years has achieved is to show how little we can say about God with any kind of certainty at all'[12] and whether:

> the increasingly destructive trail of human behaviour over the same period has finally demolished the old Christian case for a God who intervened not only in Jesus but in the history of individuals, of states, of the 'church' itself.[13]

Kent asks: 'Are we not only at the end of the line, but also at a point of no return?'.[14]

Alan Wilkinson makes a more generous judgment, but with implications similar to those of Kendall and Kent.

> . . . never in its long history has the church in England, through all its branches, tried so hard to be faithful, to proclaim and re-interpret the gospel, to pray, to serve the community and to engage in self-examination. Never before has it included so many Christians prepared to stand against the prevailing forces of public opinion. . . . [But] despite the church's many notable achievements . . . the church has been like a boat firmly stuck on a sandbank, lapped and sometimes shaken by the waves, but never able to free itself to sail out into the open sea'.[15]

Alan Gilbert relates the decline of the churches to processes in society, 'the harsh dilemmas which secularization has imposed upon British Protestantism'. And 'unless there is to be some catastrophic breakdown of modern industrial society . . . the social and psychological pressures of modernization will continue to secularize an already 'post-Christian' society'.[16]

The general picture of decline is widely held to be substantiated by statistics relating to the institutional churches. Although there are gaps in the figures, problems of comparability, and elements of guesswork in interpretation (see Chapter 8), some overall trends seem clear. From the beginning of the century until the mid-1960s the major Protestant denominations failed to maintain their numbers, the Anglican churches just about held their numbers, and the Roman Catholic population increased. In more recent years, all

The Christian Religion

three groups have shown declining membership, but not uniformly. Some of the trends can be illustrated in more detail.[17]

In 1901 the Anglican churches in England, Scotland and Wales had a membership equal to 8.5 per cent of the total population; this decreased to 4.2 per cent in 1985. The density of the Church of Scotland, the United Free Church of Scotland and the Presbyterian Church of England (expressed as percentages of the relevant total population over fifteen years), fell from 5 per cent in 1901 to 3.3 per cent in 1966. The Presbyterian Church of Wales's density fell from 0.6 per cent in 1901 to 0.2 per cent in 1985. The Methodist Church density in Britain fell from 3.1 per cent in 1901 to 1.1 per cent in 1985. More recently, English Presbyterians and Congregationalists declined by around 12 per cent in the decade 1956–66. After union, the resultant United Reformed Church declined by 22 per cent in the period 1972–80. Membership of the Society of Friends was 17,476 in 1901, 21,007 in 1966 and 16,500 (estimate) in 1985. The number of Christian Science practitioners fell from 1,104 in 1940 to 581 in 1969. There were 333 ministers in the General Assembly of Unitarian and Free Christian Churches in 1923 and 170 in 1985 (estimate).

Among religious bodies not called 'mainstream', trends have been varied. Bodies with reported increases include:

Assemblies of God 20,000 (1961), 28,000 (1966), 60,000 (1985 estimate)
Seventh Day Adventist Church 1,160 (1903), 10,884 (1966), 16,000 (1985 estimate)
Jehovah's Witnesses 6,000 (1926), 49,000 (1966), 92,000 (1985 estimate)
Elim Four Square Alliance 16,000 (1952), 20,000 (1967), 26,000 (1985 estimate)

All the main Pentecostal churches, the Church of Scientology, the African and West Indian churches, the Unification church, and the House Churches have apparently shown increases too. An increase in membership of 3,000 per cent has been reported for Dr Ian Paisley's new Free Presbyterian Church in Northern Ireland between 1956–80. The Congregational Union of Scotland had 2,298 members in 1901, and 2,200 in 1985. The Presbyterian Church of Ireland had 101,121 members in 1901 and 144,284 in 1966, declining by only 1 per cent between 1956 and 1980. Between the same years the Free Presbyterian Church in Scotland showed an estimated overall membership trend of +48 per cent.

If the modern study of religion has taught anything, it is that a religion is a multi-sided and multi-dimensional phenomenon. The few statistics cited above already begin to underline this heterogeneity and warn against the dangers of generalizing about the fortunes of Christianity in Britain. There is evidence of appreciable regional variation, with Scotland and Ireland showing signs of less numerical decline than England and Wales, and Ireland showing some increases in the traditional denominations. In all the figures there arise major questions of interpretation about attendance, adherence, membership. But, in any case, to make judgments about decreases and increases among the institutional churches only becomes at all meaningful when these are related to what has been happening to other institutions in the same society. Also, in evaluating the decline of church institutions, much depends on what is meant by 'Christianity'.

To focus narrowly upon church statistics is to decide in favour of an *institutional* definition of Christianity. This has been a common procedure in the West. Wilfred Cantwell Smith has drawn attention to the way in which some Western scholars have mistakenly tried to impose similar definitions upon, say, 'Buddhism' and 'Hinduism' as 'religions' somehow quantifiable apart from their life-setting, from their embeddedness in culture.[18] Against this, it may be argued that in all religious traditions the institutional element is fluid and partial, lacking the primary importance ascribed to it in the West. If this kind of argument is pressed in respect of Christianity in Britain, then one might for example guess that there are countless people who are not 'church members', but who, in beliefs about God and Jesus, and in ethical attitudes, may be more or less indistinguishable from 'Christian church members'. It would then be important to ask how this probably quite large segment of non-church Christianity is related both to church institutions and to other 'religions' in the British community, and how the mutual borrowings and influences could be identified and described. Though the institutional statistics do give some hint about the causes of institutional decline (war, economic hardship, social mobility), they do not say much about the nature and impact of Christian icons in the religious transactions which are taking place in and among people just below the surface of institutional life.

So statistics about all church institutions reveal more ambiguity than appears at first sight. On closer inspection there is enough evidence of change, vitality, persistence and novelty to suggest that the institutional churches deserve close attention as possible icons of the Christian religion. They will be judged as only declensions into genre if they are treated simply by analogy with other organizations, e.g. the world of business, as if that could provide a sufficient account of the nature, tasks, and iconic potential of church institutions. Thus it is exceedingly hard to determine what conclusions to draw from the ebbing numerical fortunes of much of British Christianity. Wide differences of opinion are to be found among sociologists of religion as to whether this numerical decline correlates with decline or increase of influence, with deeper or more trivial spirituality.

THE ECUMENICAL MOVEMENT

The twentieth century is often hailed as the age of ecumenism. After various efforts, by individuals (notably Archbishop Nathan Söderblom) and by groups, before and after the First World War, to bring about friendship between the churches internationally, a long history began which ultimately led, by diverse routes, to the formation of the World Council of Churches, the creation of the British Council of Churches in 1942 (and later of such councils in Wales, Scotland and Ireland), the proliferation of local councils of churches, of areas of ecumenical experiment and more recently of local ecumenical projects. In all this there resides a rich experience and a significant machinery which could not have been envisaged in 1900. By virtue of these and other developments, there is now an unprecedented degree of co-operation and goodwill between the mainstream churches (and, sometimes, other bodies) at certain levels and in certain spheres in many parts of Britain. But the declared goal of the ecumenical movement has been the organic unity of presently separated churches and a massive amount of time and effort has been expended in pursuit of this goal. Very little has come of it in concrete terms.

What of the few successes? One of the most dramatic church events in its time was the long worked-for union between the Church of Scotland and the United Free Church in 1929.[19] The motives were various, including the decline in Presbyterian membership, the pastoral challenge of the large urban centres, and the increased Irish immigrant population. The union provided a model for a non-divisive form of church establishment which has had signal advantages over the Henrician settlement in England. It also showed that a measure of disendowment could be carried through with dignity and the minimum of bitterness. But, of course, it was only a healing of historical divisions within the same family, not a union of different polities. The same may be said for Methodist union (Wesleyan, United and Primitive) in 1932.[20] It has certainly proved a genuine and solid achievement. But one of the primary aims was to rationalize grossly overlapping resources; this only happened very painfully and too slowly by far for that church's health. The only unions across denominations have been the coming together in 1972, after two earlier abortive efforts, of the Presbyterian Church of England and the Congregational Church in England and Wales as the United Reformed Church, and the union of most elements of the Churches of Christ with the United Reformed Church in 1981. What have been the ecumenical hopes unrealized?

The Lambeth Appeal to all Christian People (1920) had sounded a fairly optimistic note about accessible unity and had spoken generously of the ordained ministries of the Free Churches (though still assuming the need for episcopacy in a united church). On the other hand, the Malines Conversations (1921–5) between some Anglican catholics and some Roman Catholics showed up the divisions within the Church of England and the suspicion and puzzlement which these could generate. The scheme for a united Church of South India, involving Anglican dioceses, met with a rancorous reception in some Church of England circles and the previously generous attitude to Free Church ministries was much diluted.

A similar outcome occurred when, following successful bi-lateral conferences between Irish Anglicans and Irish Presbyterians, the Anglican home reunion committee asked its synod in 1935 to say that it 'fully and freely recognizes the validity, efficacy and spiritual reality of both ordination and sacraments as administered in the presbyterian church'.[21] The Archbishop of Dublin replaced this by a greatly watered-down statement and the matter rested there. There have been remarkably few lay attempts to challenge the clerical ecumenical paradigm and such as have taken place (e.g.

Maud Royden as an Anglican ministering at the City Temple), have occasioned episcopal thunder. The real Anglican negotiating terms were effectively restated by Archbishop Fisher in his Cambridge sermon of 1946, inviting the Free Churches to take episcopacy into their systems. Clearly, many in those churches were willing to do this. In 1955 the Church of England and the Methodist Church resolved to begin conversations; these were completed in 1963 with a Final Report. A scheme of union foundered on the predictable issue of episcopacy and ordained ministry, though there were other less palpable reasons too. 'The Methodists voted twice to accept episcopacy; but they were still rejected.'[22] Meanwhile, conversations had been taking place between Anglicans and Presbyterians. These too came to nothing. Many Scots could accept *no* form of episcopacy. Following the Anglican-Methodist débâcle, a new, multilateral approach was tried with the setting-up of the Churches Unity Commission. In 1976 the Ten Propositions were produced, but the log-jam with Anglicans about holy orders could not be broken. This may have been the last chance for substantial union between churches in Britain for the foreseeable future.

A major factor in this recent history has been the entry of the Roman Catholic Church into the Ecumenical Movement. Since Vatican II Roman Catholics and other denominations are generally treating each other as Christians and the Roman Catholics are thereby in practice conceding that their Church is one among several. The catholic sect, and others too, in the Church of England has turned its attention more and more to an ecumenical future which must include Rome. Anglican catholics can and will, therefore, go on impeding unity schemes with the Free Churches. But evangelicals can always impede catholicizing unity schemes which include, for example, consent to a 'wider papalism'. In turn the Roman Catholic Church does not have much sympathy for the democratic structures either of the mainstream denominations or of the British Council of Churches. Thus the arrival of the Roman Catholic Church has quite properly changed and complicated the style and content of the ecumenical movement in Britain.

The Church of England has played a leading role in many of the initiatives discussed above, but it has also been a chief destroyer. It has produced some notable ecumenical leaders, e.g. William Temple (1881–1944), George Bell (1881–1958) and Arthur Cayley Headlam (1862–1947), to stand alongside Free Church leaders across the period, e.g. John Scott Lidgett, Ernest Payne and Pauline Webb. But, as hinted already, the Church of England can be called 'not so much a Church as a number of sects'. These sects have worked with different notions of unity; namely catholics for the restoration of an earlier but now fragmented unity, many liberals for an idea of mutual transformation into unity, and evangelicals with an emphasis on spiritual unity which often translates into federalism. In addition, it would be wrong to underestimate the strength of conviction among some Anglicans that their church is still the church of the nation and that they will not share with others, or allow to be reduced, the status allegedly given by establishment. This point of view sits uneasily with Archbishop Manning's observation nearly a century ago that 'there is now no national church in existence . . . the Established Church of England does not contain half the English people'.[23].

Viewed in a wider perspective, it may be that a genuinely different disposition of churches is emerging. Anglican, Roman Catholic and Free Churches in fact have a great deal in common. Traditional dissent really lost its distinctive impact in the First World War when it shared with other churches in a united front of support for the war aims. The Roman Catholic Church in Britain is on 'the road to becoming just another Christian denomination'.[24] It may therefore be that the mantle of dissent is passing to a very loose grouping of independent, evangelical churches whose membership is growing and who are united by nothing so much as a deep dislike of the World Council of Churches.[25] Ian Paisley represents an extreme view when he claims that the Council is 'Doctrinally Unbiblical, Basically Unprotestant, Ecclesiastically Unclean, Practically Unchristian, and Spiritually Untrustworthy'.[26] But it is not yet clear how that dissent would manifest itself in a socially tangible form as these churches' relationships with the environing society are mostly negative.

The twentieth-century British ecumenical movement can be interpreted as both a declension into abstraction and a declension into genre. It can be judged the first of these because, despite all the goodwill and integrity, the ecumenical rhetoric in the churches and the churchly theology of ecumenism far, far exceeds the empirical reality of ecumenism. It can be judged a declension into genre because the normative picture of church life which the churches *actually* stand by is denominational. (Serious bridging of confessional loyalties and mores at the grass roots between Anglicans and Methodists was hardly attempted.) The gravity of these declensions is that the churches have settled into a polite pluralism of live-and-let-live which is also in fact a state of extreme fragmentation. It would seem that without greater organic church union, achieved with painful self-surrender, the Ecumenical Movement cannot serve as an effective icon of a depth of human unity in and beyond the prevailing secular pluralism and fragmentation. In Wales a notable feature of recent decades has been the rapprochement between Nonconformists and Anglicans which issued in a 'Covenant for Unity'. But that improvement was inseparable from the painful surrender of establishment. And 'it would be a mistake to underestimate the sense of near-disaster with which the first generation of Welsh churchmen faced disestablishment. It was a traumatic experience from which they had emerged bruised and lacerated'.[27]

CHRISTIAN PUBLIC WITNESS

The nineteenth century in Britain witnessed a growing sense of Christian responsibility in social, economic and political affairs. Examples include the Clapham Sect, the Quaker abolitionists, the Salvation Army and the Christian Socialists. Much of the general Christian response to the needs of the century was of a remedial or philanthropic nature; it did not challenge political or economic assumptions in a fundamental way. This kind of church activity displayed the churches in an increasingly false public prominence. Gilbert has argued, however, that this prominence masked the continuing impact of the cultural secularization of the church. 'Christianity's historically favourable social environment in Britain' was all the time gradually disintegrating.[28] If this thesis is correct, then it must be said that, as Christian understanding of the socio-critical role has increased, so the possibility of fulfilling that role has decreased.

Certainly the call of the Methodist Hugh Price Hughes (1847–1902) found many ready listeners in the following decades: 'Let us not only save people's souls but . . . sanctify their circumstances. It is an essential feature of [Christ's] mission to reconstruct human society on the basis of justice and love.'[29] In two rather different ways, the First World War gave impetus to this collectivist concern. Whereas the Christian doctrines of evil, guilt, repentance and forgiveness had earlier been located in an individualist, domestic framework, now the tragedy brought about by the War called for the frame of reference of Christian belief and practice to be enlarged.[30] But, as one of the five committees set up by the Anglican archbishops to take forward the concerns of the ill-starred National Mission of Repentance and Hope reported in 1919: ' . . . the [industrial] system makes it exceedingly difficult to carry into practice the principles of Christianity'.[31] But the motives expressed in the churches after the War were often lacking in altruism. They wanted to make up lost ground, to grasp a 'startling and vivid revelation of need and opportunity'. This churchly opportunism may have detracted from the necessary effort to think through, at this crucial juncture, the bases of Christian social concern. This inadequacy is apparent in the major ecumenical Conference on Christian Politics, Economics and Citizenship convened under William Temple's expert leadership in 1924, and which served as a preparation for the 1925 Stockholm Universal Christian Conference on Life and Work.

What was the emerging rationale of Christian social concern? Careful examination reveals a good measure of affinity with the theology of the Social Gospel as this had been developed in the United States towards the end of the nineteenth century up to the First World War. In Walter Rauschenbusch, for example, this theology used the notion of the 'christianization of society' which seems to mean 'applying to society those values which we associate with Jesus'. This approach presupposed the Liberal Protestant picture of Jesus whose life and teaching yields certain general values. Armed with these principles, the individual sets out to transform institutions and human relationships. But many of the American exponents of the Social Gospel were not particularly interested in the specifics of politics as such. The archetypal Washington Gladden had been above all a preacher. The 1925 Stockholm Conference was equally wary. The Kingdom of God could be to some extent achieved by human effort; but that effort does not seem to be based on anything strikingly Christian but on general humanitarian and democratic principles. How the Christian 'principles' are arrived at, how the middle ground between Christian principles and specific activity is to be understood, and how this process is related to technical-expert analysis, are questions which were, and are still, far from adequately resolved. It seems that many of those Christian thinkers who were in differing degrees indebted to the Social Gospel tradition in fact held the belief – even in the radically changed circumstances of the twentieth century – that Christianity could still supply the basis of a comprehensive social ethic, as had been the case (it was supposed) in the era of Christendom. William Temple's belief lingers that the church had the right to lay down the principles which should govern the ordering of human society, because the church possesses a divine revelation which illuminates every phase of human conduct. The Papal Encyclicals have manifested a similar outlook.

But another Christian attitude to the public realm became apparent during the period. In the 1920s and 1930s recession, unemployment, totalitarianism introduced a different mood marked by pessimism, judgment and realism. The church's task was not so much to join in the changing of society, but to preach a saving message to society about God who declared human effort to be without merit. Many sections of British churchly, denominational and sectarian Christianity have subscribed to this view in various forms, so withdrawing from a sense of Christian responsibility in the public realm.[32] Certainly the development of Christian social thought in the principal churches was thereby arrested and this neglect only compounded in the Church of England after the Second World War when, in a period of rapid and convulsive change, much nervous energy and intellectual dedication was given to canon law reform and other domestic tasks.

It is easy to criticize Christian social thought in this period. And judgments have to be tempered when it is acknowledged that social ethics in the secular sphere was itself grossly underdeveloped and was often content to parrot an earlier utilitarianism. In comparison, many of the Christian thinkers were in fact giving a lead.

The development of the Christian social concern can be seen in changes of church practice. For example, the rise of specialized ministries since the Second World War followed upon an analysis of contemporary society, with its growing disjunctions between work and home and its recognition that ministry at the place of residence does not necessarily put the church in critical solidarity with people at work. But these ministries are not without their critics. Many ministers of congregations treat specialized ministers as second-class citizens. Lay Christians may claim that their role at the front line of the church's ministry has been usurped. Not all the churches have instituted full-time specialized ministers and few have taken up the notion of worker-priests pioneered by Roman Catholics in France. It is still an open question what is the nature of the ministry/vocation of the layperson and minister at the place of work. That these questions go on being carefully asked and courageously explored in practice may be in part attributed to the work of George Macleod, founder of the Iona Community, Mollie Batten of William Temple College and others.

A crucial aspect of Christianity's role in the public realm concerns its attitude to nationalism. Some churches in Scotland, Wales and Ireland have been much identified with this question. The Nonconformist churches in Wales played an active and often belligerent part in parliament's eventual decision to disestablish the Welsh Church. The General Assembly of the Church of Scotland has served as an important focus of Scottish sentiment, especially in its Church and Nation debates. Much more fateful in its consequences has been of course the impact of the Christian religion in support of and against Irish nationalism. Several accounts have been offered of the place of the Christian religion in the Northern Ireland context. Hickey is surely correct in arguing that

> the religious divide in Northern Ireland is not based purely on the symbolic membership of a group with different political ideologies but is rooted in different interpretations of the Christian faith, which, in turn, help to form attitudes as to what 'society' and its institutions should be about.[33]

The interplay of religious and political impulses in the Orange Order reflects a society in some respects in a far less advanced state of modernization than most other parts of the United Kingdom. Will the well-advanced economic modernization in Northern Ireland hasten the political and religious modernization too? It may be an irony with which British Christians have to live that one of the conditions for the 'solution' of the Irish problem is the more rapid secularization of the Christian religion in both Ulster and the Republic of Ireland.

The matter of Christian witness in the public realm has been marked by declensions into both abstraction and genre. The two are connected. For most of the time members of Christian bodies have reflected the views of the society of which they are a part.

There have been powerful instances of individual courage in eschewing deference to the political arm, e.g. Archbishop Davidson in the First World War and Archbishop Runcie after the Falklands War. With some notable exceptions – the Free Churches and temperance, the Roman Catholic Church and abortion, the Society of Friends and pacifism – the churches have not felt under any great pressure to develop distinctive attitudes to societal issues. So most popular 'Christian' views on such issues reflect the prevailing secular wisdoms and unwisdoms and so represent a declension into genre. But, at the same time, the churches feel a responsibility to take up a position, to defend Christian values, on debated questions. This is often carried through at the highest level of abstraction – an abstraction which also conceals/reveals the problem of arriving at any degree of consensus within the churches. It has been said that justice is impossible to define, but that it is possible to recognize injustice. Is one of the lessons of the century so far that the churches may be playing their most significant social role when, at all levels, they faithfully, tenaciously, accurately and publicly draw attention to the phenomena of social injustice even if they do not generate a distinctive point of view? But the declensions into abstraction also point to a sinister phenomenon. Generalized pleas for racial harmony and justice are less likely to result in the churches dealing with racial issues in their own ranks. In 1986 the Church of England had 11,000 full-time clergy of whom just under fifty were black.

THEOLOGY

The twentieth century did not initiate a theological debate in Britain, but continued an earlier one from the nineteenth century which, in turn, received its character from the intellectual challenge posed to Christian thought by the European Enlightenment.[34] That challenge was mounted by reason against tradition, by critical analysis against the claims of self-evident authority. It revolved and revolves around whether human understanding has, in the final analysis, priority over received tradition, or whether tradition has priority over the understanding, or whether received tradition and autonomous understanding exist in a dialectical relationship. So the main lines of the debate had already been drawn. Historical-critical study of the Bible was incompatible with all kinds of fundamen-

117

talism and biblicism. Doctrine, now understood as the church's articulation of religious sentiments, was incompatible with the notion of revealed dogma. The methods and results of the scientific study of religions were incompatible with claims for the a priori superiority of Christianity. But liberal theology in the early part of the century did not want to appear simply negative, any more than J. Semler and the other pioneering *Neologen* had wanted to do in the late eighteenth century.[35] So the historical-critical method had itself to be put to work in the discovery of the authentic gospel.

The spirit of earlier Liberal Protestantism lived on in the writings of some Anglican Modernists, e.g. Henry Major (1871–1961) and Hastings Rashdall (1858–1924) who thought that it was possible to derive from the gospels an historical Jesus who could serve as the basis of an undogmatic religion and morality. Some of these writers placed reliance on the philosophy of personal idealism with its primacy of spirit and personality. Ironically that kind of idealism was itself probably a secularized version of an earlier Christian philosophy. This heavy reliance upon personalism as the basis of theological statements reappears subsequently in the period. The Roman Catholic Modernists, of whom George Tyrrell (1861–1909) and Friedrich von Hügel (1852–1925) were somewhat dissimilar representatives in Britain, also appealed to a positive use of history, this time postulating a principle of historical development which could reconcile the historical Jesus and the early church with the fully-fledged church of later times. Other liberals argued that if philosophical and scientific criticism quite rightly challenged the traditional transcendent theism, theology could properly move in the direction of a radical immanentism which would visualize God working in, through and with the natural and historical orders. A less sophisticated example of this outlook occurs in R. J. Campbell's *The New Theology*. Many writers underestimated the difficulty of correlating philosophical theology with natural science. An outstanding, but neglected, exception was F. R. Tennant whose *Philosophy of the Sciences* explored fundamental methodological problems.

But the liberal mediating positions could not hold. The unrelieved tragedy of the First World War had already eroded their intellectual and emotional basis. And the search for philosophical underpinnings had to reckon with the fact that philosophy proper in Britain was now entering upon a highly independent career as an analytical discipline (B. Russell, L. Wittgenstein, G. E. Moore, J. Wisdom, J. L. Austin). As philosophy and theology moved farther apart, liberal theology's entire undertaking was called in question. The new movement of 'crisis' theology associated with Karl Barth (1886–1968), Emil Brunner (1889–1966) and others, wanted to separate the Christian gospel from culture; to avoid all mediations with the natural sciences, psychology, religious experience and historicism; and to reinstate the central message of the otherness of God and the unique saving otherness of Christ. Barth exercised very little direct influence in England, though, as a Reformed theologian he found a much more ready following in Scotland in T. F. Torrance and others.

In Britain, the characteristic form of the new orthodoxy was Biblical Theology.[36] This approach claimed to respect the methods and findings of historical-critical Biblical study, but to use them in a positive and constructive manner.[37] The Bible was treated as a theological unity from which 'Biblical doctrines' of man (sic), sin, time, history, revelation and salvation could be extracted. This theological tendency persisted to the 1950s and was influential for the Liturgical Movement (see below) and for an emerging Protestant doctrinal consensus in the Ecumenical Movement. But Biblical Theology was built on false assumptions. It hero-worshipped so-called Hebraic thought as the authoritative bearer of revelation. It hopelessly overstated the unity of the Bible. It made the mistake of supposing that a systematic theology, apt for modern needs, can be drawn directly from the Bible. Its rhetoric was impressive; its substance elusive. It was thus both boon and bane to preachers. Yet Biblical Theology was correct to insist that theology cannot depend upon the latest theory of the Biblical critics. Also, in the hands of a theologian such as Alan Richardson, Biblical Theology brought the fruits of modern theology before a much wider lay audience.

Existentialist philosophy gained a hearing in Britain in the later 1930s, e.g. in H. R. Mackintosh (1870–1936). Under the influence of Martin Buber's *I and Thou* (tr. 1937) and of John Oman's (1860–1939) writings, a distinctive strand of theological personalism was developed in Britain. Another form came from Germany after the Second World War with the influence of Bultmann's provocative existential interpretation of Biblical 'myth'. Personalism affirmed the objective reality of subjective existence. In John Baillie and others, theological personalism could keep its feet on the ground and proved a signal gain. But it could also develop to a point where the claims of faith have no empirical reference point at all! It sometimes paid too high a price for its achievements. The existentialist concentration upon inwardness tended to withdraw theology from the political, social, economic, scientific and ecological preoccupations of the human community. In the final analysis, Christian existentialism threatened to live in a private world. To that extent it was in league with the popular, fundamentalist theology of Protestantism which continues in surprisingly unchanged form through the period.

In British theology during these decades there was a search for a new source of compelling theological authority which could satisfactorily replace the old Protestant and Catholic authorities which had been accepted as *extra controversiam*. There was also a proneness to accept passively the embargoes imposed upon theology by the secular intellectual community, and, in response, either to yield too quickly to secular criteria, or too quickly to take fright and find refuge in an arcane world of 'faith' with idiosyncratic criteria. Two features of the British scene reflect these tendencies. First, the most prominent subject of theological study in this period, at least until recently, has been the Bible! Among the least studied have been the theological disciplines of a more applied nature and those that deal with religion as a living phenomenon. This bias has been related to the distribution of power in the theological community. The prestige of biblical studies has been connected with their authoritative role in the confessional traditions coming from the Reformation and with their status as a respectable subject of scientific study in the universities. Second, theology during this period (not least, until recently, Roman Catholic theology) has existed in a high degree of intellectual isolation. In faculties and departments of theology, in theological colleges (especially of the Free Church traditions), in cathedral closes and elsewhere, the various theological disciplines have been pursued, almost entirely by men, often to very high standards. But this scholarship has not taken place at what Charles Davis has called the creative centre of a culture. It can, of course, be argued that British theology's intellectual isolation is but one outcome of the secularization of Christian belief and institutions, before which theologians are powerless. But the monolithic and all-determining character of secularization has been all too often overstated. Maybe the intellectual isolation of British theology in part arises from an unwillingness to admit that the notion of self-evident authority is now beyond recall, and that the study of theology is inseparable from the study of religion and culture. In particular, Christian theology in Britain is proving painfully and dangerously slow in taking up the indigenous dialogue with those of other living faiths.

These considerations may afford insight into what happened in the theological brouhaha of the 1960s associated with *Honest to God*. In the British society of the 1960s, certain supposedly secure moral, cultural, political and intellectual landmarks were dislodged to reveal a confused, rapidly changing, and fragmented society, not a society (as some had supposed) caught in the vice-like grip of belligerent secularism. Since the 1960s the theological scene in Britain has been confused and untidy, but there are signs of more attention being paid to present-centred criteria and to the social and moral experience of religion in a late twentieth-century advanced society. But the period as a whole has manifested a widespread declension into biblical-theological generality and abstraction in professional theology. In more popular theology declensions into genre have been common, as the beliefs current in church institutions have been taken as theological norms. (Though there has been popular apologetic of an imaginative order in, e.g. Ronald Knox, Dorothy Sayers and William Barclay.) This gulf between generality and genre has often been experienced as a fundamental clash of interests between church and academy. In fact, it is likely that neither church nor theology have adequately taken into their systems the radical transformations of sensibility and thought which have affected modern culture, which Nietzsche captured under the motif of the 'death of God'.

WORSHIP

So far, I have mainly been occupied with institutional and intellectual icons of twentieth-century Christianity in Britain. I now want to consider a phenomenon of a different order, namely Christian liturgy. Many have contended that worship is the fundamental and characteristic activity of the Christian community. If this is at all correct, it will be important, in 'taking the temperature' of Christianity in a certain period and place, to give special attention to liturgical worship.

Though there will have been many and notable exceptions, a good deal of evidence suggests that in the first three decades of the century much public worship was often sluggish, dull, individualist and sacerdotalist. In the Church of England, *The Book of Common Prayer* (1662) provided the liturgies for Mattins, with a long sermon, and for a monthly attendance at Holy Communion for many. In the Roman Catholic church the staple diet was the Tridentine low mass in Latin celebrated with close attention to rubrical detail, which may have been one factor in sending many worshippers to the warm and personal world of extra-liturgical devotions. Greater vitality in worship was experienced in some of the smaller churches, in the Salvation Army, and in the worship associated with revivalism. Reaction against the stagnancy and dullness of much worship came early from the Free Churches, but that reaction could itself become sentimentalist, subjectivist and individualist. Perhaps most significantly, the content and practice of much of the Christian worship of the era was unrelated to the emerging insights and impulses in theology, education, mission and evangelism. The striking changes in worship in the mainstream British churches since the 1930s are in the main attributable to the Liturgical Movement, though there are other antecedents and, more recently, the charismatic movement has played (some observers claim) an invigorating role.[38]

The origins of the Liturgical Movement[39] can be illustrated in the work of Prosper Gueranger (1805–75) in the nineteenth century, and its early development in the writings of Lambert Beauduin (1873–1960), Odo Casel (1886–1948), and others. Behind the desire for liturgical change lay theological, spiritual and social considerations. How could the liturgy best serve the Christian alienated in the new industrial society? In the mass, the incarnation and sacrifice of Christ should be so experienced that the corporate church could be sanctified and the requirements of social justice lived out. There was a strong outgoing impulse relating the liturgy to the 'Christification' of society. In the early Roman Catholic liturgical movement, the pioneers consciously moved behind medieval to biblical sources, seeking a balance between offering, commemoration and communion in the liturgy, especially challenging sacerdotalism by an emphasis on the participation of the people.

Some of this thinking had direct effects in the early days (e.g. bible readings in the vernacular). But the principal harvest was reaped with and after *Mediator Dei* (1947), with evening and dialogue masses, and vernacular hymns. The most radical outcome lay in Vatican II's *Constitution on the Sacred Liturgy* (1963) which consolidated the aims of liturgical renewal as seen by the pioneers, namely to keep in touch with the needs of the present age, to reunite all Christians, and to strengthen the work of evangelism. The primary motives were, therefore, of neither a historical nor an aesthetic kind. The keynotes of the revision of the mass are full, conscious and active participation, simplicity and clarity, increased use of the vernacular, more bible reading and preaching. All this has led, many attest, to a 'relaxation of rules and an access of freshness and vitality'; it has certainly introduced a 'wholesale change'.[40]

The Liturgical Movement did not influence the 1928 Prayer Book in the Church of England. Its chief route of entry was by Gabriel Hebert's *Liturgy and Society* (1935), significantly sub-titled *The Function of the Church in the Modern World*. It provided a theological basis for developments already occurring out of pastoral necessity. The first 'parish communion' had been introduced in 1927 in Newcastle. A desire was felt for a new liturgy which would express the new theology of the Church. But the various crises occasioned by the 1928 Prayer Book, not least the question as to what kind of veto, if any, parliament would exercise over further prayer book revision, delayed the process. The Liturgical Commission was finally set up in 1955; the first experimental services were put into use in 1965. These bore fruit in the *Alternative Service Book* (1980) which, though considered banal by some, seems to be preferred by a majority of clergy and laity. How far these changes at all reflect Hebert's contention that the Liturgical Movement was not primarily a set of beliefs nor a type of piety, but rather a way of life which could help to transform society, is indeed another matter.

Many of the distinguished Anglican liturgical scholars (e.g. F. E. Brightman, W. H. Frere, J. H. Strawley, Gregory Dix) were, for the reason noted above, not able to work on the revision of church services directly, though they did serve some churches of the Anglican Communion in this way. Significant historical and theological study of liturgy was undertaken by Roman Catholic scholars including Edmund Bishop (1846–1917), Anscar Vonier in *The People of God* (1937) and Illtyd Trethowan in *Christ in the Liturgy* (1952). Free Church liturgists could make a much more direct contribution to the shaping of worship. Scotland produced eminent liturgists in e.g. W.D. Maxwell (*Concerning Worship*, 1948) and Millar Patrick (*Four Centuries of Scottish Psalmody*, 1949).

The sentimentalism of the Congregationalist *A Manual for Ministers* (1936) was balanced by an emphasis on the social gospel which was to recur in several subsequent productions and which is strikingly absent from the Church of England's, *Alternative Service Book*. The Church of Scotland's *Book of Common Order* (1940) drew knowledgeably and judiciously upon traditional Reformed sources and upon other more modern sources too. It strongly influenced later books. Also significant, especially in the Free Church tradition, has been the revision of hymnbooks. The 1983 *Methodist Hymn Book* was a revision along thoroughly ecumenical lines. The Liturgical Movement made itself felt, not least through the setting-up of the Joint Liturgical Group in 1963. Many later books take up the theme of worship building community in society at large. This is apparent in *Contemporary Prayers for Public Worship* (1967). In the orders for the Eucharist appearing late in the period (*Methodist Service Book*, 1975; United Reformed Church, *A Book of Services*, 1980; the Church of England's *Alternative Service Book*, 1980) there are striking similarities to the revised Roman Catholic eucharistic rites in use in Britain today. This movement towards consensus is also apparent in luturgical theology.

Certain advantages have flowed from the general and particular effects of the Liturgical Movement in Britain. One consequence has been the increasing sense of a common Christian identity. Another consequence has been a lowering of the walls which have divided Christians in party-groups within the denominations. A striking example of this tendency has been the way in which evangelical, central and catholic in the Church of England have been able to identify themselves in good faith with the new services. Thus, on two counts, the Liturgical Movement has been the ecumenical movement which its authors hoped it would be. On the other hand, many of the criteria which have governed the changes in liturgical worship have been *historical* in character, appealing to precedent in the apostolic and post-apostolic church. It is questionable as to how far the determining icons of our rapidly changing culture have been identified and understood, and their consequences for worship grasped. In this connection, it is plain that the socio-critical function of worship has received insufficient attention. The concerns of Nathaniel Micklem and others in the symposium *Christian Worship* (1936) to restore to Christian worship its authentic biblical and theological foundations have been genuinely but selectively carried out. There is a degree of generality and abstraction about much contemporary liturgical revision, from which the prophetic aspect of worship can draw scant nourishment.

At the same time Christian worship in Britain has, since 1960, received a certain kind of revitalization from direct and indirect encounter with the charismatic movement. This movement avers that vitality in worship, if it is to be authentic, only comes through a freedom and depth which is given to it by the Spirit. But, sadly, the mainstream churches, in taking over pentecostalist beliefs and practices, have either copied their examples or appropriated them superficially in order to revive their own flagging worship; the mainstream churches have not allowed their own fundamental presuppositions about worship to be challenged. The Society of Friends has proved a small but important exception to many of these prevalent tendencies in worship. For the Quaker meeting for worship, with its relation to the Quaker business meeting, combines elements which elsewhere are often separated, e.g. social-criticism, prophecy, mysticism, silence, use of Christian and humanist tradition and also more consciously challenging sacerdotalism and sexism from which none of the other major liturgical traditions have yet significantly managed to escape.

Having said all this, the genuine dilemma must be faced that, in the extent to which Christian worship does involve itself with prevailing social icons, metaphors and rituals, it may lose its historic Christian character. There is no easy solution to this dilemma, least of all by constructing a crude opposition between past and present. It is a related question how far Christian worship should primarily be *for* the believer, the insider, and how far it should present a challenge and offer a spiritual resource to the 'outsider'. The latter function has been greatly lost sight of. As Bruce points out, most people who go to evangelical crusades are already well versed in the teachings and life of the churches.[41] Viewed from a history-of-religions perspective, it may be that the growing internal consensus about worship in many major sections of British Christianity is a mixed blessing and that a stubborn variety is the most appropriate recipe for the health of religion.

WOMEN

Although more women than men have occupied the pews in twentieth-century Britain, leadership in Church affairs, theology, worship, ecumenical matters and witness in the public realm has been firmly in the hands of men in Church, denomination and sect. The Christian histories and biographies of the modern period rarely mention women. It is likely that considerable numbers of women have left the Church in a mixture of anger and despair. But like so much of women's history in the Churches, the exodus is largely invisible. Feminist historiography has plenty of scope in this field for bringing the invisible into the light. As the history of the Free Churches has shown, the decision of a church to ordain, or otherwise officially employ, women does not necessarily advance or reflect a more enlightened attitude to women. The number of women ministers has been small and the reception to them mixed. In the Roman Catholic Church the status and role of women is also bound up with the more general question of the laity. In fact, in that church the causes of lay representation and lay consultation – let alone lay decision-making – have regressed over recent years, despite the hopes entertained by the national Congress held in Liverpool in 1980.[42] In the Church of England, the handling of theological and practical issues surrounding the ambiguous Order of Deaconesses was marked by injustice and gross insensitivity as (mainly male) church bodies tossed to and fro to each other, over decades, the questions of the deaconesses' status and conditions of service.[43]

It is noteworthy that friends and foes alike of the women's interests in the churches, including most of the women directly involved, have been at pains to disassociate themselves from the analysis and critique of sexism offered by the modern women's movement. Without the benefit of this analysis and critique it has not proved easy to withstand the excuse that the women's issue in the churches is a secondary matter. Yet the history of this issue in fact serves as a classic example of sexism at work. The primary message from the male churches has been that good Christian women do not 'campaign' for their rights, though the men campaign unremittingly for theirs. The women are patient in the face of delay and rebuff. They have as their primary concern other women, children and the elderly. They are noted for their 'spiritual' qualities. They are pastors rather than prophets or leaders. The widespread and longstanding hostility to women in the churches, in which they are stereotyped as evil Eves or virginal Marys, has surfaced at times with such ferocity as to suggest that there can be found in the churches vast subterranean reservoirs of largely repressed collective mysogyny which amounts to a severe sickness. If this be at all the case, it is alarming to speculate on the effect of such neurosis upon spirituality, ethics and pastoral care.

The distancing mechanism which treats the question of women by reference to Bible, tradition, church order and theology keeps it at arm's length from contemporary empirical analysis. Be all this as it may, the churches' contribution to the debate about the status of women in society at large in this century has been – some remarkable persons apart – deeply flawed. For the most part the churches have opted for declension into genre, uncritically accepting the received mores. More recently, in trying to avoid that, they have settled for declension into abstraction, prescribing to society very general regimens of desirable conduct but discovering all sorts of 'good' religious reasons for not attending to their own institutions. It is a sorry tale.

CONCLUSION

The contrasting nouns 'vitality' and 'hollowness' have been used to describe the state of the Christian religion in Britain as it nears the last decade of the century. Certainly the picture is more complex, and perhaps more hopeful, than the prophets of the straightforward decline of religion would have us believe. There are certainly many pockets of religious vitality in twentieth-century British Christianity, most of these in unfashionable and less than prominent places. But the charge of hollowness has to be taken very seriously too. The failures in moves to unity (it would not be so bad if they had not been attempted), the inhospitable treatment of indigenous and immigrant blacks, the systematic discrimination against women, the stultifying search for an invulnerable authority in church decision-making, and a repeated tendency of deference towards the political realm, are misleading icons of Christianity in the everyday life of the churches. The temptations to decline into abstraction, whereby a general truth is proclaimed, or into genre, whereby the present cultural forms of Christianity may be treated as absolutes, have been formidable.

But the attraction of yielding to these temptations is wholly understandable in view of the processes of loss and gain, of adaptation, in British society in which the Christian religion is ineluctably caught up. For Christianity in Britain has been facing, and still faces, the dilemma which apparently confronts many (all?) religions in societies undergoing modernization. Does the religion also modernize itself so as to remain intelligible and credible, but thereby lose its essential nature? Or, to retain its essential nature, does the religion resist modernization, thereby rendering itself incredible and unintelligible? Or does the framing of this alternative presuppose a false understanding of a religion? Is it that religions do not have 'an essential nature' but possess, lose, discover or fail to discover telling and appropriate forms of existence at different times and in different places? Is this what Richard Rothe had in mind when he asserted, provocatively, that Christianity is the most mutable of all religions, and that this is its permanent claim to fame?[44]

NOTES

1   For this discussion see Malcolm Warner, 'John Everett Millais's "Autumn Leaves": "a picture full of beauty and without subject" ', in Leslie Parris (ed.), *Pre-Raphaelite Papers*, London, The Tate Gallery/Allen Lane, 1984, pp.126–42; John Dixon Hunt, 'A Moment's Monument: Reflections on Pre-Raphaelite Vision on Poetry and Painting (1974)', in James Sambrook (ed.), *Pre-Raphaelitism: A Collection of Critical Essays*, Chicago and London, University of Chicago Press, 1974, pp.243–64; Lindsay Errington, *Social and Religious Themes in English Art: 1849–1860*, New York and London, Garland Publishing Inc., 1984, ch.7; Andrea Rose, *The Pre-Raphaelites*, London, Phaidon Press, 1977.

2   Rose, op.cit., p.5.

3   For 'genre' painting see Lionel Lambourne, *An Introduction to 'Victorian' Genre Painting from Wilkie to Frith*, London, HMSO, 1982.

4 In Warner, op.cit., p.127.
5 Walter Pater in Hunt, op.cit., p.246.
6 Cf. Rose, ibid.
7 For 'declensions' see Hunt, op.cit., p.260.
8 Elliott Kendall, *The End of an Era: Africa and the Missionary*, London, SPCK, 1978, p.6.
9 Kendall, ibid.
10 Kendall, op.cit., p.116.
11 Kendall, op.cit., pp.113ff.
12 John H. S. Kent, *The End of the Line?: The Development of Christian Theology in the Last Two Centuries*, London, SCM Press Ltd, 1982, p.x.
13 Kent, ibid.
14 Kent, ibid.
15 Alan Wilkinson, *Dissent or Conform?: War, Peace and the English Churches 1900–1945*, London, SCM Press Ltd, 1986, p.315.
16 Alan D. Gilbert, *The Making of Post-Christian Britain: A History of the Secularization of Modern Society*, London and New York, Longman, 1980, pp.156f.
17 I am indebted in this section to Robert Currie, Alan Gilbert, Lee Horsley, *Churches and Churchgoers: Patterns of Church Growth in the British Isles since 1700*, Oxford, Clarendon Press, 1977; Robert Currie and Alan Gilbert, 'Religion', in A. H. Halsey (ed.), *Trends in British Society since 1900: A Guide to the Changing Social Structure of Britain*, London and Basingstoke, The Macmillan Press Ltd, 1972, pp.407–50. I have sought roughly to update some of the statistics in the above by reference to P. Brierley (ed.), *UK Christian Handbook 1985/6 Edition*, London and Swindon, Evangelical Alliance/Bible Society/Marc Europe, 1984. But some of the *Handbook's* statistics are exceedingly speculative.
18 Wilfred Cantwell Smith, *The Meaning and End of Religion: A New Approach to the Religious Traditions of Mankind*, New York, New American Library, 1964.
19 See, for example, Ian Machin, 'Voluntaryism and Reunion, 1874–1929', in Norman Macdougall (ed.), *Church, Politics and Society: Scotland 1408–1929*, Edinburgh, John Donald Publishers Ltd, 1983, pp.221–38.
20 See Rupert Davies, 'Methodism', in Rupert Davies (ed.), *The Testing of the Churches 1932–1982: A Symposium*, London, Epworth Press, 1982, pp.32–59.
21 R. B. McDowell, *The Church of Ireland 1869–1969*, London and Boston, Routledge & Kegan Paul, 1975, p.135.
22 Peter Staples, *The Church of England 1961–1980*, Leiden-Utrecht,

Interuniversitair Institut voor Missiologie en Oecumenica, 1981, p.104.

23 Quoted in Antony Archer, *The Two Catholic Churches: A Study in Oppression*, London, SCM Press Ltd, 1986, p.70.

24 Archer, op.cit., p.258.

25 Cf. Steve Bruce, *Firm in the Faith*, Aldershot, Gower, 1984.

26 Quoted in John Hickey, *Religion and the Northern Ireland Problem*, Dublin, Gill and Macmillan, 1984, p.74.

27 David Walker, 'Disestablishment and Independence', in David Walker (ed.), *A History of the Church in Wales*, Penarth, Church in Wales Publications, 1976, p.172.

28 Gilbert, *The Making of Post-Christian Britain*, p.80.

29 In Henry D. Rack, 'Wesleyan Methodism 1849–1902', in Rupert Davies, A. Raymond George, Gordon Rupp (eds), *A History of the Methodist Church in Great Britain*, London, Epworth Press, vol.3, 1983, pp.144f.

30 Cf. Kent, op.cit., p.106.

31 Quoted in Alan Wilkinson, *The Church of England and the First World War*, London, SPCK, 1978, pp.86f.

32 See Davies, George and Rupp, op.cit., pp.210–15.

33 Hickey, op.cit., p.87.

34 Cf. S. W. Sykes, 'Theology', in C. B. Cox and A. E. Dyson (eds), *The Twentieth Century Mind: History, Ideas, and Literature in Britain: 2: 1918–1945*, London, Oxford and New York, Oxford University Press, 1972, pp.146–70; G Stephen Spinks, *Religion in Britain since 1900*, London, Andrew Dakers Ltd, 1952, chs.3,9,10.

35 See A. O. Dyson, 'Theological Legacies of the Enlightenment: England and Germany', in S. W. Sykes (ed.), *England and Germany: Studies in Theological Diplomacy*, Frankfurt am Main/Berne, Verlag Peter D. Lang, 1982.

36 Cf. Alan Richardson (ed.), *A Theological Word Book of the Bible*, London, SCM Press Ltd, 1950.

37 In this section I acknowledge a debt to Horton Davies, *Worship and Theology in England: The Ecumenical Century, 1900–1965*, London, Oxford University Press, 1965; Geoffrey Cuming, 'Liturgical Change in the Church of England and the Roman Catholic Church', Donald McIlhagga, 'Liturgical Change in the Free Churches', in Rupert Davies (ed.), *The Testing of the Churches*, pp.119–31, 159–74.

38 For pentecostalism see Walter J. Hollenweger, *The Pentecostals*, London, SCM Press Ltd, 1972.

39 See E. B. Koenker, *The Liturgical Renaissance in the Roman Catholic Church*, St Louis, Concordia, 2nd edn, 1966.

40 Cuming, op.cit., p.126.

The Christian Religion

41 Bruce, *Firm in the Faith*, p.102.
42 For laity see *In the House of the Living God* (Bishops' Conference of England and Wales), Catholic Information Services, 1982. For the Congress see *Liverpool 1980: Official Report of the National Pastoral Congress*, 1981.
43 See B. Fullalove, *The Ministry of Women in the Church of England 1919–1970*, Manchester University M.Phil. thesis, 1986, *passim*.
44 Richard Rothe, quoted in Ernst Troeltsch, *Richard Rothe: Gedächtnisrede, gehalten zur Feier der hundertsten Geburtstages in der Aula der Universität*, Freiburg i B., Leipzig and Tübingen, J. C. B. Mohr, 1899, p.30.

BIBLIOGRAPHY

In addition to the works cited in the Notes see also:

Barth, K., *The Word of God and the Word of Man*, London, Hodder & Stoughton, 1930.
Beck, G. A. (ed.), *The English Catholics*, London, Burns Oates, 1950.
Bell, G. K. A., *Randall Davidson*, London, Oxford University Press, 2 vols, 1935.
Buber, M., *I and Thou*, Edinburgh, T. and T. Clark, 1937.
Church Statistics: Some Facts and Figures about the Church of England 1985, London, The Central Board of Finance of the Church of England, 1985.
Currie, R., *Methodism Divided: A Study in the Sociology of Ecumenicalism*, London, Faber, 1968.
Edwards, D. (ed.), *Priests and Workers: An Anglo-French Discussion*, London, SCM Press Ltd, 1961.
Edwards, D., *Leaders of the Church of England 1828–1944*, London, Oxford University Press, 1971.
Hastings, A., *A History of English Christianity 1920–1985*, London, Collins, 1986.
Hebert, A. G., *Liturgy and Society: The Function of the Church in the Modern World*, London, Faber, 1935.
Hickey, J., *Urban Catholics: Urban Catholicism in England and Wales from 1829 to the Present Day*, London, Geoffrey Chapman, 1967.
Highet, J., *The Churches in Scotland Today: A Survey of their Principles, Strength, Work and Statements*, Glasgow, Jackson Son and Company, 1950.
Koss, S., *Nonconformity in Modern British Politics*, London, Batsford, 1975.
Lloyd, R., *The Church of England 1900–1965*, London, SCM Press Ltd, revd edn., 1966.

Mackintosh, H. R., *Types of Modern Theology: Schleiermacher to Barth*, London, Nisbet and Co., 1937.

Mathew, D., *Catholicism in England 1535–1935: Portrait of a Minority, its Culture and Tradition*, London, Longmans, 3rd edn., 1955.

Neill, S., *A History of Christian Missions*, Harmondsworth, Penguin, revd edn., 1986.

Norman, E. R., *Church and Society in England 1770–1970: A Historical Study*, Oxford, Clarendon Press, 1976.

Oman, J., *The Natural and the Supernatural*, Cambridge, Cambridge University Press, 1931.

Ramsey, A. M., *From Gore to Temple: The Developments of Anglican Theology between Lux Mundi and the Second World War, 1889–1939*, London, Longmans, 1960.

Temple, W., *Christianity and Social Order*, London, Shepheard-Walwyn/SPCK, 1976.

Tennant, F. R., *Philosophy of the Sciences: or, the Relations between the Departments of Knowledge*, Cambridge, Cambridge University Press, 1932.

Welsby, P. A., *A History of the Church of England 1945–1980*, Oxford, Oxford University Press, 1984.

CHAPTER FIVE

Other Major Religious Traditions

Kim Knott

The British have always been an ethnically diverse people. Over the centuries Celts, Picts and Scots, Romans, Angles and Saxons, Danes, and Normans settled here. More recently a number of ethnic groups from Europe, Asia and the Americas have made Britain their home. It is only in the last century, however, that Britain has experienced the growth of a complex form of religious as well as social pluralism. It is true that we have remains of Roman Mithraic temples which predate the arrival of Christianity on our shores. In addition, it is undeniable that Britain had a Jewish population before its expulsion in 1290. By and large, though, the countries of the British Isles have been 'Christian' for over a thousand years. It was not until the eighteenth and nineteenth centuries, with the rise in Nonconformity, the geographical spread of Irish Catholicism and the fast growth of the Jewish population following the migrations from Eastern Europe, that Britain became a nation of religious diversity.

The nineteenth century, more than any other, saw the consolidation of 'intra-religious' pluralism with the growth of Christian denominations including the Methodists, the Baptist Union, the Congregationalists, Presbyterians and Roman Catholics but also smaller groups such as the Unitarians and the Mormons. Since then, not only has Christianity in Britain encompassed Greek Orthodoxy, Polish Catholicism, the Lutheran churches of the

Baltic countries, and the black-led churches with their roots in America, the West Indies and in Africa, but also other world religions have been introduced and have begun to flourish. This new 'inter-religious' pluralism, which has developed dramatically with the arrival in Britain of South Asians from countries once a part of the British Empire, now includes not only Christianity and Judaism but also Islam, Hinduism, Sikhism, Buddhism, Jainism and Zoroastrianism. Like Christianity, all of these religions have their own subdivisions, many of which are represented today in Britain. In common with many nations in the modern world Britain has a religious profile which is complex and fascinating.

Although religious pluralism is not an unusual contemporary phenomenon, each country has a different experience of it. In India and some West African countries, for example, religious pluralism does not necessarily imply social and cultural pluralism in the way it does in Britain or North America. In those countries invasion, mission, religious diversification and syncretism over the centuries brought about the development of religious traditions which are now indigenous. The situation in Britain, however, is the result of the comparatively recent arrival and settlement of groups from geographical areas with different social, cultural and religious experiences from those of the established population. Britain, like other European and American countries also differs from some other nations in having one religion, Christianity, in a position of strength in relation to all others. Christianity, albeit denomination-ally diverse, is the religion of the majority; Judaism, Islam and the other major religious traditions are minority faiths. In addition to these major differences, Britain, like all other nations, has its own particular historical experience – political, economic and social – which has contributed to the development of the contemporary religious situation.

The nature of religious pluralism in Britain is different from that of even its neighbours in Europe with whom it has general cultural and religious similarities. For an explanation of these differences it is necessary to understand both the political, social and cultural inheritance of Britain and other European countries and the events which took place in those countries from which migrants came during the last hundred years. In Britain, the situation derives from a variety of causes including the painful growth of a tradition of religious tolerance, the need for new sources of labour in both the nineteenth and mid-twentieth centuries, Britain's colonial relationship to countries in South Asia and the West Indies, and the image projected by this nation and held by refugees and migrants in search of a safe place and an opportunity to work and to reap the rewards.[1] Other European countries, like France and Germany, with a different experience of industrial and colonial development, and with different political institutions and religious frameworks, saw a different pattern of social and religious pluralism emerge in the last century.[2]

In Britain, then, the picture is very much one of both social and religious pluralism. Far longer than the list of religions is the list of ethnic groups resident here. In the nineteenth century, conditions in Ireland and in Eastern Europe brought Irish Catholics and Russian, Polish and Austro-Hungarian Jews to Britain. This century they have been followed by Jews from Germany and other central European countries, Italians, Greek Cypriots, Poles, Eastern Europeans from the old Baltic states of Lithuania, Latvia and Estonia, Afro-Caribbeans from Jamaica and the other islands of the West Indies, South Asians from India, Pakistan, Bangladesh and the East African countries of Kenya, Tanzania, Uganda and Malawi and the Vietnamese. In addition to these there are smaller groups from West Africa, Sri Lanka, Iran and Hong Kong. They are settled throughout Britain, particularly in the big cities to which they were attracted for work.

Most of the groups have their own social and cultural centres, many their own language classes, and all their own informal networks of relations and friends as well as more formal ethnic organizations. Religion plays an important part in these activities and arrangements for many of the groups mentioned above. Some, of course, are Christian. Nevertheless, their different ethnic origins – in Central or Eastern Europe, or in the countries of the New Commonwealth – mean different cultural styles, vernacular liturgies and traditional customs. For these reasons, the non-indigenous Christian groups, like those of other religious traditions, have built up their own religious communities, purchasing buildings, developing suitable programmes of regular and festival worship, and obtaining ministers from their own ethnic group. This has gone on alongside or in conjunction with more overt social and cultural activities.

The same kind of process has occurred for those from the other religious traditions settled in Britain. In their case the goals have perhaps been clearer. Except in the case of the Jewish community, which had grown slowly since the seventeenth century and had opened many synagogues by the time the Eastern European Jews arrived in the late nineteenth century, there were no suitable religious institutions in existence which migrants from other traditions could join. For all the non-Christian religious groups settlement in Britain, sooner or later, has been accompanied by the organization of religious committees and meetings, the purchase of property for worship, new building programmes, the employment of religious specialists from within the communities here or from the community back home, and the development of religious programmes consonant with traditional requirements.[3] Not all the religions, or the groups representing them, have developed in the same way, and there has been much change both in relation to the practice of the homeland and since the early days of settlement here. This will be discussed later because it is vital not only for our understanding of the complexity of religious pluralism in Britain today, but also because of what it shows us about the individual religions, their dynamic and exciting traditions, and the way they are contributing to British life. First of all, we must learn something about the different religions which are to be found here, why they came, what forms they take, what the size of their communities is, and what their central beliefs and practices are.

THE RELIGIONS: TRANSPLANTATION AND GROWTH

Migration is inevitably a disruptive experience, and religion, like all other aspects of personal and social life, is in some way changed by it.[4] It does not necessarily encourage traditional religious and cultural roots to be laid down, although this is not uncommon, particularly for ethnic groups for whom religion has been important in the past. Some migrants do not persist with practices performed in the place of origin and do not organize themselves into groups based on religious orientation. For example, many Indian Hindu professionals and students in Britain do not become involved in local or national religious bodies or their activities. At home they almost certainly would have participated in some domestic and temple worship at important times in the Hindu calendar if not on a regular basis. A number of possible factors, in combination, may have contributed to this change in behaviour such as the temporary nature of their residence in Britain, the isolation caused by the lack of a network of relatives which other Indians settled here are part of, and the growth of a voluntaristic element in contemporary Indian Hinduism. In addition the nature of their work and the culture of their white colleagues, and the small size and scattered nature of the 'community' to which they belong add to the difficulties involved.

What we have here is a set of factors which helps to account for the formation, or in this case the lack of it, of a group's religious identity subsequent to its migration. For every migrant group the explanation for what happens to their religious identity in the new geographical and social location is different, but in all cases:

> the transplantation of a religion involves a complex relationship between tradition and interpretation, or in other words, an interplay between what is taken to be the content of the religion and the key factors in the situation which it is entering.[5]

Broadly speaking, the factors involved in this interplay are the *home traditions*, the religious and cultural baggage in all its richness and complexity, the *host traditions*, including the political, legal, social and religious frameworks in which newcomers find themselves, the *nature and experience of the migration process*, the *nature of the migrant group*, its ethnic or religious cohesiveness, size etc., and the *nature of the host response*, the experience of racism, religious prejudice or a desire for dialogue, attitudes to questions of assimilation, multiculturalism etc.[6]

How religious groups develop, the shape their religious traditions take in the new location, and the changes which occur with the passing of time and the experiences it brings depend very much on these complex factors and the way in which they interact. By looking briefly at the different religions in Britain, and then at the relationship between them and the ethnic groups which support them it will be possible to see, albeit incompletely, the results of these factors for Judaism, Islam, Hinduism, Sikhism, Buddhism, Jainism and Zoroastrianism in Britain.[7]

(i) *The Jewish community and Judaism in Britain*

Judaism has a longer history in the British Isles than the other religions to be examined in this chapter.[8] There was a small but active Jewish population here both before its expulsion in 1290 and also after 1656 when Jews again were entitled to enter and settle.[9] In the late seventeenth and early eighteenth centuries the Jewish community was comprised predominantly of Sephardi Jews with their roots in Western Europe and North Africa. Jews from Eastern Europe, Ashkenazim, increased in number, particularly during the nineteenth century. The major period of immigration by this group – brought on by pogroms in Russia and Poland – was the forty years from 1880 to 1920 during which time the Jewish population in Britain rose from 60,000 to 300,000.[10] The entry of Jews to Britain slowed down in the years following the First World War but increased in the mid to late 1930s owing to the rise of National Socialism in Germany and its policy of anti-semitism. By the 1960s the Jewish population in Britain had reached about 450,000, although it has now declined numerically to approximately 350,000 owing to such trends as migration to Israel, assimilation, marriage outside the Jewish fold and smaller family size.[11]

In 1973, Krausz recorded that there were over 100 Jewish communities in Britain, although most of these were small, numbering under 500 people. The largest communities were London (280,000), Manchester (35,000), Leeds (20,000), and Glasgow (13,000).[12] He also noted that a major demographic change had been the movement of Jews from old urban areas like the East End of London or the Leylands of Leeds to suburban areas.

Not all Jews in Britain are affiliated to religious organizations. About 60 per cent are registered members of synagogues, although the practising population is thought to be higher than this.[13] In terms of religious orientation the Jewish community is divided, although the majority continues to be Orthodox. In terms of synagogue membership, what was, 300 years ago, the largest group, the Sephardim, is now the smallest (under 3 per cent of the total GB synagogue membership).[14] Next in terms of membership size is the 'Ultra-Orthodox' or Chassidic community (just over 4 per cent, but with thirty-five congregations throughout the British Isles). The largest group of synagogues (over 200 congregations), which is generally described as 'Central Orthodox', has membership equalling 70 per cent of the total. Together these comprise the Orthodox group: around 80 per cent of the affiliated population. The main institutions serving this population are the United Synagogue (established in 1870) and Chief Rabbinate, the Federation of Synagogues (established in 1887 to serve smaller congregations developing during the period of mass immigration), and the Union of Hebrew Congregations (an ultra-orthodox organization).[15]

The 'Progressive' group, which comprises 20 per cent of the affiliated population is served by the Federation of Reform Synagogues and the Union of Liberal and Progressive Synagogues. The second organization is generally considered to be the more ideologically radical of the two.[16] Together they have about sixty congregations throughout Britain.

Taking Orthodox and Progressive groups together – both exhibit a similar pattern of general observance – recent research has suggested that, while a tenth of the affiliated population never attend a synagogue and a further tenth attend weekly, the majority, 80 per cent, attend for festivals or special occasions such as marriages and Bar Mitzvahs.[17] The most important annual festival to be celebrated in the synagogue is *Yom Kippur*.

In addition, the majority of British Jews maintain domestic practices, including the fasting and feasting of *Yom Kippur* and *Pesach*, the lighting of the *menorah* and the practice of *kashrut* (the preparation and consumption of kosher foods).

Other important aspects of Jewish belief and practice in Britain relate to the issues of Jewish education, Israel and Zionism, and social welfare.

(ii) *The Muslim community and Islam in Britain*[18]

Although Muslims did not settle until long after the Jewish community was established in Britain they now outnumber Jews by over two to one. There are Muslims here from all over the Islamic world: from South Asia, the Middle East, West Africa, Malaysia and Cyprus.[19] The largest group is that with its origins in the Indian sub-continent, particularly Pakistan and Bangladesh. There are about 371,000 Pakistani Muslims and 93,000 Bangladeshis in Britain today (as well as approximately 100,000 Indian Muslims, many of whom are from Gujarat state).[20] The former are settled mostly in Bradford and the West Midlands, and the Bangladeshis in London's East End.

Most of the research which has been conducted on the Muslim community and Islam in Britain concerns these South Asian communities.[21] They have had a presence here since the late nine-teenth century when Sylheti seamen from Bengal settled in seaports such as Liverpool and Cardiff. As with other South Asian communities, however, most Muslims from the sub-continent have settled since the Second World War, the main difference being the pace at which women and children have joined the men who came here to find work. Owing to family arrangements and religious attitudes, (particularly *purdah*, the veiling of women), Muslim family life has been slower to develop here than its Sikh and Hindu counterparts.[22] Nevertheless, in recent years Muslim organizations have grown in number to exceed those serving the other religious communities.

Socially, the Muslim community is divided into ethnic groups with their own languages and cultures. These are expressed, however, not in a multiplicity of social organizations but in the variety of mosques and other religious organizations found here. In 1960 only nine mosques were registered with local authorities (the first had been set up in 1912 in Woking) but in the twenty years that followed this grew to over 200, with many other small groups operating without formal registration.[23] Many of these mosques are either formally affiliated to, or contain leading members disposed to, various Muslim organizations. The Pakistani and Bangladeshi mosques are *Sunni* organizations, while those serving most Middle Eastern Muslims or Indian *Ismaili* Muslims are *Shi'a* in orientation.[24] Most of the Pakistani mosques fall into one of three groups, the *Sufi Barelwi* and *Deobandi* groups, or the *Jamat-i-Islami* movement, the last of which established, during the 1960s, several organizations of considerable importance in the development of Islam in Britain (the Islamic Foundation which publishes works on Islam, the UK Islamic Mission and the Muslim Educational Trust, both of which are concerned with Muslim education here).[25]

Muslims have been concerned in the last twenty years to develop a national organization which is representative of the community as a whole. The Regent's Park Mosque and Islamic Cultural Centre was opened in 1976, but this tends to receive its support from

Middle Eastern Muslims. The most recent attempt to achieve a national organization has been the establishment in 1983 of the British Council of Mosques which mosques from many ethnic and sectarian groups have joined.[26]

The main function of the mosque, whatever its theological or political complexion, is prayer. Obedient Muslims pray five times a day – at home, at work or in a mosque – and are expected to attend a mosque for communal prayer on a Friday (women are excluded from this injunction although many do attend and pray in a separate room). In addition, the mosque is the centre of activity at the times of the annual month-long fast of *Ramadan* and the festivals of *Eid al-Fitr* and *Eid al-Adha* which conclude respectively the period of *Ramadan* and the time allotted each year for the *Hajj* or pilgrimage to Mecca.[27]

(iii) *The Hindu community and Hinduism in Britain*[28]

Hinduism has been one of the most recent of the South Asian religions to develop in Britain. Although small numbers of Hindus arrived here from India during the 1950s and early 1960s, most came only as a result of policies of Africanization in the East African countries of Kenya, Tanzania and Uganda in the period between 1965 and 1972.[29] In the early 1960s Hindus comprised only one-fifth of the Indian population here, the majority being Sikh.[30] Now, although both communities number about 300,000, it is generally assumed that Hindus are slightly in the majority.[31]

As most of the Hindus who were once settled in East Africa had ethnic origins in Western India, in the state of Gujarat, most of the Hindus in Britain speak Gujarati as their mother tongue and maintain Gujarati traditions. About 70 per cent of the Hindu population is Gujarati, with 15 per cent coming from the Punjab and the remainder from other areas of India such as Uttar Pradesh, Bengal, and the Southern states.[32] Hindus are settled in most large towns and cities, particularly Greater London (Wembley and Harrow), Leicester, Coventry, Birmingham and Bradford. Research on various communities has shown that there is a tendency for members of particular caste groups to gather together in different areas.[33] In Leicester, for example, the *Lohanas*, a Gujarati trading caste, predominate; in Leeds, the *Mochis*, an artisan caste, are in greatest number.

Many Hindus in Britain belong to caste associations, and through these maintain ties with caste fellows at home and abroad. Even those who do not take an active part in such organizations, like other South Asians, consider regular gatherings of the extended family to be of great importance. This will often require a great deal of travelling in Britain as well as occasional visits to India.

Religious organizations are also of great significance, although Hindus are not required by their faith to attend a place of worship regularly owing to the practice of domestic worship. The first temple was opened in 1969 in Leicester. There are now over 100 temples in Britain, some large, some small, some in converted properties, some in people's homes, some representing mainstream Hindu practice (*Sanatan mandirs* or temples), some representing different organizations (such as the Swaminarayan Hindu Mission, the Satya Sai Baba Fellowship or the International Society for Krishna Consciousness.[34] A number of temples are affiliated to the National Council of Hindu Temples, and to the *Vishwa Hindu Parishad*, an international Hindu organization.

Large numbers of Hindus attend these temples at the time of annual festivals, particularly *Divali*, the festival of lights, *Holi*, *Janamashtami*, and *Navaratri*, a Gujarati folk dancing festival. Smaller numbers visit their local temple for regular services, for *Puja* and *Arti*, in which the deities of Hinduism are offered hospitality and light. Most families conduct similar rituals in their own homes, where they generally have a small area for worship comprising pictures and statues of favourite deities, such as Krishna, Rama, Ganesh and Ambamata, and chosen gurus, such as Satya Sai Baba, and Pramukh Swami of the Swaminarayan Mission. The varieties of practice and belief amongst Hindus in Britain are great, partly because Hinduism is a religion of diversity but also because Hindus in Britain come from a range of different geographical areas, social backgrounds and sectarian traditions.

(iv) *The Sikh community and Sikhism in Britain*[35]

Both the Sikh community and its religion are somewhat more cohesive than the Hindus and their religion in Britain. The Sikhs share a common ethnic origin in the Punjab in North India, although many came to Britain from East Africa where, like the Gujarati Hindus, they had settled for work. Their religion developed from the teachings of the fifteenth-century spiritual leader, Guru Nanak. Nevertheless, there are internal differences both in India and in Britain (which has the largest settlement of Sikhs outside the Indian sub-continent).

There are about 300,000 Sikhs in Britain, most of whom settled here in the decades following the Second World War, although pioneers had arrived as early as the 1920s.[36] Like other Indians and Pakistanis, the Sikhs were attracted to Britain by the promise of work and its financial rewards. Initially men came alone, but in the early 1960s wives and children began to join them. The prominent areas of Sikh settlement are Southall in London, Gravesend in Kent, Birmingham and Leeds with many other communities in other urban areas of England and Wales.[37]

Like the Hindus, the Sikhs are divided along caste lines although these divisions exist contrary to the teachings of the Sikh gurus. Most places of worship or *gurdwaras* are theoretically open to all Sikhs but religious and social activities are very often determined by caste allegiance. The two major Punjabi castes to which Sikhs belong in Britain are the *Jats* and the *Ramgarhias*, although there are also fairly large numbers of *Bhatras* and those traditionally seen as outside caste society, *Valmikis* and *Ravidasis*.[38] These last groups, whose relationship to Sikhism is not straightforward, have their own religious and social organizations.[39]

In addition to social divisions there are a number of Sikh sectarian groups, some of which (the *Namdharis* and *Nirankaris*) differ from orthodox Sikhism because they lay stress on the importance of living gurus in addition to the ten traditional gurus revered in Sikh teaching.[40]

The first Sikh *gurdwara* in Britain was established in 1911 in Putney, London, and it is estimated that there are now nearly 200 *gurdwaras* here.[41] Most Sikhs attend their local *gurdwara* each Sunday for a regular service of readings and prayers from the *Guru Granth Sahib*, the Sikh religious text, accompanied by singing, food sharing and rites for initiation, marriage, name-giving etc. In addition, more elaborate services are held at the time of Sikh festivals, particularly the birthday of Guru Nanak and *Baisakhi*, a spring festival, when the Khalsa fellowship, with its five Ks, was inaugurated under the tenth Guru, Gobind Singh. Sikhs are also expected to maintain a Sikh way of life away from the *gurdwara*. Most keep the five Ks, the outward signs of Sikh identity, including uncut hair, which men cover with a turban. At home many practise *nam japan*, chanting the name of God. Their religious duties are very different from those of the Hindus, for whom deity worship is common and for whom regular communal worship is unusual.[42] An umbrella organization within British Sikhism is the Sikh Missionary Society, founded in 1969 in Gravesend and now based in Southall.

(v) *The Buddhist community and Buddhism in Britain*[43]

Buddhism in Britain is quite different from the other major religious traditions because, although it has travelled here from Asia, it is not rooted in the social experiences of migration and ethnic identity. Nearly all Britain's Buddhists are ethnically English, Scottish, Welsh or Irish and do not have cultural roots overseas.[44] There are very small numbers of Buddhists here from Vietnam, Japan, Tibet, Thailand and Sri Lanka but the predominant group is native British. As a result of this it is virtually impossible to assess the size of this community of believers and adherents.

This problem is compounded by the variety of forms and styles which Buddhism takes in the British context. The first group to be started here was the Buddhist Society of Great Britain and Ireland just after the turn of the century. It revolved around the work of a British man, Allan Bennett (later known as Ananda Metteya), who, after travelling to Sri Lanka and Burma, felt called to establish Buddhism in the West.[45] In the 1920s this initiative was followed up with two further *Theravada* Buddhist ventures (see note 43): the Theosophical Society formed a Buddhist Lodge (which later became the Buddhist Society) and the Mahabodhi Society was established by the teacher Anagarika Dharmapala. It was not until the 1950s that the *Mahayana* sects of Tibet and Japan began to take root here.[46]

Two interesting developments within Buddhism here have been the development of a distinctly British form of the tradition and the recent growth of a Buddhist missionary movement somewhat different from the quietistic and individualistic groups which are most typical of Buddhism. The first, the Friends of the Western Buddhist Order, a network which supports a British Buddhist monastic order, draws on *Theravada*, Tibetan and *Zen* Buddhism for its doctrines and practices and is estimated to have attracted several thousand people to its centres in Britain.[47] The second, *Nichiren Shoshu-Soka Gakkai*, a Japanese movement, is one of the fastest growing Buddhist groups in Britain. With its emphasis on chanting and worship and on the karmic law of cause and effect, all with this-worldly goals in mind, it has attracted many young professionals who would not normally find a religious path appealing.[48]

Both of these organizations have local groups around the country. However, the hallmark of organized Buddhism is the monastery or *sangha* in which people – monks and lay followers – practise the 'middle way' of the Buddha through meditation, discipline and right livelihood. There are a number of important monastic centres in Britain: e.g., the Tibetan centres of *Samye Ling*, the Manjushri Institute and *Lam Rim*, the *Soto Zen* centre at Throssel Hole Priory, and the *Theravada* centre at Chithurst in Sussex.[49]

(vi) *The Jain community and Jainism in Britain*[50]

Jains, like the representatives of most of the South Asian religious traditions, began to arrive in Britain in small numbers earlier this century. Both before and after the Second World War they came, for business reasons, from North India. But, like the Hindus, the majority arrived by way of countries such as Kenya, Uganda and Tanzania in the 1960s and 1970s.[51] This group, like the East African Hindus, was predominantly Gujarati in ethnic origin. Today's British Jain population is comprised of about 5,000 'Indian' Jains and 15,000 'East African' Jains.[52]

Residing almost exclusively in Greater London and the Midlands' towns of Leicester, Loughborough and Coventry, this community gives the impression of being more homogeneous than the larger and more diffuse Hindu community. However, it is divided both socially and religiously. Like the Hindu and Sikh communities, Jains belong to social castes. One group in Britain is numerically dominant, comprising three quarters of the Jain population. This is the Halari Visa Oshwal, a trading caste which came here from East Africa.[53] This group, and other small social groups amongst the British Jains, is represented by a formal caste association. In religious affiliation Jains in India are divided into two groups, the *Svetambar* and *Digambar* Jains, who differ in their beliefs and practices and in their geographical spread.[54] The Jains in Britain, most of whom originated from Gujarat, belong to the former, and in addition are *deravasis* ('temple dwellers') who place importance on ritual practice in the temple and on the worship of the *tirthankaras*, the Jain saints.[55]

The main centre of religious activity for British Jains is the Jain Samaj (Europe), Leicester which was formed in 1973 and obtained a disused chapel in the city as a base in 1978. The Samaj began to publish a quarterly magazine, *The Jain*, for circulation throughout the British community, and to raise funds for the purchase of religious statues (*murti*) for the Leicester temple (*derasar*).[56] These were obtained from India and installed in August 1985.[57]

The Leicester temple hosts annual festival programmes for *Paryusan* (an eight-day celebration for the birth of Mahavir, one of the *tirthankaras*) and *Divali* (in remembrance of his enlightenment). Jains are also expected to maintain their traditions daily, not by attendance at a place of worship, but by following the example of Mahavir in truthfulness, non-violence and non-acquisitiveness.[58]

(vii) *The Parsi community and Zoroastrianism in Britain*[59]

Parsis have been coming to Britain from India for business and education for 200 years and have the longest history of settlement here of all the South Asian groups.[60] In 1861 the Religious Society of Zoroastrians in Europe was established, and, after the First World War, premises were obtained for meetings and worship. This community was organized well before other South Asian groups arrived in Britain and now contains many third and fourth generation Parsis.

Like other South Asian groups the migration pattern of the Parsis has been complex. In addition to early settlers, further migrants arrived in the 1950s and early 1960s from the Indian sub-continent and then from East Africa. The contemporary Zoroastrian community thus contains people from many different geographical and ethnic backgrounds. Many by now are socially and culturally 'British' while others still feel close ties to India, Pakistan, East Africa or Iran (a number of Iranian Zoroastrians came to Britain after the fall of the Shah in 1979).[61] Despite social differences most belong to the Zoroastrian Association, although perhaps as many as 30 per cent of Britain's 5,000 Zoroastrians remain unaffiliated.

The organizational centre of Zoroastrianism in Britain is in St John's Wood in London (purchased in 1969) where festivals and life cycle rites are conducted (including *No Ruz*, the New Year celebrations, and *Navjote*, the initiation ritual at which young Zoroastrians receive the sacred shirt and cord (*sudre* and *kusti*).[62] In addition, family practices are maintained by most in the community: prayers are said regularly, oil lamps are burnt, vernacular languages are retained, the shirt and cord are worn, and the rites of the life cycle are kept.[63] As in any established migrant community there are those who have given up their religious practices and those who, through marriage with non-Zoroastrians, have lost touch with the community.

In 1980 the World Zoroastrian Organization was set up in London to facilitate international collaboration between Zoroastrians, to defend them when under attack and to co-ordinate charitable and educational works within their community in different continents.

RELIGION, ETHNICITY AND CHANGE

Britain is not the first home of any of the seven religions described here. Each is undergoing a renewed process of institutionalization in a different location in which new religious organizations are established, traditional beliefs and practices perpetuated and often reinterpreted, and new patterns of adherence and religious behaviour developed. All of the religions, with the exception of Buddhism, have been brought here by migrant groups and are thus influenced not only by the new location itself but also by the experiences of the group in this alien milieu, that is, by the experience of their ethnic identity. Migrant groups now settled here, such as the Pakistani Muslims or the Gujarati Hindus, have had their social and cultural identity thrown into sharp focus. They have become ethnic – and religious – minorities, though back home many of them shared the culture and religion of the majority. This altered situation, of necessity, has meant change, both social and religious.

It has also meant the inevitable interplay of these two areas, the social or 'ethnic' and the religious.[64] Religion, its beliefs and practices, has influenced both the way in which migrants have organized themselves in relation to the established institutions of British society and the way they have articulated their interests. Ethnically, the experience of being culturally and socially distinct with a different language and way of life, has had an impact on the religions and the way they have developed here. Taking Islam as an example, it is not difficult to see that religion has had a serious effect on the attitudes of Pakistanis and Bangladeshis to education in Britain, particularly the education of girls. In addition, Islam and its institutional development has itself been influenced by the coming together of groups of Muslims from different geographical areas (see section (ii) above). Religion and ethnicity are far from mutually exclusive.

The relationship between them has been different for the various migrant communities in Britain. Only the Sikhs, who all originate in the Punjab, are a cohesive religio-ethnic group; all the other religious groups are comprised of people from more than one place of ethnic origin. Some of these ethnic communities have placed great value on developing religious institutions through which they can express their social and political interests *vis-à-vis* other groups. This has been true for some Pakistani Muslim and Punjabi Sikh communities. Others have put their efforts into building and supporting non-religious institutions such as caste associations (some Gujarati Hindu communities) or business networks (Parsi, Jain and some Gujarati Hindu groups).

Irrespective of the different ways in which the religions have been used for expressing ethnic interests their development has had common themes. All the traditions have centres or places of worship which are used not only for religious practice but also for social and cultural occasions. Communal worship has become important not only for its spiritual value but also as an opportunity for meeting at a social level: this would not have been necessary for many groups in their place of origin. The maintenance of the religion in the new location has become the responsibility of all those in a particular faith community, and this has focused attention on issues such as marriage inside and outside the faith, the retention of domestic religious practices, language learning, the behaviour of the young, conversion and education.

These common themes and concerns, to which can be added aspects relating not to religious but ethnic experience such as harassment, prejudice and minority status, are all that exists of unity in a situation of immense diversity. There are divisions – either ethnic or sectarian – in every one of the traditions now established here. There are differences between the traditions: some are universalizing religions like Islam and Buddhism; others are religions of a people such as Judaism or Zoroastrianism. In addition, all the religions have been changed further by the process of transplantation. All religions change over time anyway but the pace of change will be determined by the nature of the events which occur as time passes. The migration of a group of people, which brings with it the inevitable uprooting and transplanting of religious and cultural traditions, is the kind of event which brings about dramatic change. To move a religion to a new geographical location may even endanger its life, in addition to disturbing its continuity, its natural process of transmission and the unselfconsciousness of its adherents.

Most religions do survive this process, although it is only the passing of time which finally reveals the results of this period of change. As they become rooted here one question which inevitably arises is 'In what ways is the religion as it is manifested here different to the parent tradition in the place of origin?' The differences indeed will be many. In some branches of the religions established here the medium of English is now used, not only for communication with the outside world but also for some liturgical purposes (Reform and Liberal Judaism, some Hindu sects). In some cases, sectarian movements within traditions have been developed specifically for newcomers to the tradition: the Friends of the Western Buddhist Order is a good example of this, and the International Society for Krishna Consciousness, though attracting a substantial number of Indian Hindus in Britain, was set up chiefly with Westerners in mind.[65] In other cases a mission to the native British has developed successfully (in Buddhism, in certain Muslim *Sufi* groups, and in the Hindu Satya Sai Baba Fellowship). Interfaith dialogue and encounter is another area to have developed during the years of settlement in Britain: groups within the religions are involved in this at both a local and national level.[66]

In addition to these new departures, there have been many other areas in which religious groups have had to adapt the practices of their forebears. In some cases these changes have been brought on by the need to adjust to the British working week, the calendar and climate. In others they have been encouraged by the settlement patterns of adherents. One of the most critical reasons for a new approach is the young.

The next generation is always the key to the future, to the perpetuation of traditional teachings and practices. Encouraging the interest of young people in the life of a religious community often involves a willingness to accept change. Although the religions differ in their approach, many young people continue to participate in religious practice and to learn the traditional languages (the mother tongue and the language of scripture). Nevertheless there is a growing call by the young for explanation. They want to maintain their religious traditions but they need to understand them. Their sense of 'difference' in a society which is dominated by a mixture of secular and Christian values and practices requires them to go further than simply repeating the behaviour of their parents. In the classroom they are challenged not only with 'What do you do?' but also 'What does it mean?' and 'Why do you do it?'.

A new self-consciousness amongst the young about the traditions of their parents is matched by a similar experience amongst leaders within the religious communities. The contemporary experience of pluralism (and in some cases the new experience of minority status) has led those responsible for establishing religious institutions here to become aware of the theological, ethical and practical aspects of their traditions. By their communities they are demanded to develop these in programmes of worship, and in dialogue they are invited to voice them along with the views of others. This experience of social and religious pluralism is challenging not only for those within these religious communities but also for all those whose work, social relationships or own religious conviction brings them into contact with them.

Each of these religions has its own separate development in Britain. Some, like Judaism, are now well established while others are still in the process of putting down roots. All, however, are now part of the religious profile of the British Isles.

NOTES

1 See C. Holmes, 'The promised land? Immigration into Britain 1870–1980', in D. A. Coleman (ed.), *Demography of Immigrants and Minority Groups in the UK*, London, Academic Press, 1982; E. J. B.

Rose, *Colour and Citizenship: A Report on British Race Relations*, London, Institute for Race Relations/Oxford University Press, 1969; C. Nicolson, *Strangers to England, 1100–1952*, London, Wayland, 1974, for more information on the causes of social and religious pluralism in Britain.

2 S. Castles and G. Kosack, *Immigrant Workers and Class Struggle in Western Europe*, Oxford, Oxford University Press, 1985 (2nd edn.).

3 This process has not always occurred at the same pace. R. Desai, *Indian Immigrants in Britain*, London, Oxford University Press, 1963, has commented on this in relation to the major South Asian religions established here.

4 H. Mol, 'Theory and data on the religious behaviour of migrants', *Social Compass*, 26:1, 1979, pp.31–9; H. Abramson, 'Migrants and cultural diversity: on ethnicity and religion in society', *Social Compass*, 26:1, 1979, pp.5–29.

5 E. M. Pye, 'The transplantation of religions', *Numen*, 16, p.236.

6 K. Knott, 'Religion and identity, and the study of ethnic minority religions in Britain', in V. Hayes (ed.), *Identity Issues and World Religions: Selected Proceedings of the XVth Congress of the International Association for the History of Religions*, South Australia, Australian Association for the Study of Religion, 1986, pp.172–3.

7 Useful sources of information on these religious traditions are T. Ling, *A History of Religion East and West*, London, Macmillan, 1968; W. O. Cole, *Six Religions in the Twentieth Century* (with P. Morgan), Amersham, Hulton Educational, 1984; J. Hinnells (ed.), *A Handbook of Living Religions*, Harmondsworth, Penguin, 1984; the Open University course *AD208: Man's Religious Quest*, Milton Keynes, Open University Press, 1977–8 (from 1988, *A228: The Religious Quest*). The Open University course, *E354: Ethnic Minorities and Community Relations*, provides information on some of the ethnic communities referred to in this section.

8 For more information on traditional beliefs and practices in Judaism see A. Unterman, *Jews: Their Religious Beliefs and Practices;* London, Routledge & Kegan Paul, 1981; D. Goldstein, *The Religion of the Jews*, Milton Keynes, Open University Press, 1978.

9 Nicolson, op.cit.

10 J. Moonman, *Anglo-Jewry*, London, Joint Israel Appeal, 1980.

11 C. Lawton, 'British Jewry', in *World Religions in Education: Shap Mailing 1986*, London, Shap Working Party/Commission for Racial Equality, 1986, pp.16–17; E. Krausz, 'The Jews in Britain: the sociography of an old minority group', *New Community*, 2:2, 1973, pp.132–6; S. Waterman and B. Kosmin, *British Jewry in The Eighties:*

A Statistical and Geographical Study, London, Research Unit, Board of Deputies of British Jews, 1986.

12   Krausz, op.cit. These figures are now out-dated; the Jewish population of Leeds, for example, is currently estimated, by the community itself, to be approximately 16,000.

13   B. Kosmin and C. Levy, *Jewish Identity in an Anglo-Jewish Community*, London, Research Unit, Board of Deputies of British Jews, 1983. Men, as heads of household, tend to take out membership; very few married women take separate membership but nevertheless participate in the worshipping life of the congregation.

14   Waterman and Kosmin, op.cit.; S. J. Prais, 'Polarisation or decline, a discussion of some statistical findings on the community', in S. Lipman and V. Lipman (eds), *Jewish Life in Britain 1962–1977*, New York, N. G. Saur, 1981.

15   D. Cohn-Sherbok, 'Judaism in modern Britain', *Religion Today*, 3:2, 1986, pp.4–6; B. Homa, *Orthodoxy in Anglo Jewry, 1880–1940*, London, Jewish Historical Society of England, 1969.

16   Cohn-Sherbok, op.cit.

17   Kosmin and Levy, op.cit. These figures are for the Redbridge Jewish population but are assumed by the authors to be fairly representative of Anglo-Jewry as a whole.

18   Submission to God, Allah, and recognition that Muhammad is God's prophet and that the Qur'an is the word of God are central to Islamic belief. For further information on Islam see H. A. R. Gibb, *Islam*, Oxford, Oxford University Press, 1978 and K. Cragg, *Islam and the Muslim*, Milton Keynes, Open University Press, 1978.

19   P. Brierley (ed.), *UK Christian Handbook 1987–88 Edition*, London, MARC Europe, 1986; Z. Badawi, 'Islam in Britain', in *World Religions in Education: Shap Mailing 1986*, London, Shap Working Party/Commission for Racial Equality, 1986

20   These figures are from the Labour Force Survey conducted by the Office of Population Censuses and Surveys. For a discussion of this and further details see K. Knott, 'Calculating Sikh population statistics', in W. O. Cole and E. Nesbitt, *Sikh Bulletin*, No. 4, West Sussex Institute of Higher Education, Chichester, 1987.

21   For information on Pakistanis see P. Jeffrey, *Migrants and Refugees: Muslim and Christian Pakistani Families in Bristol*, Cambridge, Cambridge University Press, 1976; and M. Anwar *Pakistanis in Britain: A Sociological Study*, London, New Century, 1985 (incorporating *The Myth of Return*). Until 1971, when it became Bangladesh, Muslim Bengal was part of Pakistan (East Pakistan). For information on Bangladeshis here see. S. Barton, *The Bengali Muslims of Bradford*, Community Religions Project Monograph, Department of Theology

and Religious Studies, University of Leeds, 1986; S. Carey and A. Shukur, 'A profile of the Bangladeshi community of East London', *New Community*, 12:3, 1985, pp.405–17.

22 For further discussion see J. Nielsen, 'Muslim immigration and settlement in Britain', *Muslims in Europe Research Papers*, 21, Centre for the Study of Islam and Christian-Muslim Relations, Selly Oak Colleges, Birmingham, 1984.

23 Ibid.; A. L. Tibawi, 'History of the London Central Mosque and Islamic Cultural Centre 1910–1980', *Die Welt des Islams*, 21:1–4, 1981, pp.193–208.

24 *Sunni* and *Shi'a* are the two major divisions within Islam and arose out of groups competing over the succession to the Prophet Muhammad. For a fuller explanation of this distinction see Gibb, op.cit. and Cragg, op.cit. For *Sunni* and *Shi'a* Islam in Great Britain see P. Clarke, 'Islam in Britain', *Religion Today*, 2:3, 1985, pp.3–5.

25 D. Joly, 'Making a place for Islam in British society: Muslims in Birmingham', *Research Papers in Ethnic Relations No.4*, Centre for Research in Ethnic Relations, University of Warwick, 1987; P. Johnstone, 'Millet or minority – Muslims in Britain', in V. Hayes, (ed.), *Identity Issues and World Religions: Selected Proceedings of the XVth Congress of the International Association for the History of Religions*, South Australia, Australian Association for the Study of Religion, 1986; Nielsen, op.cit.

26 Tibawi, op.cit., Nielsen, op.cit., Johnstone, op.cit.

27 A discussion of the life of a mosque can be found in Barton, op.cit.

28 Hinduism derives from the Indian sub-continent and is most commonly understood to be a complex group of traditions with roots in Indus Valley Civilization and the religion and culture of the Aryans, both of which existed several thousand years before the Christian Era. See T. Hopkins, *The Hindu Religious Tradition*, Encino, California, Dickenson, 1971.

29 For history of settlement see K. Knott, *Hinduism in Leeds*, Community Religions Project Monograph, Department of Theology and Religious Studies, University of Leeds, 1986; H. Kanitkar and R. Jackson, *Hindus in Britain*, Extramural Division, School of Oriental and African Studies, University of London, 1982.

30 Desai, op.cit.

31 K. Knott, 'Calculating Sikh population statistics', in W. O. Cole and E. Nesbitt, *Sikh Bulletin*, No.4, West Sussex Institute of Higher Education, Chichester, 1987.

32 K. Knott, 'Hinduism in Britain', in *World Religions in Education: Shap Mailing 1986*, London, Shap Working Party/Commission for Racial Equality, 1986, pp.10–12.

33 D. Bowen, 'The evolution of Gujarati Hindu organizations in Bradford', in R. Burghart, (ed.), *Hinduism in Great Britain*, London, Tavistock, 1987; R. Jackson, 'The Shree Krishna temple and the Gujarati Hindu community in Coventry', in D. Bowen (ed.), *Hinduism in England*, Bradford, Bradford College, 1981; K. Knott, *Hinduism in Leeds;* M. Michaelson, 'Domestic Hinduism in a Gujarati trading caste', in R. Burghart (ed.), *Hinduism in Great Britain*, London, Tavistock, 1987. For an explanation of the operation of the caste system in general see S. Weightman, *Hinduism in the Village Setting*, Milton Keynes, Open University Press, 1978.

34 For temple worship see H. Kanitkar and R. Jackson, *Hindus in Britain;* K. Knott, *Hinduism in Leeds* and 'Hindu temple rituals in Britain: the reinterpretation of tradition', in R. Burghart (ed.), *Hinduism in Great Britain*, London, Tavistock, 1987. For more on these sects see R. Williams, *A New Face of Hinduism: The Swaminarayan Religion*, Cambridge, Cambridge University Press, 1984; D. Bowen, *The Satya Sai Baba Community in Bradford*, Community Religions Project Monograph, Department of Theology and Religious Studies, University of Leeds, 1988; S. Carey, 'The Hare Krishna Movement and Hindus in Britain', *New Community*, 8, 1983, pp.477–86.

35 For further information see W. O. Cole and P. S. Sambhi, *The Sikhs: Their Religious Beliefs and Practices*, London, Routledge & Kegan Paul, 1978; T. Thomas, *Sikhism: The Voice of the Guru*, Milton Keynes, Open University Press, 1978.

36 R. Ballard and C. Ballard, 'The Sikhs: the development of South Asian settlements in Britain', in J. L. Watson (ed.), *Between Two Cultures: Migrants and Minorities in Britain*, Oxford, Basil Blackwell, 1977; A. W. Helweg, *Sikhs in England: The Development of a Migrant Community*, Delhi, Oxford University Press, 1979.

37 Helweg, op.cit.; A. G. James, *Sikh Children in Britain*, London, Oxford University Press, 1974; T. Thomas and P. S. Ghuman, *A Survey of Social and Religious Attitudes Among Sikhs in Cardiff*, Cardiff, The Open University in Wales, n.d.; E. Nesbitt, 'Aspects of Sikh tradition in Nottingham', unpublished M. Phil. thesis, University of Nottingham, 1980; R. Singh, *The Sikh Community in Bradford*, Bradford, Bradford College, 1978; N. K. Singh, 'The Sikh community in Manchester', in W. O. Cole and E. Nesbitt (eds), *Sikh Bulletin*, No.3, West Sussex Institute for Higher Education, Chichester, 1986.

38 E. Nesbitt, 'Britain's Sikhs', in *World Religions in Education: Shap Mailing 1986*, London, Shap Working Party/Commission for Racial Equality, 1986, pp.18–20; Nesbitt, op.cit.; P. Bhachu *Twice Migrants:*

East African Sikh Settlers in Britain, London, Tavistock, 1985; N. K. Singh, op.cit.

39 Nesbitt, 'Britain's Sikhs'; A. Leivesley, 'Ravidasias of the West Midlands', in W. O. Cole and E. Nesbitt, (eds), *Sikh Bulletin*, No.3, West Sussex Institute of Higher Education, Chichester, 1986.

40 Nesbitt, 'Britain's Sikhs'.

41 Ibid.

42 For a discussion of Sikh religious practice in Britain see James, op.cit.

43 The Buddhist religious traditions are derived from the teachings of Gautama, the Buddha. Early in the history of Buddhism the exponents of the teachings divided into different schools and two of these are still with us today, *Theravada* and *Mahayana* (the *Theravada* school in Sri Lanka, Thailand and Burma, and the different sectarian divisions of *Mahayana* in Tibet and the Far East, particularly Japan). See R. Robinson and W. L. Johnson, *The Buddhist Religion: An Historical Introduction*, Encino, California, Dickenson, 1977, (2nd edn); J. Masson, *The Noble Path of Buddhism*, Milton Keynes, Open University Press, 1977 and Ling, op.cit.

44 To some extent the development of Buddhism in Britain has more in common with the growth of new religious movements here than the arrival of other major religious traditions. Nevertheless, it is one of the world's oldest and largest traditions and needs to be seen in this light despite the social history of its growth here.

45 C. Humphries, *Sixty Years of Buddhism in England 1907–67*, London, The Buddhist Society, 1968; P. Connolly, 'Buddhism in Britain', *Religion Today*, 212, 1985, pp.3–6.

46 These now include two forms of Tibetan Buddhism and, from Japan, *Soto Zen, Jodo Shinshu* and *Nichiren Shoshu*. See I. Oliver, *Buddhism in Britain*, London, Rider, 1979 and P. Morgan, 'Methods and aims of evangelization and conversion in Buddhism with reference to Nichiren Shoshu Soka Gakkai', in P. Clarke (ed.), *The New Evangelists*, London, Ethnographica, 1987.

47 D. Subhuti, *Buddhism for Today: A Portrait of a New Buddhist Movement*, Salisbury, Element Books, 1983; D. Ratnaprabha, 'A reemergence of Buddhism: the case of Friends of the Western Buddhist Order', in P. Clarke (ed.), *The New Evangelists*, London, Ethnographica, 1987.

48 Morgan, op.cit.; B. Wilson, 'Aims and vision of Soka Gakkai', *Religion Today*, 2:1, 1985, pp.7–8.

49 Oliver, op.cit.

50 Jainism, like Buddhism, is a tradition which emphasizes ethical questions and which is often described as atheistic in outlook. Temple practice, however, is of considerable importance in India and abroad.

See P. S. Jaini, *The Jaina Path of Purification*, Berkeley, California, University of California Press, 1979; P. Marett, *Jainism Explained*, Leicester, Jain Samaj Europe, n.d.

51 S. Shah, 'Who are the Jains?', *New Community*, 7:3, 1979, pp.369–75; M. Banks, 'A question of identity: the Srimali Jains of Leicester', unpublished paper presented at the Symposium on Gujarati Ethnicity, School of Oriental and African Studies, University of London, 1984.

52 Shah, op.cit.

53 Banks, op.cit.; M. Michaelson, 'Caste, kinship and marriage: a study of two Gujarati trading castes in England', unpublished Ph.D., School of Oriental and African Studies, University of London, 1983.

54 Jaini, op.cit.; Shah, op.cit.

55 Shah, op.cit.

56 *The Jain*, Quarterly Journal of the Jain Samaj Europe, March 1983, April and July 1984.

57 Ibid., January 1986.

58 Marett, op.cit.

59 See M. Boyce, *The Zoroastrians: Their Religious Beliefs and Practices*, London, Routledge & Kegan Paul, 1979; J. Hinnells, *Spanning East and West*, Milton Keynes, Open University Press, 1978; and *Zoroastrianism and the Parsis*, London, Ward Lock, 1981.

60 J. Hinnells, 'Zoroastrians in Britain', in *World Religions in Education: Shap Mailing 1986*, London, Shap Working Party/Commission for Racial Equality, 1986, pp.21–2. Parsis are Zoroastrians with ethnic origins in the Indian sub-continent. There is also a small number of Zoroastrians in Britain from Iran.

61 Ibid.

62 Ibid.; T. Mehta, 'Nurture in the Zoroastrian community', in *World Religions in Education: Shap Mailing 1986*, London, Shap Working Party/Commission for Racial Equality, 1986, pp.34–5.

63 A survey was recently conducted by John Hinnells of Zoroastrians around the world, including the community in Britain. Hinnells, op.cit.

64 Many scholars have been interested in one area rather than the other. Sociologists of race and ethnic relations have ignored on many occasions the importance of religion for migrant groups; educationalists concerned with religion have often failed to consider the other aspects of social life for groups here. The two areas have been discussed together in Abramson, op.cit; Mol, op.cit.; Knott, 'Religion and identity, and the study of ethnic minority religions in Britain'. In the first of these the author provides a useful definition of an ethnic group. 'Ethnic groups, or those social units with the quality of ethnicity, are those social categories or collectivities: (1) with a past-

oriented group identification, emphasizing origins; (2) with some conception of cultural and social distinctiveness; (3) which are component units in a broader system of social relations; (4) which are larger than kin or locality groups and transcend face-to-face interaction; (5) which have different meanings both in different social settings and for different individuals; and (6) which are emblematic, having names with meaning both for members and for analysts (Abramson, op.cit., p.7).

65 See Chapter 6, New Religious Movements.
66 A growing number of cities have inter-faith groups of which *Concord*, established in Leeds in 1976, is an example. At a national level the recently formed *Interfaith Network* has members from all the different faith communities.

BIBLIOGRAPHY

In addition to the works cited in the Notes see also:

Joly, D., and Nielsen, J., *Muslims in Britain: An Annotated Bibliography 1960–84*, Bibliographies in Ethnic Relations 6, Centre for Research in Ethnic Relations, University of Warwick, 1985.

Tatla, D. S., and Nesbitt, E., *Sikhs in Britain: An Annotated Bibliography:* Bibliographies in Ethnic Relations 8, Centre for Research in Ethnic Relations, University of Warwick, 1987.

CHAPTER SIX

New Religious Movements

Kim Knott

The latter half of the twentieth century in Britain is characterized by social and religious pluralism. As we have seen, many different ethnic and religious groups exist alongside an indigenous population and its traditional religion, Christianity.[1] One of the features of this contemporary pluralism is the prevalence of 'new religions', movements which are generally associated with young people and their search for spirituality and meaning.

These new movements, which have been kept in the public eye not least of all by the mass media, are often thought to represent a situation never before experienced in our religious history. This is not the case, however. In the middle of the seventeenth century, for example, Britain saw the rise of a number of new Christian groups, as well as unorthodox preachers and religious thinkers.[2] At that time too, many people were discontented with the authoritarianism of the established church and were seeking an alternative form of spirituality. The phenomenon of new religious movements, or 'cults' as they are sometimes called, is not itself new, and neither is the quest for spiritual experience. In fact, our own time, which has seen the rise of new movements like the Unification Church, the International Society for Krishna Consciousness and the Rajneesh Movement, was preceded by a period of some eighty years during which an interest in alternative religious philosophies, psychotherapy, esotericism and spiritualism was developing. The Theosophical Society, the Anthroposophical Society of Rudolf Steiner, the School of Economic Science and the Gurdjieff Society, all groups with an interest in the East and in esoteric teachings, were set up before the 1960s and the rise of the 'counter culture'.[3]

Nevertheless, it is this latest manifestation of 'new religious consciousness', perhaps precisely because it has captured the hearts and minds of the young, which has attracted journalistic and scholarly attention, parental and clerical concern.[4] In the 1960s and 1970s in America and Europe a number of young people, often disenchanted with existing social and religious institutions and ethical and behavioural norms, became involved in religious or quasi-religious groups either new to the West or at that time unheard of here.[5] Many of these followed teachers or philosophies with their roots in Hinduism or Buddhism. Others bore a relation to the Christian tradition. Some – and these multiplied in the late 1970s – were based on the need to develop the human potential, and often explored contemporary trends in psychotherapy and encounter. Others focused on more esoteric ideas including astrology, fortune-telling techniques and the occult. In the 1980s the novelty and popularity of these groups as a whole has declined although a number of the movements which arose during the time of the counter culture continue to exist and develop.

In religious and sociological terms the post-war period must be seen in the context not only of pluralism but also of secularization. Various commentators have discussed the process of secularization in relation not only to the specific decline in adherence to the mainstream churches but also to the general decline in social significance of religious institutions, beliefs and values.[6] Most have seen these trends as part of a gradual process in which the state and secular values have moved to the centre of the stage. While some sociologists have interpreted the rise of new religious movements (along with such things as the persistence of folk religion) to indicate that the dominant theory of secularization must be questioned, others have understood this phenomenon to represent no more than a rise of asocial groups marginal to society with no power to effect change or influence shared behaviour, beliefs or values.[7] Seen from this perspective, new religious movements are actually indicative of secularization and the other social processes related to it, of routinization, rationalization and fragmentation. Together, such movements are a spontaneous but ultimately hopeless demonstration against these processes, seeking as they do to provide meaning, community, authority, ritual and charisma.

The debate about secularization remains unresolved, however, and some scholars are still sceptical not only about the application of the concept of secularization and the nature of social and religious change in the West but also about new religious movements, their social and historical role and influence.[8] In recent years there has been a growing concern to see new movements in relation to their immediate social and cultural context. In the USA this has involved exploring their relationship to civil religion, fundamentalism and moral conservatism, individualism and narcissism.[9] In Britain, an interesting and useful approach has been concerned with the nature of the insertion of movements in particular societies, the controversies which result and what these reveal about the norms we create with reference to religion, society and the individual.[10]

Whatever one believes about the path of social and religious change in twentieth-century Britain, new religious movements are of interest precisely because, as all these scholarly views show, they are indicative of trends which are occurring. Like all periods of cultic flowering, the last quarter of a century has seen religious and social unrest. The proliferation of new movements and their very nature can help us to understand this unrest, its causes and effects.[11] As Bell wrote:

> When religions fail, cults appear. When the institutional framework of religions begins to break up, the search for direct experience which people can feel to be 'religious' facilitates the rise of cults.[12]

More specifically, the pattern of growth in Britain, the groups which have flourished or failed, and the nature of the public response to them (those who have joined and those who have been critical) can help us to understand what social and religious changes are taking place here and how these differ from the situation elsewhere in Europe or in the States.[13]

Most of the trends and issues highlighted by the rise and popularity of new religious movements which have been researched and discussed have been social in orientation, even where they have been concerned with religious malaise or dissatisfaction with established churches. Remarkably few scholars have focused on the religious implications of new religious movements. Less work has been done on the continuity of religious traditions in movements related to Hinduism or Christianity, on the religious, as opposed to the social, aspects of spiritual experience in new religious movements, their relation to mysticism in other historical and cultural contexts, or on religious syncretism in groups which are genuinely 'new'.[14]

NEW RELIGIOUS MOVEMENTS: HISTORY AND CONTENT

The 'horizontal' approach of sociology, which considers the phenomenon of new movements in relation to such things as the background of members, group types, and social organization, and the 'vertical' approach of religious studies or anthropology, which investigates the life of a movement in detail with particular regard to its relationship to its religious and cultural sources, are both important in the study of new religious movements.[15] In the short descriptive account which follows it is not possible to do justice to either, although reference will be made to source materials which consider the groups in more detail; neither will it be possible to explore comprehensively the scope and scale of the phenomenon as a whole.

Some 450 movements have grown up (some also have died away) in Britain since the last war, and others before it.[16] Some are related to the Hindu tradition, like the International Society for Krishna Consciousness (ISKCON), Divine Light Mission, or Transcendental Meditation (TM). Some are Buddhist in orientation like Soka Gakkai or Soto Zen. These movements, and others related to Christianity and Islam, are not all 'new' in the same way.[17] Several are only new to Britain but firmly rooted in the East whilst others take some aspects of traditional teaching or practice and develop them in an entirely new context. Many groups, though influenced by various of the world's religions (particularly Buddhism and Hinduism), are more deliberately syncretistic than those mentioned above. Some have combined elements of Eastern philosophy with esoteric teachings such as numerology, astrology or the occult (e.g., the Theosophical Society or the Aetherius Society); others with psychotherapy techniques and encounter methods (e.g., the Rajneesh Movement). Another type of group has concentrated more explicitly on these psychological approaches and has made little reference to traditional philosophies from East or West (e.g., Exegesis and est). A few groups, like Scientology, have developed their own terminology, unrelated to existing systems of thought.

Just five movements are portrayed below. They are all well known: four of them because they have attracted media attention in the last twenty years; the other, Baha'ism, because it is often considered to be the most successful new religion to have emerged since Sikhism in the sixteenth century. The Baha'i faith is old by comparison with the rest although, like the others, its major period of growth has been the last thirty years. It is not the only one of the five to have developed without the assistance of a membership both young and 'counter-cultural': Scientology recruited many interested clients, most of whom were in their late twenties or thirties, in the 1950s and 1960s before the emergence of a 'new religious consciousness'. The followers of Bhagwan Shree Rajneesh have also been recruited from an older age group. Only the members of the Hare Krishna Movement (ISKCON) and the Unification Church have been predominantly young, and in recent years these groups too have broadened their spectrum of adherence by attracting loosely-affiliated congregational members from all age groups.

Most of the movements have a relationship of some kind with an established religious tradition, although the way these relationships have developed is quite different. ISKCON stresses its direct descent from the Chaitanya movement in North India; the Unification Church sees itself as a fulfilment and development of Christian biblical teaching; the Baha'i faith focuses on the teaching of Baha'u'llah who was brought up in the Shi'a Islamic tradition of Iran; the *sannyasins* of Bhagwan Rajneesh talk of *darshans* and Buddhafields but follow Bhagwan in decrying 'religion' as a path to enlightenment.

(i) *The Baha'i faith*[18]

Despite the early history of this movement in mid-nineteenth-century Iran, the major period of expansion has been the last thirty years during which the Baha'i faith has grown to between two and four million adherents in over 300 countries.[19] Its most recent growth in membership has been in the Third World. At present it is estimated that there are over 5000 Baha'is in Britain.[20] It is said that there are some 500 local assemblies which are administered by the National Spiritual Assembly of the Baha'is in London.[21]

The sources of Baha'ism lie in Iranian Shi'a Islam. The two early leaders known respectively as the Bab, or 'gate of God', and Baha'u'llah, 'the glory of God', were both born and brought up in Iran although it was not long before the leadership was banished. Since the death of Baha'u'llah in 1892 first his son and then his son's grandson, Shoghi Effendi, took over the leadership. It was during the guardianship of this last leader, who died in 1957, that the seeds were sown for world expansion. Shoghi Effendi not only published many works in English, Persian and Arabic, he also introduced a ten-year world crusade to encourage missionary activity. In addition, he developed an Administrative Order to control the affairs of the movement, and established a World Centre of the Baha'i Faith in Haifa, Israel. After his death, authority passed to the Universal House of Justice, an elected body.

The beliefs and practices of the Bahá'í faith focus on the principle of the oneness of humanity. The oneness, according to Baha'u'llah was to evolve gradually in human consciousness as prejudice fell away and unity of purpose at the religious and social level took its place. All religions were seen as divine in origin although each had its own special historical context which made it unique. Each religion had its messenger and role for a different age, and these were all part of the process of progress towards world harmony. In line with this teaching the Baha'is have developed various global agencies and missions and have stressed the importance of universalistic plans such as world citizenship, an international language, education for all, the development of world government and ultimately of a world theocracy. In recent years, they have supported other institutions dedicated to world affairs. For example, they are involved in inter-faith dialogue at an international level and in United Nations activities.

The Baha'i faith is now recognized in many books on world religions although little is commonly known about it beyond the unfortunate fact that its Iranian members have suffered persecution at various times in the past not least under the regime of Ayatolla Khomeini. By comparison with other 'world religions', however, it is of comparatively recent origin, and like many other 'new religious movements' has experienced its major period of growth since the last war.

(ii) *The Unification Church*[22]

The Unification Church (UC) has its historical and religious roots
in Korea. It was formed by Sun Myung Moon and sprang out
of his dissatisfaction with Korean Presbyterianism and his own
revelations concerning the development of world Christianity.
Owing to Moon's background and the syncretistic nature of Korean
religion in the mid-twentieth century it also reflects aspects of
Korean shamanism, Taoism and Confucianism, and Buddhism.
Moon's teachings were formally institutionalized in 1954 when he
founded the Holy Spirit Association for the Unification of World
Christianity. During the following fifteen years the major fields of
preaching were South Korea and Japan although a woman
missionary began work in the United States as early as 1959.

It was not until the 1970s that the UC began to attract a serious
and substantial following in America, and then Europe. (It was
introduced to Britain in the early 1970s.) In 1969 it is unlikely that
there were more than 250 converts in the West, although there was
a much higher number in the Far East; by the early 1980s the
world-wide membership, including both affiliated and full-time
members, was thought to be approximately 300,000, of whom some
50,000 were American.[23] In the 1970s several important changes had
occurred which had influenced the size of membership. These had
included the public speaking tours in the USA of Sun Myung
Moon, the establishment of the One World crusade, and the development of extensive fund-raising campaigns and businesses. It is
estimated that the current British membership is about 1,400: 900
of these being 'home' members with varying degrees of commitment, and the remainder full 'centre' members working either at
centres in Britain or abroad.[24]

The philosophy and theology of the UC are too extensive and
complex to be described here. In brief, they are based upon the
teachings of Reverend Moon, which are understood to be prophetic
and are encapsulated in the *Divine Principle*. This text:

> is a systematic exposition of thought intended to complete, by
> unifying, the wisdoms of Judaeo-Christianity through a fresh
> denouement of the history of mankind's fall from divine grace
> and restoration to original perfection.[25]

As might be expected, this theology contains teachings on the relationship between God (the 'Heavenly Father') and humanity, on the complementary roles of Jesus, the first Messiah, and the second Messiah (who will establish the Kingdom of Heaven on Earth, particularly by encouraging the growth of perfect love), and on the perfectibility of human life, especially with regard to the environment and the union of marriage. The *Divine Principle* is concerned to expound the historical drama of creation, the fall and the restoration, for which the time is now right.

In line with these teachings the UC is well known for its spectacular marriage blessings in which thousands of couples are joined together. Other aspects of practical concern for the movement have been anti-communism and the facilitation, through conferences, of inter-religious dialogue and encounter. Both of these are seen as part of the means to the goal of Unificationism.

(iii) *The Hare Krishna Movement*[26]

As the popular name of this movement suggests it has links with the Hindu religious tradition. The International Society for Krishna Consciousness was formally founded in 1966 although the spiritual leader had begun his preaching mission in India several decades before. A. C. Bhaktivedanta Swami Prabhupada was himself a disciple in a Bengali movement known as the *Gaudiya Vaishnava Mission* which followed the teachings and practices of a sixteenth-century charismatic personality called Chaitanya. Chaitanya taught the importance of *bhakti*, devotion to God or Krishna. Gaudiya Vaishnavism, and later the Hare Krishna Movement, continued to spread this path, emphasizing the value of chanting the names of God, keeping a code of discipline, and worshipping Krishna and his consort, Radha.

Prabhupada's own guru had suggested that he publicize this philosophy in the West through publishing and preaching. Hence, at the age of sixty-nine he travelled to the United States where, after a slow start, he began to make followers among the young in New York. He initiated his first disciples in 1966, before sending them out to teach in other American cities and Western countries. The first disciples to travel to Britain arrived in 1968 and soon succeeded in starting a programme of devotional activities as well as attracting George Harrison of The Beatles to the philosophy and practices. A temple was opened in London in 1969. Since that time the Hare Krishna devotees have established major centres in Central London, Hertfordshire, Leicester, Belfast, Dublin and County Fermanagh, with smaller centres in other cities. The current membership consists of approximately 300 full-time members (some single and celibate, others married), 5,000 congregational or lay members, and 5,000 'life members' from the Indian community.[27]

In addition to the devotional practices mentioned above, devotees of Krishna are renowned for public displays of singing and dancing (*kirtana*) and for the distribution of their many books. Full-time members lead a very disciplined life in which they take initiation from a guru and vow to chant on beads each day, to refrain from meat, fish and eggs, from intoxicants, illicit sex and gambling. These practices and the worship they offer to Krishna are closely related to practices in other Indian religious movements. This is further highlighted by the appearance and customs of the devotees who wear Indian clothes, eat food prepared in an Indian way and keep many of the same festivals as other Hindus.

(iv) *Scientology*[28]

Scientology, though well known as a new religious movement, is different from groups like ISKCON and the UC because its origins do not lie in a world religious tradition and because it was not specifically a 'youth' religion in its early days. It did not begin as a religious movement at all but as a set of psychotherapeutic practices concerned with the nature and perfectibility of the mind. 'Dianetics' was first described in a 1948 publication by L. Ron Hubbard who, in 1950, formed the Hubbard Dianetic Research Foundation in New Jersey.

During the years between 1948 and 1952 not only did an interest in dianetics spread throughout the cities of America and Britain (where amateur groups were set up in London, Bristol and other towns) but the theory and practice developed rapidly. In 1952 the Dianetic Foundation of Great Britain was formed. In the same year the new philosophy of 'Scientology' was formally instituted in the Hubbard Association of Scientology to which most dianetics groups had affiliated by the mid-1950s. The centre of activity moved from the States to Britain in the late 1950s when Hubbard established his headquarters in East Grinstead. In 1969 he moved his administration to a fleet of ships in response to Home Office plans to limit the entry of foreign Scientologists.

Throughout the history of the movement in Britain the main practical aspect of Scientology has been the 'auditing' courses it has offered.[29] These are designed to clear away 'engrams' caused by moments of pain, emotional trauma etc., and to enable the 'analytical mind' to regain control where the 'reactive mind' has been at work. The course, which makes use of 'E meters' to register the state of the 'Thetan' (the individual life force) in relation to uncleared engrams, can be taken either individually or in succession, as part of a more serious quest for mental and emotional liberation.

The teachings and practices cannot be explained in full here but it is important to note that at a particular point in their development they began to be seen as part of a religious path, the goal being not only to 'clear' the individual but also to 'deliver mankind from a state of barbarism, and to restore the limitless creative powers to Thetans'.[30] This has involved both campaigning in areas such as human rights and mental health, and the development of religious worship for committed Scientologists. Most of those who have taken an interest in the movement, however, have participated in the courses without more formal involvement in these other areas.

(v) *The Rajneesh Movement*[31]

This movement is more informal than the others discussed here, largely as a result of the teachings of the leader, Bhagwan Shree Rajneesh. Although 'Rajneeshism' was declared a religion in 1981 by some of his disciples, this was retracted later by Bhagwan who offers 'a way of being, a different quality of existence'.[32] This way of being is all about discovering one's own 'Buddhahood' which can only be done by a process of 'letting go' – of past memories, the games of the mind, the ego. The process necessitates surrender, surrender to a Master, to Bhagwan, and this relationship is sealed by taking *sannyas* or initiation. The symbols of the relationship in the past were the *mala* or necklace on which the *sannyasin* wore a picture of Bhagwan, the spiritual name and the red clothes.[33]

Rajneesh first began to travel and teach in 1960 after his 'enlightenment' in the 1950s. His first Western disciples were attracted during a period of residence in Bombay before he moved to Pune (formerly spelled Poona) in 1974. At that time some of the main features of *sannyasin* practice were developed including 'dynamic meditation' and psychotherapy techniques. In addition, community life was established and *darshans* with Bhagwan began to be held.

Since the settled period in Pune much has happened in the life of the movement. Bhagwan began a period of silence in 1979. He moved to Oregon in the USA in 1981 and set up the community of Rajneeshpuram. Later that year various ritual practices were introduced at the community (including life cycle rites, chanting, and periods of regular reading). In 1984 the dangers of AIDS were broadcast throughout the movement (before the rest of the world had awakened to the seriousness of the problem). Then Bhagwan spoke again. This was followed by the decision that all *sannyasins* in Britain should leave for the Continent, closing down all centres except for Medina in Suffolk which would become a school for the children of members. This change, which left approximately 4,000 members in private family units, was followed by news that a group of leaders had left Oregon for Germany accusing Bhagwan of various crimes (which he in turn accused them of). Rajneeshpuram finally broke up, with Bhagwan leaving for India after a short period in prison for immigration offences and several of the renegade leaders were tried for more serious crimes.

The confusion, devastation and contradictions provoked by these events can be understood within the context of Bhagwan's teaching: 'growth still appears to be the order of the day . . . events have been of transformative value'.[34] They are all part of the process of 'letting go'.

Three of the five groups discussed here were established in Britain in the period between 1965 and 1975 when so many new movements grew up or flowered. The others, the Baha'i faith and Scientology had already begun to grow before this. All the groups continue to have a presence in Britain in the 1980s although their paths of development have not been without incident and their memberships have fluctuated according to social trends and events within the movements themselves. All have branches in other countries around the globe, although the Baha'is, ISKCON and the UC are the most widespread at an international level. Several have suffered problems related to authority and leadership. The Rajneesh Movement in Britain has, in recent years, experienced a series of destabilising events, some of which have already been referred to.

In addition to the call to close down centres and move to Germany and Holland, they have had to face the trial of an ex-leader, Ma Anand Sheela, and the disbanding of the Oregon community and return of Bhagwan to India. The International Society for Krishna Consciousness has undergone leadership difficulties at various times since the death of Prabhupada in 1977. Recently, a number of spiritual leaders have resigned and the whole issue of 'guru' status has been discussed. All the movements, with the exception of the Baha'is, have experienced some kind of harassment from British authorities in the past: Scientology in relation to the entry of foreign leaders in 1968; the UC around the time of the *Daily Mail* court case in 1980–1; ISKCON with the Charity Commissioners and courts on the issue of illegal collecting; the Rajneesh Movement over the issue of Bhagwan's desire to enter Britain in 1986. In addition, these movements were cited in the Cottrell Report to the European Parliament as examples of sects which should be controlled.[35]

There are a number of other interesting movements some of which have shared the growing pains of the groups discussed above. Two movements which were once well known but have now declined in popularity are Transcendental Meditation and Divine Light Mission.[36] Both offered meditation techniques and had their roots in India. *Raja Yoga*, another group of this kind, has continued to maintain a small but viable presence here because of its work for international peace.[37] Meditation and yoga, which were at the height of their popularity in the 1970s, have declined but not disappeared. The continuing pursuit for health and happiness has secured a place for them.

The groups which have been most successful in recent years have been the 'self religions' or 'human potential' movements.[38] These have been concerned not with rituals, texts or teachings as some of the older groups were, but with developing an awareness of the self, 'the self being the "god" that lies within'.[39] Some of the Buddhist groups have been of this kind, particularly those related to the Japanese traditions of Zen and Nichiren Shoshu. Others have included est and Exegesis, the latter claiming over 6,000 graduates from its seminar programme.[40]

Several other movements are also worthy of note. Rastafarianism is of considerable interest owing to its role in black youth sub-culture.[41] Moreover, its spirituality is rooted to some extent in the religious inheritances of Africa, the West Indies, and the 'new religious consciousness'. In recent years Britain has also seen the rise of 'matriarchy groups'.[42] These have developed Goddess-centred rituals and liturgies in addition to stressing the importance of developing women's consciousness, history and sisterhood.

CLASSIFYING NEW RELIGIOUS MOVEMENTS

It is clear from the discussion above that new religious movements are of many types with diverse philosophies and practices. In the last fifteen years several scholars have turned to the task of typologizing these movements according to their response to the world or their moral and philosophical stance.[43] An exercise of this kind had been undertaken in the 1960s by Bryan Wilson in relation to 'sects', and the variety and complexity of the groups constituting this 'new' sectarian phenomenon called for a similar approach.[44]

The most comprehensive work in this field has been done by Roy Wallis who has sought to understand the divergent forms of the new religions through the use of ideal types.[45] The three types he describes are 'world-affirming', 'world-rejecting' and 'world-accommodating' new religions, and each type has certain characteristics, such as a particular orientation towards the prevailing social order and established religious institutions, and a response towards matters of ethics, ritual and collective behaviour. A world-affirming movement, for example,

> lacks most of the features traditionally associated with religion. It may have no 'church', no collective ritual or worship, it may lack any developed theology or ethics. . . . In comparison to the world-rejecting movement, it views the prevailing social order less contemptuously, seeing it as possessing many highly developed characteristics.[46]

An example of a movement in this category would be Exegesis, one of the 'self religions'.

Wallis's typology has been criticized by several scholars because it is used to distinguish between groups on the grounds of their orientations to the world when, in fact, these orientations are themselves internally incoherent and contradictory.[47] This is not meant to be suggested as a criticism of new movements and their philosophies but as an observation of their world-views, and, indeed, of world-views in general. It is unlikely that any new religions are consistently world-affirming, world-rejecting or world-accommodating.[48] A group like ISKCON, which is classified by Wallis as world-rejecting, is seen at times as affirming the world in its positive attitude to lay participation. Some of the 'self religions', classified as affirming the world, seek rather 'transformation' within it.[49] Groups tend to fit into more than one type depending on which of their characteristics one looks at.

This typology, like others which have been proposed, is useful in so far as it facilitates description, comparison and analysis of new religious movements.[50] Bernice Martin's polar opposites of 'liminality' (the antinomian option) and 'communitas' (the total sect) are also helpful, particularly in that they enable us to recognize specific 'counter-cultural' tendencies and goals at work in various groups.[51]

NEW RELIGIONS AND CHANGE

One of the major limiting factors in the attempt to find an accurate and useful typology is the passage of time and the religious and social changes it brings with it for 'new religions' and the society in which they are located. If we look at a new movement in some depth and examine the historical process of its foundation and development it is impossible to ignore its dynamism. Groups which have not been able to respond to the changing requirements placed on them by the outside world, by the expectations and needs of members, and by the process of institutionalization have become impotent and have sometimes disappeared altogether.[52] Many spiritual teachers were able to respond to the *Zeitgeist* of the 1960s and 1970s but the real challenge came later: could the fledgling movement then harness and channel the charismatic qualities of the leader, the vibrant message and the experience of ecstacy?

This issue has been addressed in several ways in the recent study of new movements. Some researchers have looked specifically at individual religions in an attempt to describe not only their character but also the process of their development.[53] Of more theoretical interest is the application of the 'church-sect typology' to new religious movements.[54] This typology has been used not only to characterise different types of religious groups but also to assess the stages of their development. In the case of new movements, often referred to as 'cults', the question arises as to their future organizational character.[55] Will they develop the social and religious characteristics usually associated with 'denominations' or even 'churches'?

How are we to assess, for example, the universalistic character of some new religions? Might the missionary success of movements like the Baha'is, ISKCON and the UC in the Third World be indicative of a new stage of development? Another factor of relevance in relation to this is the ability of these, and some other groups, to adapt to varying geographical, cultural and social contexts. Clearly this ability must be related to a movement's chances of survival; it is also a sign of its willingness to confront the challenge of change.

Another important aspect of the process of development of new groups is their changing relationship to the other social and religious institutions with which they are in contact. In his recent study of cult controversies James Beckford's aim is to provide a framework which allows us to see the 'changing modes of insertion [of new movements] in society for the purpose of producing and reproducing the conditions of their collective mission'.[56] Understanding the public face of new movements and the response to them of state agencies, the churches, the anti-cult movement, academics, and families and friends is essential for a knowledge of movements in particular places and times.[57] Perceiving how this face and the responses to it change with time can help us to appreciate the dynamics of the process of organizational and religious development.

Whether a book similar to this one published a century hence will include a study of any of these 'new' religions in the 2080s is impossible to predict. All that can be said with certainty is that these movements had a considerable impact on contemporary religion in the late 1960s and 1970s, and that their future depends on their ability to develop strategies for growth and survival which are suited to the religious and social climate of the time.

NOTES

1 Neither the indigenous population nor its religion is monolithic in character; both are comprised of diverse groups.
2 J.Farrow, 'Spirituality and self-awareness', *The Friends' Quarterly*,

July 1984, pp. 312–23. On the history of dissent see E. Barker, 'New religious movements in Britain: the context and the membership', *Social Compass*, 30:1, 1983, pp. 33–48, and J. G. Melton, 'Modern alternative religions in the West', in J. Hinnells (ed.), *A Handbook of Living Religions*, Harmondsworth, Penguin, 1985.

3 K. Knott, *Hinduism in Leeds*, Community Religions Project Monograph, Department of Theology and Religious Studies, University of Leeds, 1986; S. Annett, *The Many Ways of Being*, London, Abacus, 1976; G. Ahern, *The Sun at Midnight: The Rudolf Steiner Movement and the Western Esoteric Tradition*, Wellingborough, Aquarian Press, 1984; P. Hounam and A. Hogg, *Secret Cult*, Tring, Herts., Lion Publishing, 1984 (an informative but sensationalist account of the School of Economic Science); J. Moore, 'Gurdjieffian groups in Britain', *Religion Today*, 3:2, 1986, pp. 1–4. The term 'counter culture' was discussed by T. Roszak in *The Making of a Counter Culture*, London, Faber & Faber, 1970 and later by B. Martin, *A Sociology of Contemporary Cultural Change*, Oxford, Basil Blackwell, 1981.

4 The 'new religious consciousness' was a term used by scholars working on new religions in the San Francisco Bay area in the 1970s: C. Y. Glock and R. N. Bellah, *The New Religious Consciousness*, Berkeley, University of California Press, 1976; R. Wuthnow, *The Consciousness Reformation*, Berkeley, University of California Press, 1976. B. Wilson comments on the special attention given to new religious movements in recent years in 'Time, generations and sectarianism', in B. Wilson (ed.), *The Social Impact of New Religious Movements*, New York, Rose of Sharon Press, 1981.

5 Annett, op. cit., lists groups of all the types mentioned in this section.

6 B. Turner in *Religion and Social Theory*, London, Heinemann, 1983, chapter 6, discusses some contemporary sociological attitudes to this question. See also B. Wilson, *Contemporary Transformations of Religion*, London, Oxford University Press, 1976.

7 Wilson, op. cit.; R. Wallis, *The Elementary Forms of the New Religious Life*, London, Routledge & Kegan Paul, 1984, chapter 4; C. Campbell, 'The cult, the cultic milieu, and secularisation', in M. Hill (ed.), *A Sociological Yearbook of Religion in Britain*, Vol. 5, London, SCM, 1972.

8 See discussion of the Stark-Bainbridge theory in Wallis, op. cit. See also T. Luckmann, 'Secularization: a contemporary myth' in *Life Worlds and Social Realities*, London, Heinemann, 1983.

9 T. Robbins and D. Anthony (eds), *In Gods We Trust: New Patterns of Religious Pluralism in America*, New Brunswick, Transaction Books, 1981.

The Twentieth Century

10 J. Beckford, *Cult Controversies: The Societal Response to the New Religious Movements*, London, Tavistock, 1985.

11 As the title of the edited volume by E. Barker suggests – *New Religious Movements: A Perspective for Understanding Society*, New York, Mellen Press, 1982 – this has become an issue of considerable interest.

12 D. Bell, 'The return of the sacred?', *British Journal of Sociology*, 28:4, 1977, pp. 419–49, p. 443.

13 Beckford, op. cit.; Barker, 'New religious movements in Britain: the context and the membership'; Martin, op. cit.

14 F. Hardy, 'How "Indian" are the new Indian religions in the West?', *Religion Today*, 1:2/3, 1984, pp. 15–18; Knott, op. cit.; P. Masefield, 'The Muni and the Moonies', *Religion*, 15:2, 1985, pp. 143–60; R. J. Z. Werblowsky, 'Religions new and not so new', *Numen*, 27:1, 1980, pp. 155–66.

15 Examples of the 'horizontal' approach are Wallis, op. cit.; Beckford, op. cit.; Barker, 'New religious movements in Britain: the context and the membership'; Martin, op. cit, chapter 10. The 'vertical' approach is exemplified by P. Clarke, *Black Paradise: The Rastafarian Movement*, Wellingborough, Aquarian Press, 1986; J. Thompson and P. Heelas, *The Way of the Heart: The Rajneesh Movement*, Wellingborough, Aquarian Press, 1986; and K. Knott, *My Sweet Lord: The Hare Krishna Movement*. Wellingborough, Aquarian Press, 1986. There are, of course, studies conducted by sociologists which also focus on one group and which describe beliefs and practices in addition to questions of membership, organization and so on: E. Barker, *The Making of a Moonie: Brainwashing or Choice?*, Oxford, Basil Blackwell, 1984; R. Wallis, *The Road to Total Freedom*, London, Heinemann, 1976.

16 P. Clarke, 'New religious movements in Britain and Western Europe: in decline?', in P. Clarke (ed.), *The New Evangelists*, London, Ethnographica, 1987.

17 Like the Unification Church, which will be discussed later in the chapter, the Children of God was a movement related somewhat unconventionally to Christianity. See Beckford, op. cit. and R. Wallis, 'Yesterday's children: cultural and structural change in a new religious movement', in B. Wilson (ed.), *The Social Impact of New Religious Movements*, New York, Rose of Sharon Press, 1981.

18 The following information is taken from D. MacEoin, 'Baha'ism', in Hinnells, op. cit., and the same author, 'Emerging from obscurity: recent developments in Baha'ism', *Religion Today*, 3:1. 1986, pp. 1–5; M. Perkins and P. Hainsworth, *The Baha'i Faith*, London, Ward Lock, 1980; Annett, op. cit.

19 MacEoin, 'Baha'ism', pp. 492–3.

20   Ibid, p. 492.
21   Annett, op. cit., p. 83.
22   The information which follows comes from Barker, *The Making of a Moonie;* Annett, op. cit. (under 'Unified Church'); Beckford, op. cit.. Further articles on the Unification Church can be found in Wilson (ed.), *The Social Impact of New Religious Movements;* Clarke (ed.), *The New Evangelists;* Barker (ed.), *New Religious Movements.* Together this represents only a small proportion of the literature on the movement worldwide though it does contain the bulk of available information on the UC in Britain. The UC also produces its own literature on the philosophy of Unificationism, etc.
23   Barker, *The Making of a Moonie*, pp. 64–5.
24   Ibid, p. 210.
25   Beckford, op. cit., p. 44.
26   For further information on the Hare Krishna Movement (ISKCON) in Britain see Knott, *My Sweet Lord;* Beckford, op. cit.; Annett, op. cit. In addition to these sources there are a number of works published on the movement in the USA and by ISKCON itself.
27   Knott, op. cit., chapter 2.
28   The following information has been gathered from Wallis, *The Road to Total Freedom;* Beckford, op. cit.; Annett, op. cit.
29   For an explanation of these terms and the teachings and practices they relate to, see Wallis, op. cit.
30   Beckford, op. cit., p. 56.
31   The information which follows comes from Thompson and Heelas, *The Way of the Heart;* B. Mullan, *Life as Laughter: Following Bhagwan Shree Rajneesh*, London, Routledge & Kegan Paul, 1983; Annett, op. cit.; Knott, *Hinduism in Leeds.*
32   Thompson and Heelas, op. cit., p. 33.
33   Originally the clothes were orange in colour, hence the name 'orange people'.
34   Thompson and Heelas, op. cit., p. 130.
35   See Knott, *My Sweet Lord*, chapter 4.
36   For information on TM in Britain see Knott, *Hinduism in Leeds* and Annett, op. cit. (There is also an article on TM in the USA in Wilson (ed.), *The Social Impact of New Religious Movements.*) For information on Divine Light see Knott, *Hinduism in Leeds;* M. Price, 'The Divine Light Mission as a social organization', *Sociological Review*, 27:2, 1979, pp. 279–96; Annett, op. cit.
37   Knott, *Hinduism in Leeds.*
38   P. Heelas, 'Self religions in Britain', *Religion Today*, 1:1, 1984, pp. 4–5.
39   Ibid., p. 5.

40 Ibid.; P. Heelas, 'Exegesis: methods and aims', in P. Clarke (ed.), *The New Evangelists*, London, Ethnographica, 1987.

41 Clarke, *Black Paradise;* E. Cashmore, *Rastaman: The Rastafarian Movement in England*, London, George Allen & Unwin, 1979.

42 K. Komatsu, 'Matriarchy groups in UK', *Religion Today*, 2:1, 1985, p. 9.

43 Broadly speaking these attempts have been part of the 'horizontal' approach described earlier. In Knott, *Hinduism in Leeds*, a system of classification adopted by T. Robbins, D. Anthony and J. Richardson, 'Theory and research on today's new religions', *Sociological Analysis*, 39:2, 1978, pp. 95–122, was used in the context of all new groups related to the Hindu tradition found in a particular geographical location.

44 B. Wilson, *Religious Sects*, London, Weidenfeld & Nicolson, 1970.

45 Wallis, *The Elementary Forms of the New Religious Life*.

46 Ibid., pp. 20–1.

47 Martin, op. cit., p. 220; P. Heelas, 'Review article: new religious movements in perspective', *Religion*, 15, 1985, pp. 79–97, p. 82.

48 Wallis does not intend these types to be mutually exclusive, and says 'empirical instances will therefore only approximate to these types, of course, often combining elements of more than one orientation', op. cit., p. 5. One critic says, however, that they do not 'approximate' enough, and that those which are supposed to approximate extremely closely to the ideal types put forward do not in fact do so: Heelas,op. cit., p. 91.

49 Heelas, op. cit., p. 90.

50 Other typologies are suggested by Robbins, Anthony and Richardson, op. cit.; and Martin, op. cit., chapter 10.

51 Martin, op. cit.

52 There are many examples of groups which have either flourished or waned with the passage of time: observation suggests, for example, that the Baha'is have successfully established their faith. ISKCON and the UC also seem to have developed strategies for survival and expansion. Groups which seem to be unable to establish a firm footing include the Theosophical Society, which though once widespread now contains an aging population, and the Divine Light Mission which seems to have disappeared from public view in recent years.

53 See Wallis, 'Yesterday's children: cultural and structural change in a new religious movement'. Also Thompson and Heelas, op. cit.; Knott, *My Sweet Lord* and Clarke, *Black Paradise*.

54 Certain scholars are identified with the study of religious organisation, particularly Weber, Troeltsch, Richard Niebuhr and Wilson.

55 R. Wallis, *Sectarianism*, London, Peter Owen, 1975; Stark and Bain-

bridge, 'Of churches, sects and cults: preliminary concepts for a theory of religious movements', *Journal for the Scientific Study of Religion*, 18:2, 1979, pp. 117–31.

56 Beckford, op. cit., p. 81.

57 Ibid. Other examples of the differing relationships new religious movements have formed with outsiders can be seen in Thompson and Heelas, op. cit., chapter 7; Knott, *My Sweet Lord*, chapter 4; C. McCann, 'The British anti-cult movement . . . a view from within', *Religion Today*, 3:2, 1986, pp. 6–8; M. Tierney, *The New Elect: The Church and New Religious Groups*, Dublin, Veritas, 1985; S. J. Gelberg, *Hare Krishna, Hare Krishna: Five Distinguished Scholars on the Krishna Movement in the West*, New York, Grove Press, 1983.

PART 3

OTHER PERSPECTIVES

CHAPTER SEVEN

'Popular Religion' 1800–1986

David Hempton

Popular religion adheres to no one definition; in different settings, in the hands of different people, the amalgam of belief that makes up its theology constantly changes.[1]

Concepts like 'popular religion' eliminate the line between past life and death and the specifics of time and place.[2]

When the editors of *History Today* recently asked the question, 'What is religious history?' an eminent array of respondents clearly found it unexpectedly difficult to give an answer. Although the study of theology and religious institutions was deemed worthwhile, there was widespread agreement among the contributors that religious history ought also to include the beliefs, motivations, experiences, rituals and practices of ordinary people in specific locations at particular times.[3] This is no easy task. Not only do historians disagree quite fundamentally about the nature and social function of religion, they are also aware of the formidable obstacles in the way of reconstructing 'popular religion', with all its behavioural and psychological complexity, from the scraps of surviving evidence. Indeed the term 'popular religion', as with its close relative 'popular culture', is easier to use than to define. It is not merely the antithesis of 'official religion', nor is it a systematic and unified alternative to it. Moreover, the traditional polarities used by historians and sociologists to get to the essence of popular religion

181

– Christian and pagan, traditional and modern, rational and irrational, religious and irreligious, internal and external – have proved to be insufficiently flexible to cope with the sheer diversity of popular belief and practice.

Religious cultures are not static, nor are they isolated from their social setting, rather they are made and remade by the people who live them, and therefore hardly ever conform to the fixed boundaries commentators have designed for them. The lost worlds of popular religious cultures can only be recovered by suspending our contemporary presuppositions about the role of religion in modern life, marginalized as it now is, and by making an imaginative leap into a very different past. To aid this process one early modern historian has urged a degree of 'profanation' to eliminate modern reverential and ideological bias, and to convey the earthiness of religious belief and practice in ordinary communities.[4] Another has suggested a rigorously contextual (family, parish and locality), comparative (sex, social class and denomination) and relational (both within and without religious structures) approach to the study of popular religious behaviour so that light comes from as many sources as possible.[5]

The aim of this chapter, then, is to build on the creative insights of early modern European historians and sociologists, who have pioneered this field of study, by trying to recapture, in however limited a degree, the flavour and texture of British popular religion in diverse locations over two centuries. Since anything approaching an exhaustive treatment of this theme is clearly impossible in such a short space, a secondary and more realistic objective is to introduce some of the new methods and approaches employed in the past two decades to illuminate the dark corners of popular belief and practice. As we shall see, the corners are dark because the religious behaviour of the great majority of men and women in the British Isles, especially after 1900, only rarely conformed to the institutional structures devised for them.[6]

It is perhaps appropriate to start where the Victorians themselves started in trying to understand the impact of industrial and urban growth on their civilization – with numbers. Indeed this Victorian obsession with statistical information, expressed in census reports, Blue Books and statistical societies unlimited, and which was satirized with such effect by Dickens in *Hard Times*, has been reawakened in religious historians searching for contours and perspective in their study of past religious behaviour.[7] The quantitative methods pioneered by Alan Gilbert and others have indeed plotted the major religious landmarks of the modern period:[8] the remarkable resurgence of popular evangelicalism and Roman Catholicism from about the 1780s; the relative weakness of the Church of England between 1780–1835, its suburban-led recovery in the Victorian era and its sorry decline, especially in inner cities in the twentieth century; the rise of evangelical nonconformity which virtually took control of culture and society in South Wales and Cornwall as did the Free Church in the Highlands and islands of Scotland; the astonishingly high mass attendance figures in the towns of post-famine Ireland; and the significant post Second World War growth rates of Jehovah's Witnesses, Latter Day Saints, Adventists and a range of pentecostal and charismatic groups.

Further refinements of the quantitative approach have shown a higher proportion of women, rural dwellers and upper– and middle-class people attending churches than their male, urban and working-class counterparts.[9] As with women, so with children, for Professor Laqueur has estimated that by 1851 over two million working-class children between the ages of five and fifteen (around 75 per cent of the total) were enrolled in Sunday schools.[10] One does not have to accept Laqueur's inference that the primary divide in nineteenth-century society was between the religious and the irreligious, not the middle and working classes, to conclude that Sunday schools played a substantial role in popular religious culture in town and country. For ordinary people the benefits of cheap literacy and self-improvement ensured that the Sunday school 'was the only religious institution which the nineteenth-century public in the mass had any intention of using'.[11] Regrettably from the churches' viewpoint only a tiny minority of pupils later made their way into full church or chapel membership.[12]

Statistical methods have not only helped confirm some old hunches and stimulate some new observations, they have shown too that religious practices do not operate in a social vacuum. It has been suggested that 'a church's power of recruitment arises from its proximity to, congruity with and utility for those whom it recruits', with the implication that church growth patterns cannot be isolated from economic and social changes or from ethnic migration and cultural identity.[13] Early Methodism, for example, grew fastest in areas of Anglican parochial weakness, where the supervision of squires and parsons was at its most rudimentary, and appealed also to particular occupational groups in closely knit communities such as small industrial, mining and fishing villages.[14] Similarly, ethnicity as a compelling force in religious adherence is only now receiving its due attention in Ulster Protestantism and Irish Catholicism, and amongst Irish Roman Catholics in Britain and Nonconformists in Wales.[15] As these examples show, religious allegiances based largely on ethnic and cultural congruities are the most durable and the least susceptible to socio-economic fluctuations. Indeed this highlights a wider European phenomenon in the modern period that attachment to the churches remained strongest in those areas, urban and rural, in which the pressures of political, social and ethnic conflict tended to reinforce rather than undermine religious loyalties.[16]

Statistics, maps and graphs are indispensable tools for social historians of religion, but we worshippers of the computer terminal need also to recognize our god's limitations. Tables and graphs create an illusion of certainty, even inevitability, about historical processes that are infinitely complex. Moreover, they set up boundaries between denominations, and between the religious and the irreligious, which are in reality less clearly defined, and thereby diminish the importance of life cycle changes and of variety in the levels of religious commitment. More prosaically in the context of the British Isles, the way in which Anglican, Catholic, Presbyterian, Methodist and Nonconformist figures are constructed makes comparisons invidious.[17] In particular, the conventional assessments of Anglican strength by numbers of Easter Day Communicants seriously undervalues the relative importance of the Church of England in English society, at least before the First World War.

Flora Thompson, in her evocative reminiscences of rural religion in *Lark Rise to Candleford* towards the end of the nineteenth century, estimates that nine out of ten Lark Rise inhabitants would have declared themselves members of the Church of England, having been christened and married in the parish church.[18] In addition, they buried their dead at church, attended festivals at Christmas, Easter and harvest time, visited the rectory on May Day, qualified themselves for the valuable charities dispensed by clerical families, paraded their finery and singing voices on Sundays, and could even be roused under certain circumstances to exhibit half-hearted displays of anti-Catholic sentiment. The majority, of course, never darkened the church's door outside festival time, unless closely bound by deference to squire or clergyman, and most of them, especially the men, resented clerical visits, particularly if the subject of religion was mentioned. According to Flora Thompson most Lark Rise residents were also perfectly at home in the world of folk tales, ghosts, haunted places and devil's stories, but rather from the point of view of rural entertainment than from dread of unfriendly supernatural visitations.[19] The kind of religion etched in by the author is a delicate mixture of social utility, rural entertainment and moral consensus in which the parish church was closely enmeshed, albeit within certain defined limits set by the community.

Quantitative methods were, of course, never intended to yield up the dark secrets of popular religion in rural Britain which until recently had been virtually ignored by social historians, despite the creative insights offered by Victorian novelists, topographers and folklorists. No doubt stimulated by the pioneering investigations of Keith Thomas into English popular religion in the sixteenth and seventeenth centuries[20] the subject has been opened up in the modern period by James Obelkevich's fine local study of South Lindsey in Lincolnshire and Sean Connolly's equally suggestive work on rural Ireland.[21] Obelkevich defined popular religion as 'the non-institutional religious beliefs and practices, including unorthodox conceptions of Christian doctrine and ritual prevalent in the lower ranks of rural society' and boldly concluded his study by advocating a 'copernican revolution' in our understanding of nineteenth-century rural religion: 'It is hard to avoid the conclusion that paganism was dominant and Christianity recessive in popular religion. Paganism was rarely Christianized but Christianity was often paganized.'[22] The evidence for this interpretation is impressive. Among Lincolnshire labourers there was scarcely a Christian observance that was not surrounded with superstitious beliefs and practices, or else ignored altogether. They were armed instead with a complete set of beliefs about the supernatural designed to bring good luck, to cure people and animals, to foretell the future and to cope with fear and death. There was also a sub-cultural world of witches and wise men, oracles and folk healers in which belief in the devil, humorous or otherwise, was more prevalent than knowledge of Jesus Christ. Obelkevich thus corroborates the brooding impression conveyed by George Eliot in *Silas*

Marner that popular rural religion was overwhelmingly pessimistic – designed more to fob off misfortune than to appropriate the remote abstractions of salvation.

> Such strange lingering echoes of the old demon-worship might perhaps even now be caught by the diligent listener among the grey-haired peasantry; for the rude mind with difficulty associates the idea of power and benignity. A shadowy conception of power that by much persuasion can be induced to refrain from inflicting harm, is the shape most easily taken by the sense of the Invisible in the minds of men who have always been pressed close by primitive wants. . . . To them pain and mishap present a far wider range of possibilities than gladness and enjoyment.[23]

It is a weakness in Obelkevich's study that the terms Christianity and paganism are accepted as the respective poles within which religious belief and practice should be studied, when the words themselves inadequately describe the complex patterns of religious inheritance, ecclesiastical penetration, community solidarity, primitive security and rural entertainment which all contributed something to rural religious life. Similarly, as Flora Thompson would no doubt have concurred, his 'three worlds of church, chapel and popular religion appear too much in isolation from one another'.[24] These are minor reservations, however, for his study of Anglicanism and Methodism in rural culture is worthy of much wider application in British society. The former lost ground steadily to the latter in many counties despite, or partly because of, its commitment to more resident and educated clergy, better maintained buildings, increased sacramental emphasis and reforms in church worship to make it more 'effete' and less 'rough'. In worship services the replacement of the village band's rough music by the more polished tones of organs and correct chants is exposed with regret in Thomas Hardy's *Under the Greenwood Tree* and Samuel Butler's *The Way of All Flesh*.[25] Such reforms made Anglican services more dignified, more feminine and more clerical, but scarcely more popular. In contrast rural Methodism, especially the Primitive connexion, was both a radical social challenge to Anglican paternalism and an alternative expression of a more fervent village religiosity.[26]

A similar pattern is discernible in the mining communities of

England and Wales where evangelical Nonconformity, particularly
Primitive Methodism, helped create a sense of community and
reassurance for people experiencing profound economic and social
changes, and for whom scarcity and disaster were ever present
threats. Choirs, classes, chapels and Sunday Schools were not
simply imposed from without, but appropriated from below, by
people searching for cohesion and a lively alternative to local tavern
culture.[27] According to Robert Colls, Methodism built 'a cocoon
of seriousness in a pub and coursing-path world of careless enjoyment and self-mockery. The cocoon provided its own reason and
reward for self-improvement – so dearly won by the miner'.[28] The
inhabitants of this cocoon were always in a minority in English pit
villages, but not so in South Wales where Nonconformists of
various denominations turned the valleys into remarkable strong-
holds of popular evangelicalism. Between 1800 and 1850 Welsh
Nonconformists built a new chapel every eight days.[29]

Popular religion in rural Ireland in the nineteenth century
presents an interesting comparison with what has been said about
mainland Britain. Before the famine, popular adherence to the
formal observances of the Catholic Church was low, but there was
considerable attachment to the rites of passage, especially baptism
and extreme unction which were almost universal. As with the
Lincolnshire labourers described by Obelkevich, the inhabitants of
rural Ireland subscribed to a whole range of beliefs and observances
only tenuously related to orthodox Catholicism. These included
superstitious interpretations of historic Christian festivals, a wide
range of magical practices from calendar customs to charms and
omens, belief in fairies, banshees and witches, and an Irish propen-
sity for squeezing the maximum amount of raucous entertainment
from festivals and wakes which the Church struggled valiantly but
unsuccessfully to control.[30] The Irish rural poor were therefore not
short of religious devotion, 'what they were devoted to, however,
was a popular religion, diverging from orthodox Catholicism in a
range of important respects'.[31]

As in England the labouring poor valued the social and psychological utility of religion more highly than confessional orthodoxy,
but the apparent similarities of English and Irish versions of popular
syncretism should not obscure some important differences. For
example, although there was a substantial gap between the worlds
of official and popular religion in Ireland, it was probably not as

wide as in England, and there was rather more overlap and mutual accommodation between the two. Indeed the relationship between Catholicism and popular religion was immensely complicated. On the one hand ancient Celtic celebrations, such as the pilgrimage to Croagh Patrick, were Catholicized, just as ancient magical springs were turned into holy wells dedicated to saints, while on the other, a whole series of quasi-superstitious beliefs and practices surrounded Catholic priests, the Virgin Mary and the relics of saints. One recent work has suggested that Irish popular beliefs in this period were closer to those held in Elizabethan England than to those of nineteenth-century English rural labourers.[32] Obelkevich in fact suggests that one of the reasons for the wide gulf between Christianity and paganism in rural Lincolnshire was the long-term success of the Reformation in undermining the sacramental framework of the medieval church.[33] This negative achievement of the English Reformation is not applicable to rural Ireland which was relatively untouched by both the Reformation and the Counter Reformation.

In Ireland the reforming energy of bishops, priests and wealthy laity, as with the Evangelicals and Tractarians in England, probably widened the gap between official Catholicism and popular customs in the first half of the nineteenth century, but unlike England, the decimation of rural Ireland by famine brought unexpected opportunities to the Catholic Church. The so called 'devotional revolution' was underway before the famine but it achieved its most striking successes among the reduced population of the post 1850 period.[34] Professor Corish's most recent estimate of mass attendance in this period is 50–75 per cent in the four Irish cities, 100 per cent in towns, 37.5–75 per cent in English speaking rural areas and 25–50 per cent in Irish speaking rural areas.[35] Such figures should give pause to those British and European historians who assume too easily that urban living was the nemesis of organized Christianity. Irish Catholicism had, it is true, special advantages. There were closer links between priests and people, religion and education, religious and political aspirations and church and national identity than could be achieved anywhere else in Western Europe. As a traditional society dragged into the modern world on the coat-tails of an expanding British economy, Catholicism in Ireland offered important symbols of culture and identity to a population determined to preserve its ties with the past.[36] Similar patterns are to be found among migrants from rural and conservative societies to the United States in the period 1850–1917.[37]

The nature of popular Catholicism in Ireland is of interest not only to Irish historians, but also to those who wish to uncover the religious experiences of Irish migrants to English and Scottish cities. By 1860 there were some three quarters of a million Irish-born inhabitants living predominantly in the industrial towns of Lancashire and Western Scotland, and in London. Most were at least nominally Catholic, but it was a Catholicism 'rooted in an ancient Gaelic-speaking tradition of native Irish spirituality and in a pre-Tridentine popular peasant culture of the home and the pilgrimage, rather than in Mass-going in a new shrine church'.[38] The ethos and atmosphere of this humble Irish culture of 'belligerent fidelity' has been vigorously brought to life by Sheridan Gilley and Raphael Samuel in England and by Bernard Aspinwall and John McCaffrey in Scotland.[39] Separated by their nationality, race, religion and poverty, the Irish clustered together in tight slums in which survived a patriotic religiosity 'which was heartily popular because it was heartily vulgar'.[40] Primitive violence was rarely far from the surface in such communities, but there existed too, warmth and generosity, humour and faith. There was, moreover, a gregarious familiarity between priests and people, in marked contrast to the prevailing relationship between clergy and laity in British denominations. Just as important in cementing community solidarity were the valuable welfare and educational facilities offered by the Catholic Church and its lay organizations. Despite these advantages however, and despite the emotional power of the close relationship between Celtic nationalism and Catholicism, only a minority of Irish migrants conformed to the prescribed devotions of official Catholicism. The Catholic Irish were nevertheless better church attenders than their English working-class counterparts, for as Hugh McLeod's study of late Victorian London has shown, Roman Catholicism was the only form of religion that integrated its adherents into a working-class environment instead of making them stand out from their neighbours.[41]

The migration of the Irish to Victorian towns and cities is but an ethnically distinctive example of a much wider social pattern in nineteenth-century Britain. The census of 1851 appeared to show, for the first time, that more people were living in urban than in rural communities and that almost half of the inhabitants of every large town had been born outside its boundaries.[42] The questions of what happened to the religious beliefs and practices of rural migrants and of what impact urban living had on the subsequent evolution of British religion have occasioned as much controversy among historians and sociologists as they did with the Victorians themselves. It was after all the much analysed 1851 Religious Census with its shocking revelation – to middle-class Victorians at least – of working-class defection from organized religion which has been the starting point of much historical enquiry into religion in urban Britain.[43] More recently these tired old debates have been given fresh life by a variety of new methods and approaches which have exposed the complexity of popular behaviour so often masked by statistics. My approach therefore is intended to be part chronological and part methodological: the period 1790–1840 will be reassessed in the light of creative new work by women historians; the early Victorian years will be viewed through the lens of literature; the later Victorian period has been illuminated by economic and structural analysis, as has the period 1890–1920 by oral evidence; finally, the modern period has been helpfully subjected to a range of sociological techniques including participant observation.

Those who attended the History Workshop on religion and society in London in 1983[44] could not fail to be impressed by the substantial proportion of papers given by women on the role of women in the history of religion. Given that many statistical surveys of religious adherence have shown a preponderance of women, and the fact that they are virtually absent from the pages of traditional ecclesiastical histories, any readjustment along these lines is to be welcomed. Regrettably much of this history, for obvious reasons, is irrecoverable, but valiant efforts have been made by the American scholars Gail Malmgreen and Deborah Valenze in the period of the early industrial revolution in Britain.[45] Dr Valenze's grandly stated aim in *Prophetic Sons and Daughters* is to uncover the sacred world view of English labourers of both sexes and relate it to the profound economic and social changes of the period 1790–1850. More realistically, her chosen terrain is the popular evangelicalism of cottage meetings which proliferated far more widely in the period of the French Revolutionary wars than the more publicized radical political clubs. Initially Wesleyan Methodism was the vehicle through which these popular religious energies were expressed but by the 1790s its increasing formalism and notorious connexional discipline alienated some of its more humble supporters. Thereafter, sectarian Methodism became the dominant, but not exclusive, expression of cottage-based religion.

Such religion threw up a kaleidoscope of practices from prophecies and healing to trances and dreams, and brought forth a sturdy independent leadership, the most striking aspect of which was the relatively high proportion of women. This was facilitated by the domestic setting of cottage religion, the sense of autonomy women gained from their labouring experiences and the receptivity of men to female leadership when social and economic changes threatened to dislocate families and kinship networks. Moreover, the women brought to life in Dr Valenze's study are far removed from the idealized domestic angels we encounter in Victorian fiction. Acquainted with grief and hardship from an early age, and made even more independent by geographical mobility and late marriage, these women were remarkably young – around eighteen years of age – when they started their preaching mission and were not easily controlled by any authority. Indeed they were the embodiment of a 'world turned upside down' which repudiated the formalism of churches and chapels and the disciplines of economic and social control. There is much here that is reminiscent of the millenarian groups of the French Revolutionary period described by Professor Harrison and of the Civil War and Interregnum Puritanism brought to life by Christopher Hill.[46]

In several impressive case studies Dr Valenze shows too how popular evangelicalism could re-create the world of cottage industry, village familiarity and household unity in an increasingly urban and factory dominated environment. Successive waves of rural migrants into manufacturing towns eschewed employer-sponsored Anglican churches and Nonconformist chapels in favour of a more intimate and informal religious atmosphere in which the professional preachers had no part. This era of cottage-based religion declined rapidly from the 1850s when towns, institutions – including churches – and railways spread into most corners of British society, and cottage religion virtually disappeared with the household economy which had sustained it.

Aside from pointing up the importance of women in this humble culture, before they were shuffled aside in the 1840s by a Nonconformity dominated by theologically educated preachers, respectable laymen and chapel business, Dr Valenze also touches on themes of wider significance. For example, it is still not clear how much of the urban-based popular evangelicalism of Victorian Britain had its roots in the rural revivalism of the previous half century.[47] E.T. Davies has shown how much of nineteenth-century Welsh Nonconformity had its origins in the religious and social protest of tenant farmers and small-holders in the countryside and among the proto-industrial workers of Glamorgan and Monmouthshire against predominantly Anglican landowners and entrepreneurs. Similarly, the remarkable strength of the Free Church in the northern highlands and islands of Scotland was built around a population living in near destitution by engaging in a subsistence agriculture with the minimum of tenurial security. Moreover, the Church of Scotland had become associated in many minds with landlordism, clearances and cultural supremacy.[48] Thus revivalism and poverty lived in a symbiotic relationship. In England too, early Wesleyan and later Primitive Methodist revivals were part religious, part social, protest against Anglican paternalism. Even in Ireland much of the popular evangelicalism, which has exercized such a profound influence over the northern part of the country, had its origins in the rural revivals among the small tenant farmers and outworkers of southern and south-western Ulster between 1780 and 1820. Here the story is yet more complex, for much of this rural revivalism was directed not so much against the episcopal Established Church but against Roman Catholic competition in the land and linen markets.[49] This rural sectarianism was brought into Belfast by migrant workers in the early nineteenth century and has done much to set the tone of politics in that resilient but unhappy city.[50]

Religion, it seems, sinks its deepest roots into popular culture when it helps give expression to the social, economic, ethnic and cultural homogeneity of populations facing rapid change or oppression. But to take the additional step, as some socialist historians do, of suggesting that religion is primarily a form of social control is to minimize the way in which humble people make and remake the religious traditions to which they give their allegiance.[51]

If, as has been suggested, popular evangelicalism achieved its greatest successes in British society in the period of transition from community to class and from traditional recreations to the advent of mass leisure, there has also been widespread agreement that Victorian towns and cities hastened these changes and produced a working class whose religious apathy was in marked contrast to the institutional religiosity of the middle and upper-middle classes. Indeed, virtually every statistically based analysis of Victorian religion, from Horace Mann's reflections on the Religious Census of 1851 to Hugh McLeod's and Jeffrey Cox's treatment of London at the turn of the century, have drawn attention to a class differential in religious practice in modern Britain.[52] Why this was the case and, more particularly, what kind of religion, if any, survived among the urban working classes are difficult questions to answer. There is as yet no study of popular urban religion to match the quality of Obelkevich's rural insights, and working-class Anglicanism in particular has been strikingly under-researched by comparison with the work done on the Nonconformist and Catholic churches.[53] So peripheral is religion alleged to have been in the lives of working-class Britons, outside the regional exceptions already mentioned, that some social historians have virtually ignored it altogether in their descriptions of popular life before the First World War.[54] Two recently exploited sources, literature and oral evidence – with all their attendant flaws – have shed a glimmer of light on urban popular religion.

Nineteenth-century novels, because of their quantity and quality, have been irresistible quarries of information for social historians, especially those, who like the Victorians themselves, are interested in religion.[55] Quarrying is, of course, rough work and is generally more concerned with extracting raw materials then in appreciating the landscape within which they are found. Literary critics have therefore been rightly suspicious of certain kinds of historical approaches to literature – most notably the cuckoo method – which has been described by E.M. Forster as a kind of pseudo scholarship. Conversely, empirically-minded historians have often had their nerves set on edge by the amateurish historical methods employed by some literary critics. Interdisciplinary study, to coin Michael Wolff's phrase, seems to teeter on the brink of becoming anti-disciplinary study.[56] Nevertheless, despite the effects of distorting lenses, both deliberate and unintentional, of much Victorian fiction, novelists are, on the whole, sensitive observers of the society in which they lived. Even their misconceptions can be revealing, as are the features of their society they took for granted. Disraeli's fiction, for example, which was strongly influenced by the view of English history propagated by R.H. Froude and other early leaders of the Oxford Movement, exaggerated the religiosity of England's medieval past and thus over-reacted to the popular infidelity of the early Victorian period.[57] By isolating the problem of religious decline, romantic medievalists were partly responsible for creating new problems of explanation which have dominated the historiography of religion in this period.

Conversely, George Eliot in *Silas Marner* creatively inverts the conventional pattern of a historically religious countryside contrasted with the new irreligious towns which seemed to have been irrefutably demonstrated by the census of public worship in 1851. What is hinted at through Silas, however, is that the religion of the countryside was a rather pale mixture of deference, dependency, custom and community solidarity whereas popular urban religion, albeit a minority taste, was based more on voluntary commitment to religious associations. The local studies of social historians have indeed shown that although church-going was a vulnerable habit of rural migrants to Victorian towns and cities, most of those who came from large 'open' villages had already little to lose.[58]

What then does Victorian literature reveal about the beliefs and practices of those who lived in nineteenth-century urban Britain? The so-called industrial novels of the 1840s and 1850s suggest that the relative absence of formal religious observances did not necessarily mean that religion was redundant in popular life. Religious belief, according to these sources, could be important in facing up to death and disaster, in establishing a rudimentary moral code, in developing neighbourly concern in times of economic hardship and depression, in nurturing a sturdy respectability in family life and in providing a Biblical justification for attacking the oppression of the rich and the lack of justice in labour relations.[59] Conversely religion was repudiated when it concentrated on eternal rather than temporal objectives,[60] when it condemned popular leisure activities[61] and when it introduced unnecessary tensions into the family and the workplace. Above all, and this has been corroborated by working-class autobiographies and city mission reports, any form of religion which reinforced rather than diminished class distinctions was unpopular with the urban poor.[62] Indeed, the sheer 'respectability' of much pre-First World War religion with its sabbatarianism and temperance, its clerical professionalism and opposition to popular recreations, systematically eroded the base of working-class support for official religion.[63] What was left has been described as 'proletarian parochialism', which was founded on community solidarity and a homespun morality of not doing anybody any harm.[64] Such religious apathy was largely beyond the reach of both the plebeian ultra-evangelicalism of Brethren, Baptists, Salvationists and city missioners, and the more colourful rituals of High Church Anglicanism and ethnic Catholicism. In short, popular adherence to Victorian churches was limited by a powerful combination of class and culture conflict with which readers of Dickens and Samuel Butler will already be familiar.[65] Churches were still used for rites of passage, watch night and harvest thanksgiving services – and outright scepticism was remarkably rare – but increasingly they were seen in working-class culture as places suitable only for women, children and the aged. For the majority of working-class men, especially those with an emerging political consciousness, religious institutions seemed to be antithetical to their lifestyles and indifferent to their interests. Nevertheless, criticisms of the churches from this source 'often reflected not so much irreligion or indifference as disappointed expectations'.[66]

The impression conveyed by Victorian novelists that the religion of the people could have a whole range of private and social meanings, quite apart from institutional adherence is supported by a new source available to students of popular religion in the late nineteenth and early twentieth centuries: taped interviews with controlled samples of old people who were brought up in that period. The pioneering work of Elizabeth Roberts, Paul Thompson and Thea Vigne, and Stephen Humphries has been helpfully synthesized and reinterpreted by Hugh McLeod in *Oral History*.[67] Oral evidence helps to do justice to the complexity and fluidity of the religious outlook of ordinary individuals, but however well chosen are the samples and the questions put to respondents, this method, as with any other, has its limitations. Samples probably over-represent the more respectable elements of the working class and may reflect life cycle changes, exaggerated by nostalgia, of greater religiosity among the young and the aged. Samples are also too small to be conclusive and questions tend to focus more on habits and affiliations than on beliefs and experiences.

With such slender evidence McLeod may be hasty in revising upwards his previous estimates of working-class church attendance, but there can be no doubt that proportions were higher in Scotland and Wales, and in Lancashire and Yorkshire, than they were in London. Women were also more likely to attend church than men. But religion was not confined to the institutionally religious. Even non-churchgoers sent their children to Sunday School, dressed up on Sundays, used religion to get jobs and welfare relief, sang hymns as a means of cementing community solidarity, extolled 'practical Christian' virtues, relied heavily on Christian sexual ethics (not least as a point of departure), derived comfort from religion in times of suffering or disaster, accepted that church and chapel or Protestant and Catholic were fundamental social divisions, and used the churches' social facilities without feeling any need to attend more overtly 'religious' activities.

One important, but often neglected, aspect of popular religion amplified by oral evidence is the emotional resonance achieved by the religious music of hymns and choirs, and the happy memories of church- or chapel-organized seaside treats and social gatherings. None understood the raw edge of nostalgic emotionalism in popular religion more than the predominantly American-technique revivalists of the late nineteenth and twentieth centuries unless it be those more recent producers of mellow religious pop on Sunday television.[68] But not all religious emotion is artificially produced. In the late Victorian era churches and chapels, even within the same denominations in different parts of the same town, produced 'atmospheres' of attraction or repulsion, warmth or stiffness. With rare exceptions historians are not good at capturing the emotional flavour of popular religious assemblies. Edmund Gosse and Flora Thompson have done it better. 'I wish I could paint', writes Gosse of his father's little Devonshire Brethren assembly,

> in colours so vivid, that my readers could perceive what their little society consisted of, this quaint collection of humble, conscientious, ignorant and gentle persons. In chronicle or fiction I have never been fortunate enough to meet with anything which resembled them. The caricatures of enmity and worldly scorn are as crude to my memory, as the unction of religious conventionality is featureless.[69]

This is in the same spirit as Flora Thompson's treatment of Lark Rise Methodists, or 'Devil dodgers' as they were called for their practice of attending parish church on Sunday morning and

Methodist chapel in the evening. Her account of these meetings
rings with the authenticity of mingled sympathy and gentle criticism. She captures the warmth of religious enthusiasm transmitted
through extempore prayer, lively singing and mutual confession.
The weekday reserve and godly discipline of the Methodists gave
way on Sunday evenings to shining eyes and gentle expressions.
On the other hand she pokes fun at the highly coloured personal
testimonies of Methodists fleeing from sin to grace – the religious
equivalents of public house yarns – and at the uneducated preachers
basking so self-consciously in their religious limelight.[70]

Lest Victorian nostalgia take over it is well to be reminded, as
David Clark has done recently in his study of a Yorkshire fishing
village, that popular religion could also be crass, bigoted, sectarian
and disruptive of human relationships.[71] 'These cramping cults',
wrote H.G. Wells in *The New Machiavelli*, 'do indeed take an
enormous toll of human love and happiness . . . they make frightful
breaches in human solidarity'.[72] Religious emotions can be characterized by aggression as well as nostalgia.

Before leaving the oral evidence of pre-First World War working-
class religion it should be pointed out that it does make a contribution to the current debate of whether or not it makes sense to
divide the urban working class into the 'rough' and the 'respectable'. Here the evidence is predictably inconclusive. Regular and
devoted pub-goers did not attend churches and vice versa, but there
were various shades of commitment in between. The real value of
oral evidence, however, has been to show that religion was
important to non-church-goers in a variety of ways. It frequently
intersected with other social frameworks including politics,
employment, leisure, community identification and differentiation,
values, emotions and ethics. It shows too that secularization,
however it is to be defined, was a more gradual and complicated
process than is sometimes supposed.

Just how closely religion could interact with other social frameworks has been the subject of a number of outstanding local studies
of religion in British industrial towns and cities in the period
1850–1930. Although not specifically concerned with the characteristics of popular beliefs and practices Maclaren, Joyce, Foster and
Yeo have tried to relate religious cultures to much wider economic
and structural changes in Victorian Britain.[73] Indeed industrial
Britain, and its by no means ideologically uncommitted historians,

has thrown up a bewildering range of religious patterns from Joyce's description of orange-coloured popular Protestantism in Lancashire to Foster's treatment of *petit bourgeois* Nonconformist liberalism in Oldham; and from Maclaren's portrayal of sturdy Scottish Presbyterian respectability in Aberdeen to Yeo's picture of religious organizations in Reading, in common with other voluntary associations, coming in and going out with the tide of liberal capitalism. What they have in common is a conviction that religion in industrial society is inseparable from the class, employment, community, ethnic and cultural interests of its adherents. This is no mere reductionist argument, however, for religion was itself an active agent in the creation of wider cultural frameworks. The Methodist miners of Durham, for example, developed a style of politics, trade unionism and wage negotiations with their Nonconformist employers which owed more to their religious beliefs than to the pursuit of narrow class interests as such. Similarly, class antagonism in late Victorian Lancashire was overlaid by religious and ethnic identities which often resulted in an 'unreasoning sectarianism in popular politics'.[74] This pattern survives in a more acute form in twentieth-century Ulster.

Despite the proliferation of excellent case studies of urban religion in the late nineteenth and early twentieth centuries, including those by Hugh McLeod and Jeffrey Cox in different parts of London, the actual *beliefs* of the urban working class remain tantalizingly opaque. Indeed the oral evidence already discussed, for all its methodological problems, is at least as insightful as the recorded impressions of clergymen, city missioners and autobiographers. A number of consistent themes do nevertheless emerge from such sources. Although thorough-going scepticism was rare, most working-class Londoners had only the dimmest perceptions of Christian doctrines or of eternal life, whether heavenly or hellish. Strictly speaking they were not unbelievers, nor were they anxious doubters, but Christian supernaturalism played as little part in their lives as did the semi-pagan and magical ideas which were held by some inhabitants of the English countryside. Whether this was due, as Cox suggests, to the rise of a new class society and the spread of popular scientism, or whether it was the result of the churches' own supernatural tameness, by comparison, for example, with eighteenth-century Methodism and twentieth-century Pentecostalism, is not entirely clear.[75] According to Cox not all was lost from the churches' viewpoint, however, for they were able to promote a 'diffusive Christianity' through education, welfare relief, clubs and rites of passage, at least until the state spread its collectivist tentacles. Notwithstanding such competition the churches were able to further diffuse a 'diffusive Christianity' through religious broadcasting and services at school assemblies.[76] Here indeed, as consumers of such religion will testify, is religious diffusion to the power of infinity.

Working-class Londoners could still urge their womenfolk to set decent religious standards for their children, and they could still be roused to displays of religious patriotism during wars and royal jubilees; but Hugh McLeod is right to emphasize the further erosion of working-class religiosity in twentieth-century London as more puritanical restraints were cast off and the terrors of hell were seen as nothing compared to the sins of social inequality.[77]

London is, of course, far from typical of the nation as a whole, and there remains in the twentieth century higher levels of popular religious adherence in other parts of the British Isles, particularly in the Celtic fringes. Understandably, but regrettably, there has been far more written by both historians and sociologists of religion on the reasons for, and characteristics and consequences of, secularization than there has on the content of the popular religion which has survived. One recent and entertaining exception is David Clark's *Between Pulpit and Pew*, a study of folk religion in Staithes, a North Yorkshire fishing village. The method employed is participant observation and the author set out with clear distinctions between 'official' and 'folk' religion which proved easier to define in theory than to observe in practice.[78] For villagers the two cultures, popular and sacred, became a seamless web in the personal cycle of birth and death, and in the annual community cycle of Sunday School and chapel anniversaries, and the New Year, Easter, Harvest and Christmas celebrations. In addition, the occupational dangers of a fishing community spawned its own sub-culture of superstitious practices which were adhered to with a mixture of embarrassment and deadly seriousness. The inhabitants of Staithes could also display local cantankerousness in their opposition to that familiar triad of twentieth-century religion, ecumenism, bureaucratic centralization and ministerial professionalism. Ironically, local chapels came to mean more to the villagers when threatened with amalgamation or extinction than they did as going concerns.

Staithes religion then was composed of a complex mixture of local custom, half-belief, occupational superstitions, cyclical rituals and rhythms, community identification and differentiation, chapel loyalties and nostalgic religious emotions. Many of these features coexisted not only within the same small community but also within the minds of the individuals who composed it.

Staithes is, of course, a most unrepresentative sample of modern popular religion. Although not immune from modernizing trends, including the hospitalization of birth, sickness and death, its geographical location and economic function have cocooned it in a time warp. As Clark suggests what is needed now are more studies of folk religion in an urban setting to see how far popular culture has been demystified by the secularizing forces of the twentieth century.

It is tempting to get embroiled in the prolific debates on secularization, but in the limited space available it would be impossible to add anything fresh to the historically based work of Yeo, Gilbert and McLeod or to the sociological approaches of Berger, Martin and Wilson.[79] Besides, the problems with the term itself are well known, since religion is not amenable to precise definition, and the base line from which secularization is assumed to have proceeded constantly shifts with the impressive body of new research on late medieval and early modern popular religion.[80] Yet with all the attendant difficulties of using the term properly it is clear that both institutional religion and popular religiosity, of whatever hue and texture, has declined significantly in the twentieth century. It may have been partly diffused into other channels as Cox suggests or partly replaced by sacralized alternatives as Lyons has it,[81] but outside Ireland and pockets of Scotland and Wales much of Victorian religion has simply ebbed way. The speed, characteristics and extent of 'secularization' have varied considerably in different communities, among different social classes and in specific regions. Indeed its effects have been as complex as the religion it has undermined. It would be a mistake, moreover, to suggest that 'secularization' is unilinear or irreversible. International Pentecostalism, charismatic renewal and new religious movements, whether epiphenomenal and culturally marginal as some suggest, or major new landmarks on the world's religious landscape, testify to the stubborn refusal of religion to move quietly aside, even in technologically-advanced Western societies.[82] Here, the 'strange gifts' of the charismatic renewal may indeed be examples of 'the incoherence of confused enthusiasm' as one critic has called it,[83] but such language is strikingly similar to the remarks of Anglican bishops and clergy on revivalistic Methodism in Devon and Cornwall in the 1740s.[84]

A century later a worldwide Methodism with several million adherents was still regarded as a heresy by some Anglican High Churchmen,[85] but it was no longer perceived to be a localized and transitory phenomenon. There are, of course, substantial dissimilarities between early Methodism and the charismatic renewal, not least in their social constituencies, but they do suggest that popular enthusiasm for the raw edges of spiritual authenticity, however irksome to those with more traditional views of the role of religion, is remarkably resilient to secularizing forces.

What conclusions then can be drawn from this rapid survey of almost two centuries of popular religion in the British Isles? The first and most important, as the introductory quotations suggested, is that the concept 'popular religion', like its cousin 'popular culture', is potentially misleading. There was in fact no such thing as a distinctive and definable popular religion in Britain in this period. Rather there were many complex individual and communal expressions of belief and practice among the mass of people in different settings and at different times. More local studies, especially of non-metropolitan urban religion, are therefore desirable, but they are not of themselves sufficient; for as Professor Ward has rightly pointed out:

> The consequence of the increasing precision of local studies is to force attention upon the fact that the major international movements in Protestant (and for that matter, Catholic) history are not to be explained upon a local basis, any more than they are upon the institutional presuppositions which ecumenical historians share with denominational ones. There will be no explaining the shared responses to shared perceptions until historians recognize that such things exist.[86]

In the same way as Obelkevich has stated that religious life cannot be 'reduced' to its social foundations, but is unintelligible without them, so too popular religion cannot be 'reduced' to its local setting however necessary it may be to explore local peculiarities.[87] Professor Ward's own work on the international dimensions of popular pietism in the eighteenth and nineteenth centuries, and

Dr McLeod's forthcoming comparative study of religion in major western cities are welcome attempts to investigate modern religion on a much wider canvas than has been the recent fashion.[88] If done sensitively, to avoid either a crude form of historical dispensationalism or social and economic determinism, such an approach opens up the way for far more creative analytical frameworks than is possible from the growing mountain of empirical local studies.

Second, the boundaries and categories constructed by historians to make sense of religion – official and popular, Christian and pagan, religious and irreligious, secular and sacred, rough and respectable, traditional and modern, imposed and indigenous – are insufficiently flexible to describe a much more complicated reality. There must be enough scope to include life cycle changes, distinctions between male and female religiosity and the survival of religious frameworks and meanings in communities, ethics, even politics, long after formal religious adherence has declined. In particular, more needs to be said about the role of women and children, and the importance of class and ethnicity in the development of religious cultures.[89]

Third, and perhaps most difficult of all, more comparative and relational studies are required to highlight both the massive continuities of 'popular religion' and the important periods of change and adaptation. The religious geography of the British Isles, and of large parts of continental Europe for that matter, shows clearly enough the historical continuities of belief and practice over several centuries. Equally important are the profound changes of the periods 1730–50 when popular evangelicalism took root in the British Isles; 1790–1830 when English and Welsh Nonconformists and Irish Catholics substantially undermined the Anglican confessional supremacy at popular if not at elite level; and the 1880s when it became clear that Victorian religion, at least outside the Celtic fringes, was a declining, if far from spent, force. The developments of the twentieth century further undermined institutional and popular religion. Only time will tell if the pentecostal, charismatic and new religious movements on the one hand and the resilience of conservative Protestantism and Roman Catholicism on the other can arrest the general demise of British Christianity.

Finally, as Trexler has suggested, we commentators need to divest ourselves of a whole range of twentieth-century perceptions about the nature of past religion and its social function.[90] Both the older denominational historians and the more recent sociologists and social historians of religion, through lack of imagination, have been guilty of minimizing the complexity and diminishing the humanity of quite humble people and their communities.

NOTES

1. D.M. Valenze, *Prophetic Sons and Daughters. Female Preaching and Popular Religion in Industrial England*, Princeton, Princeton University Press, 1985, p.245.
2   R.C.Trexler, 'Reverence and profanity in the study of early modern religion', in K. von Greyerz (ed.), *Religion and Society in Early Modern Europe*, London, Allen & Unwin, 1984, pp. 245–69.
3   C. Brooke et al., 'What is religious history?', *History Today*, vol. 35, August 1985, pp. 43–52.
4   Trexler, op. cit., pp. 245–69.
5   N.Z. Davis, 'Some tasks and themes in the study of popular religion', in C. Trinkaus and H. A. Oberman (eds), *The Pursuit of Holiness in Late Medieval and Renaissance Religion*, Leiden, Brill, 1974, pp. 307–36; and N.Z. Davis, 'From "Popular Religion" to religious cultures', in S. Ozment (ed.), *Reformation Europe: A Guide to Research*, St Louis, Center for Reformation Research, 1982, pp. 321–41.
6   For church attendance figures in the British Isles since 1700 see R. Currie, A. Gilbert and L. Horsley, *Churches and Churchgoers*, Oxford, Clarendon Press, 1977.
7   A. Briggs, 'The human aggregate', in H.J. Dyos and M. Wolff (eds), *The Victorian City: Images and Realities*, London, Routledge & Kegan Paul, 1973, vol.1, pp. 83–104.
8   Currie, op. cit.; A. D. Gilbert, *Religion and Society in Industrial England: Church, Chapel and Social Change 1740–1914*, London, Longman, 1976; and J. Bossy, *The English Catholic Community 1570–1850*, London, Darton, Longman & Todd, 1975.
9   J. Cox, *The English Churches in a Secular Society: Lambeth, 1870–1930*, Oxford, Oxford University Press, 1982; D.N. Hempton, 'Bickersteth, Bishop of Ripon: the episcopate of a mid-Victorian Evangelical', *Northern History*, vol. 17, 1981, pp. 183–202; K.S. Inglis, 'Patterns of religious worship in 1851', *Journal of Ecclesiastical History*, vol. 11, 1960, pp. 74–86; and H. McLeod, *Class and Religion in the Late Victorian City*, London, Croom Helm, 1974.
10 T.W. Laqueur, *Religion and Respectability: Sunday Schools and Working-Class Culture 1780–1850*, New Haven and London, Yale University Press, 1976.

11 W.R. Ward, *Religion and Society in England 1790–1850*, London, Batsford, 1972, p. 13.
12 For this and other controversies surrounding Sunday schools see D. Hempton, *Methodism and Politics in British Society 1750–1850*, London, Hutchinson, 1984, pp. 86–92.
13 R. Currie, op. cit., pp. 21–123.
14 Hempton, *Methodism and Politics*, pp. 14–16; and A. Everitt, *The Pattern of Rural Dissent: the Nineteenth Century*, Leicester, Leicester University Press, 1972.
15 S. Connolly, *Religion and Society in Nineteenth-Century Ireland*, Dundalk, The Economic and Social History Society of Ireland, 1985; E.T. Davies, *A New History of Wales: Religion and Society in the Nineteenth Century*, Dyfed, Christopher Davies, 1981; A.D. Gilbert, *The Making of Post-Christian Britain*, London, Longman, 1980, pp. 75–6; R.F.G. Holmes, *Our Irish Presbyterian Heritage*, Belfast, Presbyterian Church in Ireland, 1985; R. Swift and S. Gilley (eds), *The Irish in the Victorian City*, London, Croom Helm, 1985; and R. Wallis, S. Bruce and D. Taylor, *'No Surrender!' Paisleyism and the Politics of Ethnic Identity in Northern Ireland*, Belfast, Department of Social Studies, Queen's University Belfast, 1986.
16 Connolly, op. cit., pp. 58–9; and H. McLeod, *Religion and the People of Western Europe 1789–1970*, Oxford, Oxford University Press, 1981.
17 It is, for example, difficult to compare figures based on Episcopalian communicants, Presbyterian communicants, Methodist and Nonconformist membership, and either the estimated Roman Catholic population or Mass attenders, since they clearly measure different aspects of religious adherence and commitment.
18 F. Thompson, *Lark Rise to Candleford*, Penguin Modern Classics, 1973, ch.14.
19 For suggestive comments on the complicated relationship between official and popular religion in nineteenth-century rural England see H. McLeod, 'Recent studies in Victorian religious history', *Victorian Studies*, vol.21, no.2, 1978, pp.245–55.
20 K. Thomas, *Religion and the Decline of Magic*, London, Weidenfeld & Nicolson, 1971.
21 J. Obelkevich, *Religion and Rural Society: South Lindsey 1825–1875*, Oxford, Clarendon Press, 1976; S.J. Connolly, *Priests and People in Pre-Famine Ireland 1780–1845*, Dublin, Gill and Macmillan, 1982.
22 J. Obelkevich, op. cit., pp.305–6.
23 G. Eliot, *Silas Marner*, London, Collins, 1953, ch.1.
24 McLeod, 'Recent studies', p.250.
25 S. Butler, *The Way of All Flesh*, Penguin English Library, ch. 14; T.

Hardy, *Under the Greenwood Tree*, Penguin English Library, pt.2 ch.4.

26 Obelkevich, op. cit., pp. 220–58; J.M. Turner, *Conflict and Reconciliation: Studies in Methodism and Ecumenism in England 1740–1982*, London, Epworth Press, 1985, pp. 82–8; N. Scotland, *Methodism and the Revolt of the Field: A Study of the Methodist Contribution to Agricultural Trade Unionism in East Anglia, 1872–96*, Gloucester, Alan Sutton, 1981, pp. 9–10.

27 R. Moore, *Pit-Men, Preachers and Politics: The Effects of Methodism in a Durham Mining Community*, London, Cambridge University Press, 1974; R. Colls, *The Collier's Rant: Song and Culture in the Industrial Village*, London, Croom Helm, 1977; and Hempton, *Methodism and Politics*, pp. 214–6.

28 Colls, op. cit., p. 100.

29 Davies, op. cit., p. 26. See also, E.T.Davies, *Religion in the Industrial Revolution in South Wales*, Cardiff, University of Wales Press, 1965, pp. 44–96.

30 Connolly, *Priests and People*, pp. 74–218; P. Corish, *The Irish Catholic Experience: A Historical Survey*, Dublin, Gill and Macmillan, 1985, chs 4–7; D. Keenan, *The Catholic Church in Nineteenth-Century Ireland: A Sociological Study*, Dublin, Gill and Macmillan, 1983: J. O'Shea, *Priest, Politics and Society in Post-Famine Ireland: A County Study of Tipperary, 1850–1891*, Dublin, Wolfhound Press, 1983; D. Hempton, 'Irish religion', *Irish Economic and Social History*, vol.13, 1986, pp. 108–12; and D.W. Miller, 'Irish Catholicism and the historian', *Irish Economic and Social History*, vol.13, 1986, pp. 113–16.

31 Connolly, *Religion and Society*, p. 49.

32 Keenan, op. cit., p.23.

33 Obelkevich, op. cit., pp. 271–4.

34 E. Larkin, *The Historical Dimensions of Irish Catholicism*, New York, Arno Press, 1976; and Larkin, *The Making of the Roman Catholic Church in Ireland 1850–60*, Chapel Hill, University of North Carolina Press, 1980.

35 Corish, op. cit., p.167.

36 L.M. Cullen, *The Emergence of Modern Ireland 1600–1900*, London, Batsford, 1981, pp.135–9, 254–6.

37 W. Herberg, *Protestant-Catholic-Jew: an essay in American religious sociology*, Garden City, New York, Doubleday, 1956; O. Handlin, *The Uprooted*, Boston, Little, Brown and Company, 1973; and K.A. Miller, *Emigrants and Exiles: Ireland and the Irish exodus to North America*, New York, Oxford University Press, 1985.

38 Swift and Gilley, op. cit., p.10.

39 Ibid., see the articles by O'Tuathaigh, Aspinwall and McCaffrey, Connolly, Gilley and Samuel; S. Gilley, 'The Roman Catholic mission to the Irish in London', *Recusant History*, vol. 10, 1969–70, pp.123–41; Gilley, 'Protestant London, No-Popery and the Irish poor, 1830–60', part 1, *Recusant History*, vol.10, 1969–70, pp.210–30, and part 2, *Recusant History*, vol. 11, 1971–2, pp.21–46; and H. McLeod, 'Building the "Catholic Ghetto": Catholic organisations 1870–1914', in W.J. Sheils and D. Wood (eds), *Voluntary Religion*, Oxford, Basil Blackwell, 1986, pp. 411–44.

40 S. Gilley, 'Vulgar piety and the Brompton Oratory, 1850–1860', in Swift and Gilley, op. cit., p.263.

41 McLeod, *Class and Religion*, p.72.

42 J.A. Banks, 'The contagion of numbers' and R. Samuel, 'Comers and goers', in Dyos and Wolff, op. cit., pp. 105–60.

43 For a more sophisticated approach to the use of statistical evidence based on regional and local variations see N. Yates, 'Urban church attenders and the use of statistical evidence, 1850–1900', *Studies in Church History*, vol.16, 1979, pp. 389–400.

44 J. Obelkevich, L. Roper and R. Samuel (eds), *Disciplines of Faith*, London, Routledge & Kegan Paul, 1987.

45 D.M. Valenze, op. cit.; G. Malmgreen, 'Economy and culture in an industrializing town: Macclesfield, Cheshire, 1750–1835', unpublished Ph.D. thesis, Indiana University, 1981; E.K. Brown, 'Women of Mr Wesley's Methodism', *Studies in Women and Religion*, vol.2, 1983; E.K. Brown, 'Women in Church History: Stereotypes, Archetypes and operational modalities', *Methodist History*, vol.28, 1980, pp.109–32; and F. Prochaska, *Women and Philanthropy in Nineteenth-Century England*, Oxford, Clarendon Press, 1980.

46 J.F.C. Harrison, *The Second Coming: Popular Millenarianism 1780–1850*, London, Routledge & Kegan Paul, 1979; E.P. Thompson, *The Making of the English Working Class*, London, Victor Gollancz, 1963, pp. 116–20, 382–9 and 797–803; and C. Hill, *The World Turned Upside Down: Radical Ideas during the English Revolution*, London, Temple Smith, 1972.

47 W.R. Ward, 'The religion of the people and the problem of control, 1790–1830', *Studies in Church History*, vol.8, 1972, pp.237–57 and *Religion and Society*, pp. 75–85; J. Baxter, 'The great Yorkshire revival 1792–6; a study of mass revival among the Methodists', in M. Hill (ed.), *A Sociological Yearbook of Religion in Britain*, vol.7, 1974, pp.46–76; J. Kent, *Holding the Fort: Studies in Victorian Revivalism*, London, Epworth Press, 1978, ch.2; and R. Carwardine, *Transatlantic Revivalism: Popular Evangelicalism in Britain and America, 1790–1865*, Westport, Connecticut, Greenwood Press, 1978.

48   A.A.MacLaren, *Religion and Social Class: The Distruption Years in Aberdeen*, London, Routledge & Kegan Paul, 1974, pp.1–49; A.L. Drummond and J. Bulloch, *The Scottish Church 1688–1843*, Edinburgh, The Saint Andrew Press, 1973, pp.114–41; and A.L. Drummond and J. Bulloch, *The Church in Late Victorian Scotland*, Edinburgh, The Saint Andrew Press, 1978, pp.126–214.

49   Cullen, op. cit., chs. 6 and 9; M. Elliott, *Partners in Revolution: The United Irishmen and France*, New Haven, Yale University Press, 1982, pp.19–20; P. Gibbon, 'The origins of the Orange Order and the United Irishmen', *Economy and Society*, vol.1, 1972, pp.134–63; and D. Hempton, 'Methodism in Irish society 1770–1830', *Transactions of the Royal Historical Society*, 5th Ser. vol.36, 1986, pp.117–42.

50   Connolly, *Religion and Society*, pp.31–41; and P. Gibbon, *The Origins of Ulster Unionism: The Formation of Popular Protestant Politics and Ideology in Nineteenth-Century Ireland*, Manchester, Manchester University Press, 1975.

51   This point is made with particular clarity by J. Rule, 'Methodism, popular beliefs and village culture in Cornwall 1800–50' in R.D. Storch (ed.), *Popular Culture and Custom in Nineteenth-Century England*, London, Croom Helm, 1982, pp.48–70. See also E. Yeo and S. Yeo (eds), *Popular Culture and Class Conflict 1590–1914*, Brighton, Harvester Press, 1982.

52   H. McLeod, *Religion and the Working Class in Nineteenth-Century Britain*, London, Macmillan, 1984, pp. 57–66; MacLaren, op. cit., pp.121–43; C.G.Brown, 'Religion and the development of an urban society: Glasgow, 1780–1914', unpublished Ph.D. thesis, University of Glasgow, 1981; S. Yeo, *Religion and Voluntary Organisations in Crisis*, London, Croom Helm, 1976, pp.117–62; and E.R. Wickham, *Church and People in an Industrial City*, London, Lutterworth Press, 1957.

53   The Church of England in Lancashire is particularly under researched. For helpful introductions to aspects of Anglicanism in Victorian cities see O. Chadwick, *The Victorian Church*, pt.2, London, A.&C. Black, 1970, ch.5; N. Yates, *Leeds and the Oxford Movement*, Publications of the Thoresby Society, vol. lv, 1975; Hempton, 'Bickersteth'; and D.E.H. Mole, 'The Victorian town parish: a rural vision and urban mission', *Studies in Church History*, vol.16, 1979, pp.361–71.

54   J. Rule, *The Labouring Classes in Early Industrial England 1750–1850*, London, Longman, 1986, pp.162–5; and S. Meacham, *A Life Apart*, London, Thames & Hudson, 1977, pp.199–200.

55   Although the dangers are only too obvious, both literary criticism and historical understanding have been advanced by sensitive books

on this theme. See W.E. Houghton, *The Victorian Frame of Mind, 1830–1870*, New Haven, Yale University Press, 1957; V. Cunningham, *Everywhere Spoken Against: Dissent in the Victorian Novel*, Oxford, Oxford University Press, 1975; E. Jay, *The Religion of the Heart: Anglican Evangelicalism and the Nineteenth Century Novel*, Oxford, Oxford University Press, 1979; and D. Hempton, 'Popular religion and irreligion in Victorian fiction' in T. Dunne (ed.), *The Writer as Witness: Literature as Historical Evidence (Historical Studies)* vol.16, Cork University Press, 1987.

56   M. Wolff, 'Victorian study: an interdisciplinary essay', *Victorian Studies*, vol.8, no.1, 1964, pp.59–70.

57   D.R. Schwarz, *Disraeli's Fiction*, London, Macmillan, 1979.

58   D.M. Thompson, 'The churches and society in nineteenth-century England: a rural perspective', *Studies in Church History*, vol.8, 1972, pp.267–76; and the articles by Rogers, Robson and Thompson in D. Baker (ed.), *The Church in Town and Countryside*, Oxford, Basil Blackwell, 1979, pp.335–59, 401–14 and 427–40.

59   These examples are taken from a range of so-called 'social problem' novels in the 1840s and 1850s including *Mary Barton* and *North and South* by Elizabeth Gaskell, *Alton Locke* and *Yeast* by Charles Kingsley, *Sybil* by Benjamin Disraeli, and *Bleak House* and *Hard Times* by Charles Dickens. For a brief introduction to these themes see M. Wheeler, *English Fiction of the Victorian Period 1830–1890*, London, Longman, 1985, pp.32–41.

60   *The Deliverance of Mark Rutherford*, London, 1893, ch.6; and E.P. Thompson, 'Anthropology and the discipline of historical context', *Midland History*, vol.1, no.3, 1972, pp.41–55.

61   G. Moore, *Esther Waters*, Everyman's Library, London, Dent, 1962, ch.3, where the heroine's father refers to the Brethren as 'your hymn-and-misery lot'; B. Harrison, 'Religion and recreation in nineteenth-century England', *Past and Present*, vol.38, 1967, pp.98–125; and J. Kent, 'Feelings and festivals', in Dyos and Wolff, op. cit., pp.855–72.

62   D. Vincent, *Bread, Knowledge and Freedom: A Study of Nineteenth-century Working Class Autobiography*, London, Europa Publications, 1981; and S. Budd, *Varieties of Unbelief: Atheists and Agnostics in English Society 1850–1960*, London, Heinemann, 1977.

63   McLeod, *Class and Religion*, pp.216–23.

64   Ibid., pp.49–50 and 279–87.

65   See especially Dickens, *Hard Times* and Butler, *The Way of All Flesh*.

66   Hempton, *Methodism and Politics*, pp.212–13; and H. McLeod, 'Religion in the British and German labour movements *c.* 1890–1914: a comparison', *Bulletin of the Society for the Study of Labour History*, vol.51 no.1, Spring 1986, pp.25–35.

67   P. Thompson, *The Edwardians: the Remaking of British Society*, London, Weidenfeld & Nicolson, 1975; P. Thompson, *The Voice of the Past: Oral History*, Oxford, Oxford University Press, 1978; E. Roberts, *A Woman's Place: an Oral History of Working-Class Women, 1890–1940*, Oxford, Basil Blackwell, 1984; and H. McLeod, 'New perspectives on working-class religion: the oral evidence', *Oral History*, vol.14, no.1, 1986, pp.31–49. McLeod's references contain a fuller bibliography of works on this subject than is possible here.

68   Kent, *Holding the Fort*, chs 5 and 9.

69   E. Gosse, *Father and Son*, Penguin English Library, 1983, ch.6.

70   Thompson, *Lark Rise to Candleford*, Penguin Modern Classics 1973, ch.14.

71   D. Clark, *Between Pulpit and Pew: Folk Religion in a North Yorkshire Fishing Village*, Cambridge, Cambridge University Press, 1982, ch.5.

72   H.G. Wells, *The New Machiavelli*, London, Penguin, 1946, bk.1, ch.3.

73   MacLaren, op. cit.; Yeo, op. cit.; J. Foster, *Class Struggle and the Industrial Revolution: Early industrial capitalism in three English towns*, London, Weidenfeld & Nicolson, 1974, ch.7; and P. Joyce, *Work, Society and Politics: The culture of the factory in later Victorian England*, London, Methuen, 1982, ch.7.

74   Joyce, op. cit., p.261.

75   Faith healing, for example, has enhanced the popularity of various religious traditions including early Methodism, Roman Catholicism and international pentecostalism. See W.J. Sheils (ed.), *The Church and Healing*, Oxford, Basil Blackwell, 1982.

76   Cox, op. cit., chs. 4 and 8.

77   McLeod, *Class and Religion*, pp.279–87.

78   Clark, op. cit., pp. 65–6. For a helpful introduction to folk religion and its literature see D. Yoder, 'Toward a definition of folk religion', *Western Folklore*, vol.33, 1974, pp.2–15.

79   A.D. Gilbert, *The Making of Post-Christian Britain: A history of the secularization of modern society*, London, Longman, 1980; D. Martin, *A General Theory of Secularization*, Oxford, Basil Blackwell, 1978; and for a helpful select bibliography of recent work on secularization see D. Lyon, *The Steeple's Shadow*, London, SPCK, 1985, pp.153–61.

80   For recent introductions to European religion in these periods see K. von Greyerz (ed.), op. cit., and J. van Engen, 'The Christian Middle Ages as an historiographical problem', *The American Historical Review*, vol.91, no.3, June 1986, pp.519–52.

81   Lyon, op. cit., pp.96–113.

82   D. Martin and P. Mullen (eds), *Strange Gifts? A Guide to Charismatic Renewal*, Oxford, Basil Blackwell, 1984; E. Barker (ed.), *New*

Religious Movements: a Perspective for Understanding Society, New York, Edwin Mellen, 1982; and R. Wallis, *The Elementary Forms of the New Religious Life*, London, Routledge & Kegan Paul, 1983.

83   P. Mullen, 'Confusion worse confounded', in Martin and Mullen, op. cit., pp.97–106.

84   Lambeth Palace Library Mss., Secker Papers, vol.8 (Methodists). This includes the Lavington correspondence parts of which are reproduced by O.A. Beckerlegge in *Proceedings of the Wesley Historical Society*, vol.42, 1980, pp.101–11, 139–49 and 167–80. See also G. Lavington, *The Enthusiasm of Methodists and Papists Compar'd*, London, 1749–51; and E. Gibson, *Observations upon the Conduct and Behaviour of a Certain Sect usually distinguished by the Name of Methodists*, London, 1744.

85   Hempton, *Methodism and Politics*, pp.164–6.

86   W.R. Ward, Review of H. McLeod, *Class and Religion in the Late Victorian City*, *Journal of Ecclesiastical History*, vol.26, 1975, pp.424–5.

87   Obelkevich, op. cit., p.313.

88   W.R. Ward, 'The relations of enlightenment and religious revival in Central Europe and in the English-speaking world', *Studies in Church History*, subsidia 2, 1979, pp.281–305; Ward, 'Power and Piety: the origins of religious revival in the early eighteenth century', *Bulletin of the John Rylands University Library of Manchester*, vol.63 no.1, 1980, pp. 213–52; H. McLeod, 'Building the "Catholic Ghetto": Catholic organisations 1870–1914', in W.J. Sheils and D. Wood (eds), *Voluntary Religion*, Oxford, Basil Blackwell, 1986, pp.411–44; H. McLeod, 'Religion in the British and German labour movements'; and U. Gäbler and P. Schram (eds), *Erweckung am Beginn des 19. Jahrhunderts: Referate einer Tagung an der Freien Universität Amsterdam 26–29 März 1985*, Amsterdam 1986.

89   S. Mews (ed.), *Religion and National Identity*, Oxford, Basil Blackwell, 1982.

90   Trexler, op. cit., pp.245–69.

CHAPTER EIGHT

How Religious Are The British?

Kenneth Thompson

The question 'How religious are the British?' seems, at first sight, relatively straightforward. It appears to call for a recital of relevant statistics, which we assume to be readily available. Here, at least, the social scientist might be expected to lead us on to safely factual ground, away from the realm of mere speculation. Unfortunately, the question and the answers are not so simple or straightforward. Those social scientists who have taken an interest in this question soon discovered that it poses formidable problems of definition concerning the nature and dimensions of religiousness, and with respect to measurement. Why should this be so? In order to answer this question, and to arrive at an appreciation of the findings that are available, we will consider the theoretical issues and then some of the different sorts of data that have been collected.

DEFINING RELIGION AND RELIGIOSITY

The problem of defining religion and other social phenomena was discussed in some detail by the founding father of French academic sociology, Emile Durkheim. He began his work on *The rules of sociological method* (1895) by stating:

> We are still so accustomed to solving questions according to commonsense notions that we find it difficult to dispense with them in sociological discussion. . . . Precisely because it deals

with things that we talk about constantly, such as the family, property, crime, etc., it often appears unnecessary for the sociologist to give a rigorous, preliminary definition of them. We are so accustomed to using these words, which constantly occur in conversation, that it seems pointless to specify the meaning being given to them. We simply refer to the popular notion of them, but this is often ambiguous. This ambiguity causes us to classify under the same name and with a single explanation things which, in reality, are very different.[1]

It was for this reason that Durkheim devoted so much space to defining religion when he came to write his classic on the sociology of religion, *The Elementary Forms of the Religious Life* (1915). It also explains why his definition seems so long and complicated, stating in carefully considered terms that:

A religion is a unified system of beliefs and practices relative to sacred things, that is to say things set apart and forbidden, beliefs and practices which unite into one single moral community, called a Church, all those who adhere to them.[2]

By using the term 'moral community' he emphasized two features: the element of moral obligation, and the social quality of religion, in which belief and action are held and practised in common by a group. (The additional reference to this as a 'church' should not necessarily be understood as narrowing down the notion of a moral community to an organized religious body, as Durkheim was mainly discussing elementary forms of religion in primitive societies where religion and society were virtually co-terminous.) But, above all, the definition is notable for the primacy it gives to the notion of the sacred as the distinguishing feature of the content of religion. By deliberately avoiding reference to the supernatural or a deity in his definition, Durkheim allows for the inclusion within the orbit of religion of beliefs and practices which he acknowledged were *laiques en apparence*, such as the mother country, the French Revolution, the cult of the individual, and the nation.[3]

One stream of thought in the sociology of religion has continued to follow Durkheim's 'inclusive' definitional approach and has continued to look for beliefs, experiences and practices which have on them the stamp of the sacred. Sometimes these have been referred to as functional alternatives or surrogates for religion as more narrowly or conventionally understood. The preferred methodology of such studies tended, until recently, to be descriptive and analytical, rather than quantitative. They have analyzed the ways in which various modern meaning-systems serve as the basis of 'moral communities', with a view to discerning their socially integrating effects – the ways in which they exercise a moral constraint that functions to maintain the established social order, and offer the individual a shield against the psychic threats of meaninglessness.

The other major stream of thought which will enter into our considerations, derives from the German sociologist Max Weber, who is known to a wider public through the popularization of his concept of the 'Protestant ethic', as described in his book *The Protestant Ethic and the Spirit of Capitalism* (1904/1930). However, Weber's most important treatise on the sociology of religion entitled *Religionssoziologie (The Sociology of Religion)* forms part of his vast systematization of the social sciences, *Wirtschaft und Gesellschaft (Economy and Society)*. In that work he appears to suggest that it is impossible to define religion, or at least that it can only be defined after empirical inquiry and discussion.[4] It becomes clear from his discussion, however, that in practice he operated with an 'exclusive' and substantive definition of religion which largely coincided with the popular understanding of what constituted religion – an institutionalized set of fundamental beliefs (a cosmology) and practices which have a supernatural reference or grounding. Subsequent work in this Weberian tradition has tended to utilize a quantitative methodology and has concerned itself with the process of secularization; it has attempted to plot the decline of religious institutions empirically.[5]

Although there has been a great deal of crossover between these Durkheimian and Weberian approaches, it is worth distinguishing them for the purpose of appreciating the different definitions and methodologies that can be brought to bear on this subject. The distinction is also useful for understanding the various meanings that have been given to the concept of 'secularization', which has featured prominently in discussions of the social changes that bring about religious decline. Broadly speaking, the Weberian focus tends to be on processes of rationalization in modern society – what Weber described as 'disenchantment of the world' – in which the

213

rationality of technology and calculation takes over from recourse to the supernatural or a super-empirical, transcendent reality, in human thinking. The sphere of the religious is constantly shrinking, according to this view, as religion as an institution shrinks and finds its functions taken over by other institutions, and even the internal life and organization of the Church increasingly conforms to this secular rationality.[6] The only exceptions to this inexorable trend, in Weber's view, are to be found in those sectarian movements created by charismatic leaders, which react against such worldly compromise. But even these exceptions are likely to be short-lived, as the second generation of sect members face the problems of ensuring organizational continuity.

The Weberian approach to the study of religion is often characterized by a pessimistic and fatalistic tone. Such studies plot the decline of religious involvement – as indexed by participation rates in religious activities and the gap between religious norms and the attitudes and conduct of members with respect to beliefs, rituals and morals. They also describe the shrinking scope of religious organizations compared with other institutions in society, and the internal 'secularization' of religious groups as they are brought into conformity with patterns of thought and organization characteristic of the secular world outside. However, analyses of the various meanings attached to the concept of secularization have served to reveal its multi-dimensionality. This means that religious trends have to be discovered by empirical analysis, they cannot be assumed to exist as part of some universal process. Variations in these trends over time, and between societies, have to be explained by more culturally-specific theories, rather than assuming that secularization is a unitary process experienced uniformly in all societies.

Leaving aside, at this point, the complicated question of variations in secularization between societies,[7] a glance at British statistical surveys makes it clear that it is quite possible to find decline on one dimension of religiosity co-existing with stability or growth on another dimension. For example, we will find that church membership and participation in religious rites is declining in Britain, whilst belief in God remains at a high level. The various dimensions of religiosity and their relationship to the different meanings attached to the concept of secularization must be distinguished in order to make sense of the religious statistics that are available. Thus, the American sociologists Charles Glock and

Rodney Stark distinguished five dimensions of religiousness: belief, practice, knowledge, experience, and consequences.[8] Whilst a study of the use of the concept of secularization in empirical research, by Shiner, identified six different types of secularization: decline of religion, conformity with this world, disengagement of society from religion (differentiation), transposition of religious beliefs and institutions, desacralization of the world, and a general concept of social change (from 'sacred' to 'secular' society).[9]

In the Durkheimian tradition there is a corresponding theoretical and methodological problem, and that is to distinguish the various types of meaning-systems, moral communities, and ways of being religious. In this respect, Thomas Luckmann's *The Invisible Religion* has been described as the most influential monograph in the Durkheimian tradition dealing with meaning-systems.[10] Like Durkheim, Luckmann looked for fundamental meaning-systems that provide people with a 'sacred cosmos', but he adopted a more voluntaristic model than Durkheim, forsaking the search for a single set of ideas which are treated as sacred by all the members of a society, and preferring to speak of the sacred cosmos of modern industrial societies as 'assortments of ultimate meanings' from which people make their choice. Despite the success of Luckmann's book, subsequently most of the sociologists who have focused on ultimate meaning-systems have tended to restrict the term 'religion' to those meaning-systems which refer to the supernatural. This narrowing down of the definition of religion may have the virtue of tidiness, but it also has the negative effect of taking away the impetus that Durkheim's focus on 'moral community' gave to the search for sets of ultimate beliefs which symbolically bind people in a shared commitment and sense of like-mindedness because of what they hold sacred. Frequently, in a modern society, those beliefs will carry traces of traditional religion or folk-belief, but now transposed into a discourse where they articulate with other, non-religious, elements. This is most evident in modern national-isms, in immigrant minority cultures or ethnic communities, and in what some sociologists have called 'civil religion' – beliefs and rituals that reaffirm the sacred unity of the nation.[11]

Finally, even operating with a narrow definition of religion, it can be argued that there are different ways of being religious, and that we can only discover what these are by empirical research. In this connection, Towler has analyzed the thousands of letters received by the late Bishop of Woolwich in response to the publication of his controversial book *Honest to God* (1963), with a view to disclosing the different ways of being religious that exist even within the terms of conventional religion (that of mainstream Christian churches or denominations – mainly the Church of England in this case). Towler claims to have found five different types of conventional religiousness: exemplarism, conversionism, theism, gnosticism, and traditionalism.[12] Whether this is an exhaustive typology only further research will show. However, it is useful by virtue of the fact that it is empirically derived from spontaneous statements rather than being based on a set of categories imposed by the researcher or a conventional categorization of theological positions.

Having indicated some of the attempts made by sociologists to define religion and the different types or dimensions of religiosity, we will now turn to examining some of the following sorts of data: (i) statistics on religion in the United Kingdom; (ii) survey data on beliefs and values; (iii) exploratory studies of meaning-systems, moral communities, civil religion, and other forms of 'sacralization' that persist within a supposedly secular society.

(i) *Statistics on religion in the United Kingdom*

The first thing to note about the available statistics on religion in the UK is that they are not up-dated very frequently, at least not in any standardized form that facilitates comparative analysis. The most comprehensive set of comparative religious statistics is that in the *UK Christian Handbook*, but even this relies on estimates for some years, thus, the following statistics taken from the 1983 edition refer to 1980.[13] On the basis of those figures, one of the most striking findings is the contrast between the low proportion of the adult population of the United Kingdom actively maintaining membership of a Christian church and the relatively high proportion claiming some sort of loose allegiance. (See Tables 8.1–8.8.)

Less than a fifth (17.4 per cent) of adults in this nominally Christian nation are members of a church, although there is a considerable regional variation ranging from a membership of 13 per cent in England to 23 per cent in Wales, 37 per cent in Scotland and 80 per cent in Northern Ireland. In terms of loose allegiance,

TABLE 8.1 **Summary Church Statistics for the whole of the United Kingdom**

	Members				Ministers				Churches			
	1970	1975	1980	1985[4]	1970	1975	1980	1985[4]	1970	1975	1980	1985[4]
Episcopal	2,558,497[2]	2,271,957[2]	2,158,888	2,040,000	17,456	15,931[2]	14,686	13,400	20,338[2]	19,816[2]	19,525	19,200
Methodist	673,434[2]	596,406	536,416	470,000	4,500[2]	4,215[2]	3,855	3,600	9,972[1]	9,138	8,483	7,800
Baptist	293,172	267,081[2]	251,425	240,000	2,465[1]	2,354[2]	2,593	2,800	3,657[1]	3,572[2]	3,484	3,400
Presbyterian[3]	1,896,166	1,722,543	1,579,982	1,430,000	5,657[1]	5,367	5,230	5,000	7,162	7,012	6,709	6,500
Other Churches[3,5]	561,193[2]	611,355	648,005	710,000	9,111[2]	9,779[2]	10,893	11,900	7,204[2]	7,914[2]	9,043	9,700
TOTAL PROTESTANT[5]	5,982,462[2]	5,469,342[2]	5,174,716	4,890,000	39,189[2]	37,646[2]	37,257	36,700	48,333[2]	47,452[2]	47,244	46,600
Roman Catholic	2,524,373[2]	2,433,740	2,341,801	2,260,000	8,164[2]	8,037[2]	7,681	7,400	4,048[2]	4,114[2]	4,151	4,200
TOTAL CHRISTIAN	8,506,835[2]	7,903,082[2]	7,516,517	7,150,000	47,353[2]	45,683[2]	44,938	44,100	52,381[2]	51,566[2]	51,395	50,800
Percentage of adult population[6]	20.2%	18.3%	17.4%	16.4%								

Millions	1971	1976	1981	1986
England	35,101	35,859	35,978	37,681
Wales	2,073	2,142	2,154	2,268
Scotland	3,874	3,950	3,938	4,081
N. Ireland	1,079	1,099	1,103	1,181
Total UK	42,127	43,050	43,173	45,211

[1] Estimate
[2] Revised figure
[3] Congregational figures now included in Independent churches
[4] Figures calculated on all three previous items on individual churches and then totalled.
[5] Includes Orthodox Churches
[6] Based on the following population figures for adults aged 15 and over taken at 1971 Census and subsequent official mid-year estimates the 1986 figures being a 1979-based projection.

TABLE 8.2 **1980 Summary figures by individual country**

	Members				Ministers				Churches			
	England	Wales	Scotland	N Ireland	England	Wales	Scotland	N Ireland	England	Wales	Scotland	N Ireland
Episcopal	1,820,444	133,000	40,961	164,483	13,317	800	235	334	17,050	1,675	333	467
Methodist	463,051	25,963	8,190	39,212	3,562	100	42	151	7,636	553	77	217
Baptist	159,088	66,904	17,888	7,545	1,950	407	153	83	2,211	1,010	173	90
Presbyterian	147,438	157,317	993,491	281,736	1,594	664	2,488	484	1,829	2,035	2,257	588
Other Churches[1]	551,668	26,461	51,410	18,466	9,860	312	564	167	7,411	473	796	383
TOTAL PROTESTANT[1]	3,132,939	409,645	1,111,940	511,442	30,283	2,283	3,482	1,219	36,117	5,746	3,636	1,745
Roman Catholic	1,574,793	90,008	310,972	366,028	5,672	262	1,178	569	3,036	206	477	432
TOTAL CHRISTIAN	4,716,482	499,653	1,422,912	877,470	35,955	2,545	4,660	1,788	39,153	5,952	4,113	2,177
Percentage of adult population[2]	13%	23%	37%	80%								

[1]Includes Orthodox Churches   [2]Based on the figures in footnote 6 in the table above

TABLE 8.3 **1980 Summary rates of change**

	1980 Attendance	1980 ratio of Members per ch	1980 ratio of Ministers per ch	Rate of change per annum of Members 1970–75	1975–80	1980–85[3]	Rate of change per annum of Ministers 1970–75	1975–80	1980–85[3]	Rate of change per annum of Churches 1970–75	1975–80	1980–85[3]
				%	%	%	%	%	%	%	%	%
Episcopal	69%	110	0.8	−2.4[2]	−1.0	−1.1	−1.8	−1.6	−1.2	−0.5	−0.3	−0.4
Methodist	89%	63	0.5	−2.4[2]	−2.1	−2.5	−1.3	−1.8	−1.6	−1.7	−1.5	−1.7
Baptist	91%	72	0.7	−1.8[2]	−1.2	−1.2	−0.6	+2.0	+1.4	−0.5	−0.5	−0.3
Presbyterian	59%	236	0.8	−1.9	−1.7	−1.9	−1.0[2]	−0.5	−0.7	−0.4	−0.9	−0.8
Other Churches[1]	85%	72	1.2	+1.7	+1.2	+1.8	+1.7	+1.2	+1.8	+1.9	+2.7	+1.4
TOTAL PROTESTANT[1]	71%	109	0.8	−1.8	−1.1	−1.1	−0.8[2]	−0.2	−0.3	−0.4	−0.1	−0.3
Roman Catholic	95%	564	1.9	−0.7	−0.8	−0.7	−0.3	−0.9	−0.7	+0.3	+0.2	+0.2
TOTAL CHRISTIAN	78%	146	0.9	−1.5	−1.0	−1.0	−0.7	−0.3	−0.4	−0.3	−0.1	−0.3

[1] Includes Orthodox Churches   [2] Revised figure   [3] Based on total figures for each category

TABLE 8.4 African/West Indian Church Statistics for the whole of the UK

| | Members | | Ministers | | Churches | | 1980 | Rate of change per annum of | | | 1980 Ratio of | |
	1975	1980	1975	1980	1975	1980	Attendance	Members %	Ministers %	Churches %	Members per ch	Ministers per ch
Aladura International Church	300	300[1]	10[1]	10	1	1[1]	90%[1]	0.0	0.0	0.0	300	10.0
Church of Cherubim & Seraphim	2,000	2,000[1]	80	80[1]	3	3[1]	90%[1]	0.0	0.0	0.0	667	27.0
Other African Churches	20,000[1]	20,000[1]	1,000[1]	1,000[1]	100[1]	100[1]	90%[1]	0.0	0.0	0.0	200	10.0
Church of God of Prophecy	2,800	5,290	150	341	15	33	98%	+13.6	+17.9	+17.1	160	10.3
New Testament Church of God	4,466[4]	6,369[4]	167	190	41	47	95%[4]	+7.4	+2.6	+2.8	136	4.0
Wesleyan Holiness Church	1,588	2,337	6	7	19	19	75%	+8.0	+3.1	0.0	123	0.4
Other West Indian Churches	50,000[1]	70,000[1]	2,000[2]	2,400[2]	500[3]	560[3]	93%[1]	+7.0	+3.7	+2.3	125	4.3
TOTAL AFRICAN/WEST INDIAN	81,154[1]	106,296[1]	3,423[1]	4,028[1]	679[1]	763[1]	92%	+5.5	+3.3	+2.4	139	5.3

[1]Estimate   [2]Estimate includes many part-time ministers
[3]Communities not church buildings   [4]Official figures, actual church attendance is considerably greater – perhaps five times the number of members

TABLE 8.5 Pentecostal/Holiness Church Statistics for the whole of the UK

| | Members | | Ministers | | Churches | | 1980 Attend'ce | Rate of change per annum of | | | 1980 Ratio of | |
								Members %	Ministry %	Churches %	Members per ch	Ministers per ch
	1975	1980	1975	1980	1975	1980						
Apostolic Church	4,826	4,904	50	58	187	180	85%	+0.3	+3.0	−0.8	27	0.3
Assemblies of God	50,000[1]	55,000[1]	536	662	541	571	100%	+1.9	+4.3	+1.1	96	1.2
Elim Pentecostal Church	25,000	25,000	152[2]	152	349	366	73%	0.0	0.0	+1.0	68	0.4
Emmanuel Holiness Church	251	370	14	10	9	8	90%	+8.1	−6.5	−2.3	46	1.3
Church of the Nazarene	3,665	3,792	78	87	94	95	80%	+0.7	+2.2	+0.2	40	0.9
TOTAL PENTECOSTAL/ HOLINESS	83,742	89,066	830	969	1,180	1,220	92%	+6.4	+3.1	+0.7	73	0.8

[1]Estimate   [2]Revised figure

TABLE 8.6 Non-Trinitarian Church Statistics for the whole of the UK

	Members 1975	Members 1980	Ministers 1975	Ministers 1980	Buildings 1975	Buildings 1980	1980 Attend'ce	Rate of change per annum of Members %	Rate of change per annum of Ministers %	Rate of change per annum of Buildings %	1980 Ratio of Members per Building
British Israelites	1,175[1]	1,075[1]	–	–	0	0	100%	–1.8	–	–	–
Christadelphians[3]	25,000[2]	22,000[1]	–	–	400	360	67%	–2.5	–	–2.1	61
Church of Christ, Scientist	17,000[2]	15,000[1]	–	–	294	261	100%	–2.5	–	–2.4	57
Jehovah's Witnesses	79,586[2]	85,321	7,090[2]	8,109	624[4]	1,163	105%[4]	+1.0	+2.7	+13.3	72
Church of Jesus Christ of Latter-Day Saints (Mormons)	79,717[2]	91,032	5,260	7,331	160	197	40%	+2.7	+6.9	+4.2	462
New Church	2,533	2,190	35	30	44	40	70%	–2.9	–3.0	–1.9	55
Church of Scientology	20,000	30,000	250	450	12	16	n/a	+8.4	+12.5	+5.9	1,875
Spiritualists[3]	56,766[1]	52,404[1]	233	290	594	578	73%	–1.6	+4.5	–0.5	91
Theosophists[3]	5,359[2]	5,122[1]	–	–	13[2]	13[1]	70%	–0.9	0.0	0.0	391
Unification Church	150	570	–	–	10	28	100%	+30.6	–	+22.9	20
Unitarian and Free Christian Churches	15,000[1]	11,000	129	155	257	247	20%	–6.0	+3.7	–0.8	45
The Way	400[1]	1,000[1]	1[1]	5[1]	20[5]	50[5]	100%	+20.1	+38.0	+20.1	20
Worldwide Church of God	1,880	2,159	21	16	0	0	100%	+2.8	–5.3	–	–
TOTAL NON-TRINITARIAN CHURCHES	304,566[2]	317,073	13,019[2]	16,385	2,428[2]	2,953	74%	+0.8	+4.7	+4.0	107

[1]Estimate   [2]Revised figure   [3]A composite figure comprising several associations or groups
[4]Indicating more attend Kingdom Halls than belong as members   [5]Estimated communities not buildings

TABLE 8.7 Other Religions Statistics for the whole of the UK

	Members		Ministers		Buildings		1980 Attend'ce	Rate of change per annum of			1980 Ratio of Members per Building
								Members %	Ministers %	Buildings %	
	1975	1980	1975	1980	1975	1980					
Buddhists	13,000[2]	17,000[1]	150[2]	210[1]	36[2]	50[1]	25%[1]	+5.5	+7.0	+6.8	340
Hindus	100,000[1]	120,000[1]	100[4]	120[1,4]	120[1]	125[1]	25%[1]	+3.7	+3.7	+0.8	960
International Society for Krishna Consciousness	10,000	35,000	100	250	2	5	15%	+28.4	+20.1	+20.1	7,000
Muslims[5]	400,000[1]	600,000[1]	1,000[1]	1,540	1,000[2]	1,520	67%	+8.4	+9.0	+8.7	395
Ahmadiyya Movement	8,000[1]	10,000[1]	5	7	5	7	75%	+4.6	+7.0	+7.0	1,429
Sikhs	115,000[1]	150,000[1]	–	–	75	105	100%	+5.5	–	+7.0	1,429
School of Meditation	3,862	4,820	–	–	2	2	15%	+4.5	–	0.0	2,410
Others	50,000	80,000[1]	80[1]	100[1]	80[1]	100[1]	63%[1]	+9.9	+4.6	+4.6	800
Jews	111,000[3]	110,915	400[1]	416	315	321	25%	0.0	+0.8	+0.4	346
TOTAL OTHER RELIGIONS	810,862	1,127,735	1,835	2,843	1,637	2,235	60%	+6.8	+7.6	+6.4	505

[1]Estimate [2]Revised figure [3]Heads of households, male and female [4]Including many part-time priests [5]Including non-South Asians

TABLE 8.8 **Approximate Community Sizes (throughout whole of UK)**

	1975 Millions	1980 Millions
Church of England	27.5	26.6[1]
Other Episcopal	0.7[1]	0.7[1]
Baptists	0.6[2]	0.6[1]
Methodists	1.5	1.5
Presbyterian[4]	1.9[1]	1.7[1]
Roman Catholics	5.2[2]	5.2
Other Trinitarian Churches[4]	1.1[1]	1.3[1]
TOTAL CHRISTIAN CHURCHES	38.5[2]	37.6

	1975 Millions	1980 Millions
Jews	0.4	0.4
Church of Scientology	0.3	0.5
Other Churches (JWs, Mormons etc.)	0.7[1]	0.7[1]
Hindus	0.2[1]	0.3[1]
Muslims	0.5[2]	1.0
Sikhs	0.2	0.4
Other religions	0.1[1]	0.2[1]
TOTAL OTHER	2.4[2]	3.5
TOTAL ALL RELIGIONS	40.9[2]	41.1
Percentage of population[3]	73%	74%

[1]Estimate   [2]Revised figure
[3]UK population was 56.0 million in 1975 and 55.9 million in 1980
[4]Congregational figures now included with 'Other Trinitarian Churches'

(From: Brierley (ed.), 1982)

TABLE 8.9 **Indicators of religious commitment, Great Britain compared with the European average/percentages**

Indicators of Religious Disposition:	Great Britain	European average
Often think about meaning and purposes of life	34	30
Never think life meaningless	50	44
Often think about death	15	18
Often regret doing wrong	8	10
Need moments of prayer, etc.	50	57
Define self as a religious person	58	62
Draw comfort/strength from Religion	46	48
God is important in my life (6–10)	50	51
Have had a spiritual experience	19	12

Indicators of orthodox belief	Great Britain	European average
Believe in personal God	31	32
(Believe in a spirit or life force)	39	36
Believe in:		
God	76	73
Sin	69	57
Soul	59	57
Heaven	57	40
Life after death	45	43
The Devil	30	25
Hell	27	23
Personally fully accept Commandments demanding:		
No other Gods	48	48
Reverence of God's name	43	46
Holy Sabbath	25	32

Indicators of moral values:	Great Britain	European average
Absolute guidelines exist about good & evil	28	26
Personally fully accept Commandments prohibiting:		
Killing	90	87
Adultery	78	63
Stealing	87	82
False Witness	78	73
Agree with unrestricted sex	23	23
Terrorism may be justified	12	14
Following acts never justified:		
Claiming unentitled benefit	78	
Accepting a bribe	79	
Taking marijuana	81	
Homosexuality	47	
Euthanasia	30	
Political assassination	77	
Greater respect for authority: good	73	59
Willing to sacrifice life	34	33

Indicators of Institutional Attachment:	Great Britain	European average
Great confidence in Church	19	21
Church answers moral problems	30	35
Church answers family problems	32	33
Church answers spiritual needs	42	44
Attend church monthly	23	35
Denomination:		
Roman Catholic	11	54
Protestant (Established	68	29
Free Church/Non-conformist)	6	2
Believe religion will become:		
More important in future	21	19
Less important in future	40	34
Believe in one true religion	21	25
Religious faith an important value to develop in children	14	16

(From: Abrams et al., 1985)

it is said that the Church of England can claim roughly half the UK population, while the 'Other Protestant' groups and the Roman Catholic Church can each account for about one person in ten. But the figures for actual membership show that the 'Other Protestant' groups have a total membership greater than the other two religious communities, whilst the Roman Catholics have outnumbered active Anglicans since the first half of the 1970s.[14] There was a steady decline in overall membership of these churches throughout the 1970s, averaging just over 1 per cent per annum. This contrasts with a spectacular growth in some sects and new religious movements, and the religions of immigrant groups. However, the entire category of these 'Other Churches' amount to less than 9 per cent of the total membership of all the Christian churches. Furthermore, as Barker points out, 'The growth in membership of non-Christian groups from a total of 800,000 in 1975 to one of just over a million (2.6 per cent of the total UK adult population) in 1980 can mainly be accounted for by a rise from 400,000 to 600,000 Muslims.'[15]

The 1987/88 edition of the *UK Christian Handbook* reveals a continuing decline in the major Christian churches' active membership and an increase in membership of non-Christian churches. Whereas Christian churches lost half a million members in the previous five years, Muslims increased by more than a third to 852,000, Sikhs increased from 150,000 to 180,000, Hindus went up by a third to 30,000 and Buddhists increased by 35 per cent to 23,000. And whereas the number of mosques increased from four in 1960 to 314 in 1985, 750 Christian church buildings closed and there were 1,500 fewer Christian ministers. The trend towards a more pluralistic religious situation in Britain is highlighted by the fact that Muslims now outnumber the combined strength of Methodists and Baptists by 152,000. Membership of Christian churches declined to just under 7 million in 1985, compared with nearly 7.5 million in 1980 and 8.5 million in 1970. Furthermore, of the 15 per cent of the population registered as Christian church members, the majority were predominantly young or old people, with a much lower representation of age groups in between. Women consistently outnumber men in membership and attendance in Christian denominations, suggesting that they have a greater need or willingness to be involved in voluntary communities. An interesting trend revealed by the latest statistics is that a far greater proportion of Muslim women attend mosques in Britain than in traditional

Muslim countries. This suggests an enhanced use in this country of the mosque as a focus of social life; for women it is a place where they can receive instruction in English.

(ii) *Survey data on beliefs and values*

The limitations of membership and participation statistics are evident if we try to formulate comparative judgments about the religiosity of different societies. For example: Is Britain less Christian than the United States, or more so than Sweden? In the United States roughly 70 per cent of the population claims membership of a church or synagogue, and about 40 per cent attend a place of worship each week.[16] Whilst in Sweden, the vast majority of the population is nominally in membership of the Church of Sweden, but less than 3 per cent are likely to be found in church on any Sunday.[17] And yet the widespread image of America is that of a society with high rates of crime and family breakdown, a society where the Ten Commandments are more widely and flagrantly offended against than in societies where church-going is much less common. A possible explanation for the discrepancy may be found in the suggestion of some sociologists that Americans attend church because it is the approved way of behaving – part of the 'American way' and so socially useful, or that it is a means by which later generations rediscover their ethnic roots and find a community identity.[18] More recently, there have been attempts to explain the upsurge of religious activity in America as simply part of a more general conservative reaction against political and social events of the 1960s and early 1970s – civil rights campaigns, student counter-cultures, the Vietnam War and then the Watergate political scandal. Whatever the explanation, it is clear that membership statistics alone cannot tell us whether one population is more religious than another. There has to be some attempt to discover what people's actual beliefs and values are, and whether these beliefs affect their everyday actions and behaviour. Indeed, the possibility cannot be ruled out that there may be some truth in the remark frequently encountered by researchers in this field to the effect that: 'I am a better Christian than many of those who go to church.'

The most comprehensive and up to date international study of beliefs and values is that reported on by the European Value Systems Study Group in 1985.[19] The section of their report dealing with religious attitudes and values in Britain begins by drawing attention to the contrast, which we discussed earlier, between the generally low rates of religious participation and the still fairly high levels of belief and of identification with a particular Church:

> In Britain, over 70 per cent of the population seldom or never read the Bible . . . and no more than one person in seven attends church weekly. Yet, more than three-quarters of respondents to the Values Study expressed a belief in God and 85 per cent reported membership of one of the main Christian denominations.[20]

This survey of a sample of the British population numbering 1,231 persons carried out in 1981 revealed that three-fifths identified themselves as 'religious persons' and half regularly felt the need for prayer, meditation or contemplation. Only 4 per cent identified themselves as atheists. On the other hand, there was evidence that 'spiritual experience' was not widespread: only one in five reported having a profound spiritual experience. The evidence suggests that general expressions of religious commitment vary both with the degree of orthodox belief and practice and with important socio-demographic characteristics such as age, sex and occupational status. Religious commitment is higher the older the respondent, women are more religious than men at any age, occupation is only significant in the case of working women, who have a higher commitment than non-workers until well into middle-age; the least religious group is composed of young women at home with young children, and these also score low on measures of psychological well-being. Subjective perception of the importance of God – the single most useful summary indicator of religiosity emerging from the multi-variate analysis of the data – seems to vary with the intensity of church attendance, the conception people have of God (an orthodox Christian view of a personal God contrasted with some sort of spirit or life force), and the degree of comprehensiveness of the orthodox beliefs held. Whilst some form of religious commitment appears to be widespread, it seems doubtful that there is a dimension of religiosity which varies independently of the degree of attachment to traditional beliefs. This is in line with American studies which suggest that non-doctrinal commitment varies *directly* with traditional beliefs.[21]

At the heart of traditional Christian doctrine is the belief in a personal God. It is revealing, therefore, that the survey found that two-fifths of the population conceive of God as some sort of spirit or life force, whereas under one-third believe in a personal God, one-fifth are unsure, and a further 10 per cent profess no belief in either. Furthermore, little more than a quarter of the population accept absolute, as opposed to relative, guidelines concerning good and evil, and only a quarter accept the full range of Christian beliefs when these are taken to include both hell and the devil. Not surprisingly, there was a high correlation between belief in a personal God, acceptance of the full range of traditional Christian beliefs, and acceptance of absolute moral rules. What is perhaps more surprising is the high proportion of the population reporting that they personally accept and observe the moral precepts of the Ten Commandments concerning social behaviour, whilst doubting that others do so. There is a contrast between the low proportion accepting the first three commandments, which are specifically religious – i.e., to have no other Gods, reverence God's name, observe the sabbath – and the last seven commandments which are concerned with social behaviour – to honour parents, not to kill, not to commit adultery, not to steal, not to bear false witness and to covet neither one's neighbour's spouse nor their goods. When compared with other European countries, the British seem to be more moralistic than the European average (see Table 8.9).

However, the fact that the British people who were questioned also stated overwhelmingly that they believed their fellow citizens did not share their own high moral standards, raises questions about the nature and possibility of moral community in Britain. On the one hand, it might seem as if there is a basic moral community, assuming that widespread acceptance of the same fundamental values is all that is necessary to constitute it; but, on the other hand, such a moral community cannot be very cohesive if people do not trust others to accept the same moral constraints. It also has to be admitted that a survey of values such as this has many limitations, and that it cannot tell us very much about the meanings which people attach to the questions asked, nor about the real extent of shared understandings and like-mindedness that may constitute various sorts of community. A sociological approach to religion must dig beneath the surface that is only partly mapped out by questionnaire surveys of values if it is to discover the nature and extent of moral communities in contemporary society.

(iii) *Meaning-systems, moral communities, and civil religion*

The concept of *community* carries a wide variety of meanings and has had a checkered career in the social sciences. As Anthony Cohen explains in his recent book, *The Symbolic Construction of Community:*

> Over the years it has proved to be highly resistant to satisfactory definition in anthropology and sociology, perhaps for the simple reason that all definitions contain or imply theories, and the theory of community has been very contentious. At its most extreme, the debate has thrown up ideologically opposed propositions which are equally untenable. For example, it used to be claimed that modernity and community are irreconcilable, that the characteristic features of community cannot survive industrialization and urbanization. It is a spurious argument for its opposition of 'community' and 'modernity' rests only upon ascribing stipulatively to community those features of social life which are supposed, by definition, to be lacking from modernity. . . . Others have suggested that the domination of modern social life by the state, and the essential confrontation of classes in capitalist society, have made 'community' a nostalgic, bourgeois and anachronistic concept. Once again, the argument is based entirely upon a highly particularistic and sectarian definition. However, its redundancy can be claimed not only on philosophical grounds, but also as being evident in the massive upsurge of community consciousness – in such terms as ethnicity, localism, religion, and class itself – which has swept the 'modern' world in recent years.[22]

Cohen recommends that we follow Wittgenstein's advice and seek not the lexical meaning of the word but its use. The word community seems to be used to imply that the members of a group have something in common with each other and that this distinguishes them in a significant way from the members of other putative groups. It expresses a relational idea: the opposition of one community to others. It is not necessary to equate community with locality and face-to-face interaction. There are communities of the mind, or of like-mindedness, composed of people who share symbols, beliefs and values in common, which makes them feel different from those who do not share these. Such symbolic communities, or moral communities, have discernible boundaries, sometimes of a physical nature, such as territorial boundaries, others may be racial, linguistic or religious, whilst others exist purely in the mind.

The symbolization of likeness and difference is frequently expressed through rituals, which serve to confirm and strengthen social identity and provide a means through which people experience community. This was a basic theme of Durkheim's sociology of religion, although he mainly focused on face-to-face communities of primitive societies and could not anticipate the growth of the mass media, which have enabled people to participate in rituals and symbolic performances at second-hand, as exemplified by mass media coverage of ceremonies in which the Royal Family are involved. Symbolic communities in modern societies are frequently reproduced and reaffirmed through the agency of the mass media – print, radio and television. Consequently, unlike the anthropologists who studied community through participant observation of face-to-face interaction in local communities, the sociologist must also study the processes and effect of mass communication. This is a natural development of Durkheim's sociology, for he did not suggest that community based on like-mindedness ('mechanical solidarity' in his terms) would be totally squeezed out as a result of the increase in modern society of social integration based on impersonal exchange of specialized services ('organic solidarity'). The balance between these two forms of social solidarity might change, Durkheim argued, but they would always coexist as two aspects of any society.

The symbolic discourses that constitute communities can manifest 'religious' elements in two ways. First, they may contain traces of religious symbols in the narrow sense of religion as referring to the supernatural as, for example, in the various elements of Judaeo-Christian culture that still persist in many fields of social life. Second, the symbols may be religious in the broader sense referred to by Durkheim, in that they express and activate a sense of something that is sacred to the community. For Durkheim, that sense of the sacred derived from the fact that the symbols represented the essence of the community itself – that which set it apart and made it different from a real or imagined other group or social entity. Hence, although they may be false gods, according to orthodox religious teaching, it is quite possible for 'imagined communities' like the nation, or ethnic groups, to be considered sacred by their adherents. The oppositional way of thinking that sustains a sense of community distinctiveness also sustains the sense of the sacred as against the profane – in their extreme forms both nationalism and racism seek to preserve the pure essence of their community from pollution by the alien other.

A sociological answer to the question: 'How religious are the British?' will be superficial and incomplete if it does not include some discussion of these issues concerning symbolic communities. Many of the fiercest conflicts as well as the most passionate emotions in our society are concerned with these issues, as for example, in the inter-communal strife in Northern Ireland, Scottish and Welsh nationalism, racial tensions, and, less controversially, the devotion shown towards the Royal Family. Historically, the transmission of an ideology depended to a large extent on religion, but there have been problems because Christianity is divided and no church has been able to claim a majority of the people in all parts of the British Isles. Indeed, religion has been one of the major sources of division with respect to national identity. As one ecclesiastical historian put it:

> . . . modern British history, perhaps more than the history of any other European state, discloses a complex inter-relationship between political attitudes, ecclesiastical allegiances and cultural traditions. The Christian religion in the British Isles, in its divided condition, has in turn been deeply involved in the cultural and political divisions of modern Britain and Ireland. Churches have been, in some instances and at some periods, vehicles for the cultivation of a 'British' identity, corresponding to the political framework of Great Britain and Ireland. They have also been instrumental, in part at least, in perpetuating and recreating an English, Irish, Scottish or Welsh identity distinct from and perhaps in conflict with 'British' identity, both culturally and politically.[23]

It is interesting to compare the relation between religious and national community in Britain with that of America. Both societies are characterized by religious diversity. In the British Isles there are different established or majority churches in its constituent parts, such as the Presbyterian Church of Scotland, the Presbyterian (Calvinistic Methodist) Church in Wales, the Protestant churches in Northern Ireland, and the Church of England. This has created problems for the transmission of a unifying ideology of national identity and community. In America the 'civil religion' that fosters national community is not closely associated with the institutional religion, but it does benefit from the high level of religiosity throughout the country. However, as befits a country in which Church and State are officially separate, the main symbols and ritual events of the civil religion are concerned with the Presidency, national anniversaries, and sites where the heroic past is remembered, such as Gettysburg and Arlington National Cemetery.

In Britain, although there may be a lower degree of religiosity, this is balanced by the fact that the monarchy unites Church and State, so that ceremonies and celebrations involving royalty can combine the symbolic discourses of religion and politics to promote a sense of national community. These civic rituals featuring royalty are dramatizations of the nation as a symbolic or imagined community. It is *imagined* because the members will never know most of their fellow members, 'yet in the mind of each lives the image of their communion'.[24] The Queen is spoken of as head of the great family of the nation, or as head of a family of nations in the case of the Commonwealth. Many of the civic rituals also celebrate points in the lifecycle of members of the Royal Family, such as the marriages of the royal Princes, Charles and Andrew, and the annual celebration of the Queen's birthday. They frequently involve, and cement, a link with other institutions, as when the Queen as Head of State takes part in the State Opening of Parliament, or engages in the military ritual of the Trooping of the Colour on the monarch's official birthday. Not the least important function is the link forged with the nation's past by ceremonies such as that on Remembrance Day, when members of the Royal Family lay wreaths at the Cenotaph, and veterans of past wars are on parade. All of these events, combining religious symbols with those drawn from other institutions and discourses, contain 'manufactured' or invented traditions, many of them of quite recent origin, which are broadcast 'nationwide' in such a way that members of the audience are drawn to identify with the imagined community and its past.[25]

Studies of the development of the coronation in Britain as a televised event provide illustrative data on the process of inventing tradition and on the manufactured nature of communalization. They reveal how the ostensibly traditional religious ceremony was adapted to the needs of television, whilst the BBC took upon itself the responsibility for deciding what kind of tone and impression should be created and transmitted, even down to the specification of what sorts of camera shots and which objects should be given prominence.[26] However, this does not mean that the sense of community and awe which is evoked is any less genuine or deeply felt, it cannot be so easily dismissed. It lends support to the case for there being a continuing capacity for sacralization in modern society. At such times, as Durkheim explained when he equated religion with the socially sacred, the heightened sense of collective life gives people the sense that they are in contact with an ideal world, which has a sacred property because it contrasts with the profane world of everyday experience.

The nation is only one of the 'imagined' or symbolic communities which, on ceremonial occasions, or in periods of perceived external threat, provide evidence of the continuing presence of the sacred in the modern world. There are many sub-cultures, ethnic groups, and regions (such as Northern Ireland) where this is even more evident. Studies of many of the ethnic groups in Britain reveal a flourishing community life in which elements of the sacred co-exist with individual participation in the secular activities in which rational calculation predominates. But perhaps even more important than the persistence of the sacred is the phenomenon of symbolic adaptation, in which religious symbols are combined with elements from other discourses, to articulate community identity and give meaning to life. Modern forms of cultural transmission may be used as vehicles for this purpose, including such seemingly secularized forms as popular music, disc-jockeys and the record industry, clothing and hair fashions. A striking example is that of Rastafarianism, which not only spread from Jamaica to diffuse a particular blend of religious and political symbols among second and third generation blacks in Britain, but also interpenetrated the sub-cultures of white youth. As Stuart Hall notes in his account of the ideological character of Rastafarianism and its spread to Britain:

The Rastafarian 'case' allows us some concluding reflections

235

on the nature of religious ideology. Ideologies are not fixed doctrines or belief systems. They can be adapted to express different meanings in different historical circumstances. A second point is the multi-accentual character of ideology. The same repertoire of concepts, symbols, imagery and doctrine can articulate a variety of meanings and positions, depending on how the elements are combined and accented. Symbols – like 'The Promised Land' – do not carry a single, unilateral meaning. They belong to rich connotational chains of meaning, which can be differently inflected or positioned. Rastafarianism, for example, imposes its own set of connotations on many well-established signifiers (e.g. Moses, Babylon, Israelites, Zion) which it has 'stolen' from other discourses (e.g. that of white Biblical interpretation), dissociated from their original meanings and position, imported as elements into a different, signifying chain, deflecting the terms to a new meaning in the process.[27]

Symbols, including those originating in religious meaning-systems, seldom die out. They are intrinsic to communities. However, they are versatile and adaptable, and it is the task of sociology and its kindred disciplines (such as social anthropology) to trace the shifts in meanings and their functional relations with other elements of culture and social structures. This can be done not only with respect to the political sphere, as in the studies of civil religion and its relation to the nation, but also with respect to age groups, e.g., youth sub-cultures,[28] the family and sexuality,[29] economics and work,[30] immigrant and ethnic groups, and other areas of culture and social relations. Instead of starting with the fatalistic premise that religion is dying out, and secularization is the only significant trend, the sociology of religion is beginning to adopt a more positive stance and focus its efforts on analyzing the many forms of moral community or symbolic community that exist in a modern society such as Britain.

NOTES

1 K. Thompson (ed.), *Readings from Emile Durkheim*, London, Tavistock and Ellis Horwood, 1986, p.76. From E. Durkheim, *Les règles de la méthode sociologique*, Paris, Alcan, 1895.
2 E. Durkehim, *Les formes élémentaires de la vie religieuse*, Paris, Alcan,

1912/1915, trans. J.W. Swain as *The Elementary Forms of the Religious Life*, London, Allen & Unwin, 1915, p.47.

3 See examples in Durkheim's writings as cited in W.S.F. Pickering, *Durkheim's Sociology of Religion*, London, Routledge & Kegan Paul, 1984, p.179.

4 M. Weber, *The Sociology of Religion*, trans. E. Fischoff, London, Methuen, 1922/1965, p.1. (German original 1922).

5 R. Towler, *The Need for Certainty: A Sociological Study of Conventional Religion*, London, Routledge & Kegan Paul, 1984, p.2.

6 See K. Thompson, *Bureaucracy and Church Reform: The Organizational Response of the Church of England to Social Change, 1800–1965*, Oxford, The Clarendon Press, 1970, for a discussion of the dilemmas posed by bureaucratization in the Church of England.

7 See D. Martin, *A General Theory of Secularization*, Oxford, Basil Blackwell, 1978.

8 R. Stark and C.Y. Glock, *American Piety: The Nature of Religious Commitment*, Berkeley and Los Angeles, University of California Press, 1968.

9 L. Shiner, 'The concept of secularization in empirical research', *Journal for the Scientific Study of Religion*, vol.6, pp.207–20. Also in Kenneth Thompson and Jeremy Tunstall, *Sociological Perspectives*, Harmondsworth, Penguin Books and The Open University Press, 1971, pp.460–74.

10 R. Towler, op. cit., p.2.

11 See R.N. Bellah, 'Civil Religion in America', *Daedalus*, 96 (Winter), 1967, pp.1–21.

12 Op. cit.

13 P. Brierley (ed.), *UK Christian Handbook 1983*, London, Evangelical Alliance, Bible Society, MARC Europe, 1982.

14 Cf. the discussion by E. Barker, 'Religion in the UK Today: A sociologist looks at the statistics', P. Brierley, op. cit., pp.5–9.

15 Ibid.

16 See E. Barker, op.cit., and Princeton Research Center, *Emerging Trends*, vol.4, no.2, February, 1982, Princeton N.J., Princeton Research Center.

17 B. Gustaffson, 'Sweden', in H. Mol (ed.), *Western Religion*, The Hague, Mouton, 1972.

18 W. Herberg, *Protestant, Catholic, Jew*, Garden City, Doubleday, 1956.

19 M. Abrams, D. Gerard, and N. Timms (eds), *Values and Social Change in Britain*, London, Macmillan, 1985, in association with the European Value Systems Study Group.

20 D. Gerard in Abrams et al., op. cit., pp.50–1.

Other Perspectives

21 H.H. Nelson, and R.F. Everett, 'A Test of Yinger's Measure of Non-Doctrinal Religion: Implications for Invisible Religion as a Belief System' in *Journal for the Scientific Study of Religion*, vol.15, 1976, pp. 263–7. Also W.C. Roof et al., 'Yinger's Measure of Non-Doctrinal Religion: A Northeastern Test', in *Journal for the Scientific Study of Religion*, vol.16, 1977, pp.403–8.

22 A.P. Cohen, *The Symbolic Construction of Society*, London, Tavistock and Ellis Horwood, 1985, pp.11–12.

23 K. Robbins, 'Religion and Identity in Modern British History', in S. Mews (ed.), *Religion and National Identity*, Oxford, Basil Blackwell, 1982, pp.465–87.

24 B. Anderson, *Imagined Communities: Reflections on the Origin and Spread of Nationalism*, London, Verso, 1983, p.15.

25 See D. Cannadine, 'Context, Performance and Meaning', in E. Hobsbawm and T. Ranger (eds), *The Invention of Tradition*, Cambridge, Cambridge University Press, 1983, pp.101–64, for a discussion of the invention of traditions with respect to broadcasting and civic rituals.

26 See D. Chaney, 'A Symbolic Mirror of Ourselves: civic ritual in mass society', in *Media, Culture and Society*, vol. 5, no.2, 1983, and in R. Bocock and K. Thompson (eds), *Religion and Ideology*, Manchester, Manchester University Press, 1985, pp.258–66.

27 S. Hall, 'Religious ideologies and social movements in Jamaica', ch.19 in Bocock and Thompson, op. cit., p.293.

28 See D. Hebdige, *Subculture: The Meaning of Style*, London, Methuen, 1979, and S. Hall and T. Jefferson (eds), *Resistance through Rituals: Youth Subcultures in Post-war Britain*, London, Hutchinson, 1976.

29 See V. Beechey, and J. Donald (eds), *Subjectivity and Social Relations*, Milton Keynes, Open University Press, 1985, and J. Brown, M. Comber, K. Gibson and S. Howard, 'Marriage and the Family', ch.5 in M. Abrams et al. op. cit. 1985.

30 See, for example, the discussion of values and voluntary work by Gerard, in Abrams et al., op. cit., ch.8.

BIBLIOGRAPHY

In addition to the works cited in the Notes see also:

Ferard, D., 'Religious Attitudes and Values', ch. 3 in M. Abrams et al, *Values and Social Change in Britain*, London, Macmillan, 1985.
Luckmann, T., *The Invisible Religion*, London, Collier Macmillan, 1967.
Robinson, J., *Honest to God*, London, SCM, 1963.

Weber, M., *The Protestant Ethic and the Spirit of Capitalism*, trans. by Talcott Parsons, London, Allen & Unwin, 1930 (German original, 1904).

Index

Index

Index

Index

Index

Index

Index

trade unionism, 198
tradition, 117
trance, 191
Transcendental Meditation (TM), 161, 169
Trinity, Holy, 53, 59, 74
Tulloch, John, 66
Tyndall, John, 62
typology, 170–1, 215, 216
Tyrrell, George, 39, 67, 118

UC, 107, 158, 162, 164–5, 166, 168, 172
UK Christian Handbook, 216, 227
Ultramontane, 21, 31, 34–5, 66–7
Under the Greenwood Tree, 186
Unification Church, *see* UC
Union of Hebrew Congregations, 139
Unitarian, 11–12, 28–9, 34, 37, 39, 133
Unitarian and Free Christian Churches, 107
United Free Church of Scotland, 107, 109
United Methodist Free Church, 27
United Presbyterians, Scotland, 29
United Reformed Church, 107, 110, 124
United Synagogue, 139
utilitarianism, 115

Vatican Council, First, 36; Second, 39, 67, 123
Vedanta Advaita, 89
Vedas, 85–6
Victoria, Queen's Proclamation, 92
Vie de Jesus, 55
Virgin Mary, the, 21, 188

von Hügel, Baron F., 39, 118

Ward, W. G., 31, 66
Ward, W. R., 201
Watts, Isaac, 22
Way of All Flesh, The, 186
Webb, Benjamin, 33
Webb, Pauline, 112
Weber, Max, 213–14
Wellhausen, J., 66
Wesley(s), 12, 19, 22
Wesleyan Connexion, 26–8
Westcott, B. F., 54, 59, 67
Westminster, Cardinal Archbp of, 32, 66
Westminster Review, 70
Whately, Archbp R., 56, 70
Whitefield, George, 19
Wilberforce, Bp Samuel, 30, 62, 64
Wilberforce, William, 21, 30
Williams, Rowland, 60, 66, 80, 82–5, 93, 95
Wilson, H. B., 54
Wiseman, Nicholas, 32–5, 37
witches, 185, 187
women, 126–7, 170, 190, 191, 196, 202, 227, 228–9
Wordsworth, William, 32
worker-priest, 116
worship, 121–6, 150

Yom Kippur, 139
Young, Brigham, 28

Ziegenbalg, Bartholomew, 74
Zionism, 139
Zoroastrian(s), 134, 146, 147, 149

247